TRAPPED

IN FOUR SQUARE MILES

A Novel by

SAM WAZAN

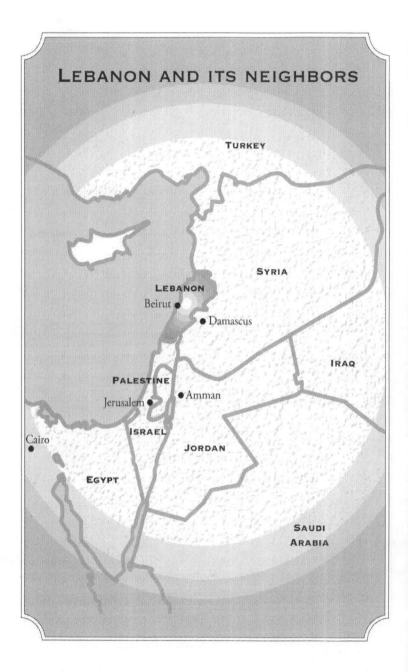

LEBANON AND ITS NEIGHBORS

TURKEY

SYRIA

LEBANON

Beirut ●

● Damascus

IRAQ

PALESTINE

Jerusalem ●   ● Amman

ISRAEL

JORDAN

Cairo
●

EGYPT

SAUDI
ARABIA

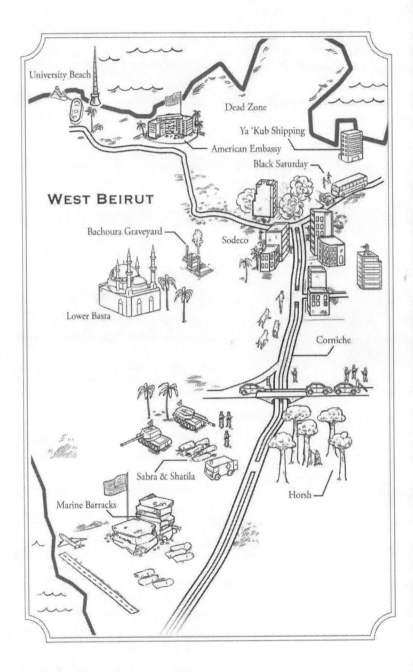

University Beach

Dead Zone

Ya 'Kub Shipping

American Embassy

Black Saturday

WEST BEIRUT

Bachoura Graveyard

Sodeco

Lower Basta

Corniche

Sabra & Shatila

Horsh

Marine Barracks

In memory of M. Sharif, my fifth grade best friend, who was killed during the first year of war.

Contents

Read with open minds,
Connect with compassionate hearts,
&
Act for a peaceful world.

CHAPTER 1

THE WILL
1975

At age thirteen, I prayed for my grandmother to die. I detested her disregard for me and my brother, Nabil, who was one year my junior. Grandmother had suffered a stroke that had rendered her partially paralyzed for the past three years. She used her infirmity to justify every miserable thing she did to us.

The night I killed her, she sneezed yet again during dinner. In spite of the faint glow of the twenty-five-watt light bulb that dangled from the ceiling, Mama, Nabil, and I saw her spit fly. Wet chunks landed in the hummus, yogurt, and cheese, and on the dinner plates. At the sight of the looks of revulsion on our faces, Grandmother broke into hysterical laughter while her dentures rested on her lower lip. My baba laughed right along with her.

Mama scurried to salvage the food with a little spoon. Nabil and I pushed away from the table, fighting nausea. I retreated to my bedroom and prayed for Allah, Glorious is He and He is exalted, to take her. He answered.

After Grandmother went to bed, I heard sobbing in her room, which was next to mine. I got up and cracked open her door. I saw Baba kneeling at Grandmother's bedside. Mama stood at the end of the bed, covering her mouth with her hand.

Grandmother died around ten o'clock that Sunday night, October 12. I squeezed next to Mama in front of the massive antique armoire. A large oval mirror caught my reflection. I recoiled. *Oh, my Allah! You responded to my prayers!* The angel of death, Izrael, dwelled in my eyes. I held the power to summon him!

Baba held Grandmother's hand. He nudged and shook her. Her body was limp.

"Mama! I want Mama." Baba wept. That was the first and last time I saw him cry. The image remains locked in my memory.

Moments later Baba stood up. He wiped his tears with his sleeve, squeezed by me with determination, and opened a drawer in the armoire. Mama leaned over to see what had tempered Baba's anguish. He retrieved a large envelope and an ink pad and then returned to Grandmother's bedside and pulled out some documents. He pressed Grandmother's thumb on the ink pad and then rolled it on a piece of paper.

He turned to me. "Call this number. *Now!*" He recited a phone number.

"W-what is happening?" Nabil stood in the doorway. Mama grabbed his hand and whisked him to her bedroom in the east wing.

I went to the living room and dialed the number. "It's ringing," I said.

Baba hustled to the phone. Mama approached. I made eye contact with her, hoping for an explanation. She ignored me.

"The time is now," Baba said into the phone. "She is gone."

Pause.

"*In sha'Allah*- God willing.*"

Pause.

"See you in an hour!"

Pause.

"*In sha'Allah*- OK."

An hour later, Baba asked me to wait in the foyer. "If it is any of your uncles, don't open the door," he demanded. "It will be bad if any of them decides to visit."

I stood in the foyer and found myself gazing at the handmade shell-inlaid plaque with the inscription: WHAT ALLAH WILLED, which hung over the elevator door. Minutes later, the bell rang. Baba didn't need to be alerted. He had heard the elevator's motor running during the long ascent to our penthouse. He flinched as if an invisible bullet had been fired, and it hushed all of us. I peeked through the peephole.

"Not my uncles," I whispered.

"What are you waiting for, then? Hurry! Open!" Baba said.

The elevator door opened into our vestibule. A man—it turned out to be Baba's attorney—arrived with three other men: a notary and two soon-to-be witnesses. A few thumps of date and notary stamps and numerous signatures later, my father and his cast had produced an authentic post-mortem will, all certified, legitimized, and valid.

Not only did Baba circumvent the *sharia*, Islamic law, with this maneuver, he preempted any reversal of the will by the civil courts. Had he not done so, he would have had to share the inheritance with his five siblings. Each of my four uncles would have received one-sixth, and my aunt, one-twelfth of Grandmother's assets. The other one-twelfth of my aunt's share would have been distributed equally among the male survivors. Now Baba had revised what Allah willed in the sharia.

"Dial your uncle Ramzi," Baba asked me after the elevator descended with the will team. He broke the news to Uncle Ramzi first, as he was the eldest, and then the rest of his brothers and his sister, Najat.

Only Aunt Najat arrived that night. She entered holding a purse in one hand and a plastic bag in the other. A loquacious mouthpiece of Prophet Muhamad's narratives, she made a declaration from the foyer. "According to sharia and in Muhamad's words—Allah prayed for and saluted him—we should expedite burial." Her loud proclamation terrorized Nabil and pleasured Baba.

"Here, Ayda!" She handed Mama the plastic bag. "Say Allah! Play the Qur'an. We must finish the Qur'an recitation within a week."

Mama pulled a cassette player out of the bag and played it.

Aunt Najat collapsed in a chair. When she saw Nabil, she stretched her arms to him. She forced him to sit on her lap, and she jumbled up baby talk with narratives to soothe his fears. Uncle Ramzi, being the rightful decision maker, called back. His remote directives validated my doubts. Had it not been for Grandmother living with us, he would never set foot in our home.

While Baba and Uncle Ramzi discussed the timing and location of the burial, Nabil whispered into Aunt Najat's ear and pointed at Grandmother's room. I heard him say, "... men came. They signed papers and then left."

Baba hung up with Uncle. He said, "We will bury Mama tomorrow after the noon prayer at the Lower Basta Mosque next to the Bachoura Graveyard."

The gravesite was the least pricey in all of Beirut.

After what she had gleaned from Nabil's innocent remarks, Aunt Najat's emotions transformed from sorrow to outrage. She pushed Nabil off and stormed out of the flat without saying a word.

CHAPTER 2

VOTES FOR SALE

After the dawn prayer the next day, my eldest cousin, Nazih, and I picked up the obituaries from the print shop. We plastered the notices in the neighborhoods where relatives lived and worked, and hung more than ten notices under the marble sign at the entrance to our building. The inscriptions on the gray granite sign there read, ALLAH IS THE LANDLORD. On the second line, HADHARI TOWER.

Four hours later in the flat, the burial proceedings began. My job entailed greeting the mourners and segregating women and men to separate wings. Mama lit charcoal incense in an open-top thurible and then toured both wings of our penthouse to expel the evil spirits. Meanwhile, two women cleansed Grandmother's body in the bathroom.

In a brass tray next to an ashtray full of stubbed-out cigarettes, Mama offered aspirin and Panadol. I took two pills for my severe headache and then returned to the vestibule—once a hall between the two flats that Baba had combined to form the expansive penthouse—to open the back door for the laborers coming from the funeral home.

They maneuvered a scratched wooden coffin through the doorway. They wore dirty gray coveralls and shoved the cuffs of their pants into cheap muddy black boots. I figured they had just dug her grave. The workers placed the coffin in the hallway outside the bathroom and lit cigarettes.

Seconds later, the women emerged from the bathroom. "*Pray for the prophet!*" they cried out. The mourners responded, "May Allah pray for our master Muhamad."

I hustled to the end of the hallway to watch. The women handed Grandmother's body, wrapped in a shroud, to the men. They sprinkled a handful of leftover smelling salts on the shroud.

With my uncles, Aunt Najat and Baba gently lowered Grandmother's body into the coffin. My cousins and I lifted the coffin and marched to the stairs. We climbed down, leaving the women behind. We knew sharia dictated that no women would be allowed at the graveyard.

The hearse idled in the alleyway, while all the cars in the cortege parallel-parked on the main road, causing a traffic backup. In the alleyway and under the weight of the coffin, my cousins and I splashed through the overflowing sewage. The stench and humidity moved us faster.

Nazih took the wheel of Baba's Simca. An uncle sat in the front. I squeezed in with Baba and Uncle Ramzi in the backseat. We drove right behind the hearse, which blasted the Qur'an from two large, gray bullhorns.

The twenty-car procession to the mosque moved deliberately slowly, keeping pace with the hearse. In the half-mile stretch to the mosque, drivers hustled in and out of the cortege. Some swore at the deceased while others sounded their horn, agitated by the inconvenience. At the Sodeco intersection—the only intersection we had to cross but one of the busiest in Beirut—the policeman admonished the driver of the hearse for going through a red light.

Three minutes later, we arrived at the mosque. My eighteen cousins converged at the back of the hearse. I eagerly followed. We slid the coffin out and lifted it onto our shoulders. My uncles and Baba waited atop the stairs. Caretakers opened only one side of the decorative black wrought-iron gates. Muslim brothers who attended just to pray had to maneuver around my uncles to enter.

At the gate I got goose bumps. To get through the door, my cousins shouted random orders at those standing in our way. At times the weight of the coffin crushed my collarbone. I leaned with the sways and kept touching it when I felt irrelevant. Grandmother's body shifted, and I felt it bump against the side of the box. The thump terrified me.

"Let's not disturb her," an uncle begged

After some awkward shoe-removal acrobatics, we entered the mosque and went straight to the altar, where a platform awaited the coffin. We gently hefted it onto the cradle and dispersed to the ablution area.

The mosque had a rectangular shape. Massive, symmetrically arrayed gray marble columns created open, expansive halls. About forty feet above, ornate calligraphy—a completely unintelligible verse from the Qur'an—encircled the dome. Around the perimeter, sunlight beamed through arched stained-glass windows, streaming colorful light through its panes.

Just as the sharia dictated, the cleric stood at the center of the room with the coffin. We assembled in lines and faced the coffin, east. Each man squeezed in, leaving no room for the devil to get between them, just as prophet Muhamad instructed in a narrative.

We, the immediate family members, formed the first line. I stood on Baba's right, since I was the "heir to the throne," as he had always introduced me. Nabil leaned his head on my shoulder. The sight of the coffin frightened my younger brother. I winked at him with a weak smile.

Behind us, I saw my best friend, Sharif, next to his father, Abu Sharif, a high-ranking bank executive. He wore a dark suit, white shirt, and a colorful tie. He pursed his lips and nodded at me. Sharif waved from his hip.

Othman, our grocer, stood dripping with sweat next to Abu Sharif. He gave himself the authority to redirect my gaze. He almost popped his eyes out of their sockets to get my attention and then he used the pupils to point at the altar, ordering me to turn around. Before I did, I saw my twenty-four-year-old bearded cousin, Jamil. He was yelping at the beggars at the gate—the men and women who loafed outside mosques and exacted prayers on special occasions for maximum payouts. I wondered what Jamil was doing with them.

The cleric tapped on a microphone mounted on a chrome stand. It was dead. He turned around and said loudly: "We will perform the noon prayers first, then the funeral prayer. I want to remind you, my Muslim brothers, that the funeral prayer is different than all other prayers. There will be four *takbeerat*-calls that God is Greatest. After the first, we will read 'Al-Fatiha' chapter. Second, we pray for our master Muhamad—Allah prayed for and saluted him—and third, pray for Allah to forgive the deceased. Fourth, we will pray for Allah to forgive you and your loved ones and ask for the salvation of Allah's chosen, the Muslims. There will be no prostrating. After the prayer concludes, I ask that only those related to the deceased lift the coffin."

He turned to the altar. "Let us pray."

During the funeral prayers, my shirt sent up fumes of Grandmother's smelling salts. I shivered. I wished that the foul odors that emanated from the shoe stand and the ablution area would overpower the stench of death.

Right after we saluted the angel on the left shoulder to conclude the prayers, someone called out, "Pray for the prophet."

Along with everyone, I repeated the obligatory "May Allah pray for our master Muhamad."

In the center of the mosque, Jamil stood in the only ray of sunshine beaming from the dome. He glowed. He had found the perfect audience for a grave torture or day-of-reckoning speech.

I tried to swallow my resentment. My father mumbled a few curses. My uncles turned slowly, their eyes pinned on the coffin as if Allah watched.

Four years before, Mama rescued me and Nabil from Jamil. We sat in the kitchen as Mama paced between the sink and the range. Jamil asked us if we prayed five times a day. Nabil and I shook our heads.

"It is the most important pillar of Islam." He waved his index finger. "You will be hell bound if you don't! You come with me to the mosque and ask Allah for forgiveness. Now!"

Mama intervened. "They are too young. When they reach puberty, come back!"

"They are never too young to know about their religion."

"Go inside and torture your uncle," Mama told him, and Jamil left.

"Your cousin! *Ach!* He is a talk addict," she said.

"B-but, Mama, we don't pray five times a day." Nabil was unconvinced.

Mama wiped her hands with her apron. "Allah said, 'Worship none but Him and show kindness to your parents. If one of them or both of them attain old age with thee, never say unto them any word expressive of disgust nor reproach them, but address them with excellent speech.' That is all you need to know."

Jamil had no chance of receiving respect. Aunt Najat had eloped with a Shia. Grandmother shunned her for marrying down. His father's family had implored him to enter a temporary for-pleasure marriage, lawful among Shias.

Accordingly, throughout the years Baba condemned Jamil with

the heretics. "The Shias. They are de facto Muslims!" he said, "agitating anarchists!"

"That doesn't make them *heretics*, Baba. Does it?" I had said.

"Our master Muhamad—Allah prayed for and saluted him—said, 'O People! No prophet or apostle will come after me, and no new faith will be born. Reason well, therefore, O People! And understand words which I convey to you. I leave behind me two things, the Qur'an and my Sunnah.'" My father had been emphatic. "Sunnah, as in *Sunni*, not Shia! Only Muhamad is the leader of the entire nation of Islam. Not Ali! Ali was just a caliphate."

Jamil, on the other hand, followed Prophet Muhamad's *and* Ali's teachings. He capitalized on his mixed bloodline to reach both sects. While with Shias, he wore a black cloak over whatever he had on. With us, he flaunted his appearance: no moustache, a bearded face shaved only under the jaw line to expose the skin on his neck. To add more authenticity, he wore a white satin hat embroidered with the Dome of the Rock.

Now, at the mosque, Jamil invoked his Sunni righteousness to connect. He looked out at the gathering, his eyes dark with fervor. He said, "I am here to ask you to support our candidate Professor Ali Adwan."

He elevated a Shia man to a professor! Baba must be infuriated. In a Sunni mosque and *during a funeral?* May Allah curse your father.

I leaned into my father and whispered, "Can he do this?"

Baba dropped his arm on my chest violently. *"Shh!"*

Jamil continued, "Professor Adwan said that the *government* should bear the cost of Sunni *and* Shia funerals."

Suddenly my uncles and Baba formed a circle around Jamil. Mourners followed. I stayed behind, next to the cleric.

"Professor Adwan said that our schools should teach not only the Qur'an, but also for our children to stand up for Islam and Palestine against the Jews worldwide."

I noticed some nods in agreement.

"The *Christians* are flocking to claim more government ministries. I am telling you now; we must get behind Professor Adwan before we lose our voice in this country!"

"*Allahu akbar!*" Allah is Greatest! The cleric beside me shouted. He startled me.

"Allahu akbar!" the beggars echoed at the entrance.

"The Arab leaders!" Jamil continued. "Traitors! They signed up with the big *Satan America.*" His face flushed at the mention of Arabs forming alliances with the Satan, America. "We, here and now, should fight alongside our Palestinian brothers and kill the Jews and their Christian cohorts. We, the *real* Muslims here, will honor and dignify Allah."

"Allahu akbar!" the cleric yelled into the microphone, which crackled to life. The beggars and a few men shouted the same.

Abu Sharif looked annoyed. He shook his head and nudged Sharif. They left.

Othman, the grocer, plowed his way to the center of the circle. Husam, my mother's witty cousin and favorite relative, approached Baba while holding Nabil's hand.

"We'll see you outside the gates at the graveyard," Husam told Baba.

Jamil continued, "We get *attacked* for supporting our Palestinian brothers when they bravely do Allah's work in Israel. December 1968! Who in the Lebanese government, eh? E*h*? Which Muslim protested against the bombing of the airplanes? Not *one*! *We* must annihilate the Jews, but *you* stand on the sidelines. The Phalange party and more Christian militias are getting armed. We have one political party and not one pistol to fend off their aggressions. Professor Adwan led the students' movement. Students were martyred. Allah said, '... and as for those who strive in our path, we will surely guide them in our ways. And verily Allah is with those who do good ...'

Support Professor Adwan against the enemies of Islam! Do good! Vote for Islam!" Jamil punched the air.

Almost all those in the mosque chanted, "Allahu akbar!"

Jamil referred to the predominantly Christian Maronites' armed party, the Phalange. In some ways my cousin was right. Arab leaders drove golden cars and lived in castles. We in Beirut took Jewish fire and dealt with the Christians robbing us of government positions. Baba and my uncles always recognized that point.

In a more solemn voice Jamil said, "When the time comes, remember this: Professor Adwan will pay three dollars more than other candidates. Sign up today! Go to the booth by the falafel stand on the way to the graveyard. But don't go there for *him*. Go there for Allah." He strode to the exit. All the mourners except my uncles and Baba followed.

"What did you want?" Baba asked me.

"W-what? This is scary. Isn't it?"

"That the mourners left?" he said.

"That the Jews bombed the airport. That no one responded. That Muslims are dying in marches. We should go sign up, like Jamil says."

"After the burial."

As I put on my shoes, I glanced inside the mosque. Jamil handed the cleric and the beggars—those who were the most passionate—folded bills. Apparently those who left to vote for Professor Adwan moments before deserved heavenly rewards.

I rushed to join the funeral procession, which, on the steps of the graveyard would earn us, the Hadhari family, the reputation as "the most disgraceful survivors in the history of Beirut."

CHAPTER 3

DISGRACEFUL SURVIVORS

The graveyard gates opened two hundred yards down a one-way street. Baba and my four uncles marched just behind the rear bumper of the hearse. I followed them. Without meaning to, we caused traffic to back up to the Sodeco intersection a quarter mile behind. The noise from horns and the loudspeakers on the hearse overpowered the calls of the three-wheeled cart vendors who swerved in and out of our cortege, hawking their wares.

The guards at the graveyard gates came into view. They had two well-known tasks: to fend off the beggars from accosting the mourners and, more importantly, secure the graveyard from the greedy survivors.

A few months before, one heir exhumed his father's corpse, cut a thumb off, and reinterred the body. The clever son then fingerprinted a will post-mortem. His claim won an indisputable ruling in the courts. His wife bragged, and the in-laws discovered the scam. They sued and won. Now the graveyard had turned into a fenced fort.

Baba had gotten Grandmother's thumbprint on her deathbed, I marveled. Was it so unethical? Where were my uncles and aunt when Baba was sitting on the bidet in the bathroom across from my grandmother, waiting for her bowel movement so he could help her to the bidet afterwards?

The funeral car slowed to a stop before the gates. My cousins and I stooped and lifted the coffin. It squeaked. Right when we climbed the steps, my uncles and Baba, in a show of affection, insisted they carry it forward.

In that brief moment, I looked around. Mourners who left the mosque were returning from the voting booth and joining us. Othman cycled down on his front-loading platform tricycle with a grin on his face. Abu Sharif and Sharif stood grimly by. To them, this occasion was a funeral, not a payout day for votes. Husam hugged Nabil as if to shield him from the gravity of mortality.

My father and uncles became the pallbearers. They worked in perfect harmony.

Grandmother had raised them only to love her, not one another.

Death heals, I thought.

My cousins and I rushed to help them with the coffin's considerable weight. When I ducked to get under it, I heard my uncles utter profanities.

What was going on? I felt anxious and confused.

Because of where I stood, the coffin blocked my view of my uncles. The booming loudspeakers smothered their voices.

"The pimp did *what?*" Uncle Ramzi cried out.

An uncle shouted, "He has a will."

"The mutt!" Uncle Ramzi lunged at Baba. The rest of my uncles struggled to balance the coffin. Nazih jumped under it to compensate, but the coffin rocked back and forth.

"You have a will?" Ramzi shouted. "I am going to kill you!"

Baba froze in place.

"You son of a bitch!" my youngest uncle yelled.

"Take it! *Now!*" my uncles barked at their sons.

The instant my uncles felt their sons take the weight of the coffin, they abandoned their position. They punched and kicked Baba as he continued to hold on. He tried in vain to dodge the blows. I jumped to shield him. They threw me aside.

"May your sons die in the ugliest ways!" Ramzi shouted.

You, pimps! I thought, infuriated.

I swung and threw punches. I slugged Uncle Ramzi first. Nazih ducked from under the casket and lunged at me. He pinned me with a chokehold and pounded my face with his fist. Suddenly both Nazih and I were knocked down. Nazih let go to defend himself.

I looked up. Othman tackled and punched Nazih mercilessly. Then he took off his shoe and hammered my cousin's skull with it. A loud *thud* sounded behind him.

Atop the stairs, the front end of Grandmother's coffin slammed onto the ground. The lid popped off and slid to the sidewalk. Onlookers gasped. My uncles could not have cared less.

Baba battled to keep the back end up. Punches landed all over his body, and he lost his balance. He couldn't prevent the inevitable. The back end of the coffin crashed to the ground and shattered. The side panels collapsed. Grandmother's shrouded body flew out and rolled down to the street. Either her head or feet rested on the curb, it was hard to tell. Everything stopped. The silence was absolute. The speakers and horns were mute as mourners stood by, spellbound. Nabil disappeared behind Husam. I felt a sudden knot in my stomach. I crossed my arms and hunched over.

Husam zoomed in on the moment and shouted, "How could you?"

Abu Sharif approached Husam, and together they gently lifted the corpse. Grandmother's head dangled from Husam's arm.

"Get back!" Ramzi shouted at them. "It is forbidden for other men to touch her!" He reached under Husam and took Grandmother.

"May Allah forgive you for this, Hadharis," Husam said.

I looked up to find my hero, Baba. He dusted his coat and frantically scanned the ground for the buttons missing from his shirt. The rest of my uncles shoved past him and hurtled down the stairs.

The security guards went to Baba, for he appeared injured. "Shame on you!" one guard shouted from atop the stairs at my uncles. "May Allah forgive you and exemplify you to Muslims worldwide."

"You disgrace Islam," the other guard yelled. The veins in his neck bulged.

Baba stood behind the guards and said a few words of his own. "Allah will remember this on Judgment Day! Allah doesn't forget."

My uncles mumbled to each other. They took charge of the funeral proceedings, making Baba and me irrelevant.

My uncles lowered Grandmother's body to the gravediggers, who stood in the grave, irritated by the delay. Baba asked me to join him and grip the shovel. We tossed one shovelful of dirt over Grandmother and left.

CHAPTER 4

THE SECTARIAN CHASM

Early the next morning, my uncles reprinted Grandmother's obituary, omitting Baba's name as a survivor. Word had it that one of them was prepared to shoot Baba if he had made an appearance at Uncle Ramzi's house.

In our penthouse later that afternoon, Baba ended Nabil's childhood violently. It all unfolded in the family room. I stole glances at Baba. He squinted into space and dabbed his chin. Mama smoked her one-hundredth cigarette. Nabil, who feared Grandmother's ghost might haunt him in our bathroom, went to use the bathroom in the master suite. Baba followed him with his eyes and then shouted, "Stop!"

Instantly Nabil started to bite his nails.

Baba got up from the "man of the house" chair, retrieved the beating cane from under the cushion, and charged at Nabil.

Between strokes Nabil screamed, "What did I do?"

Mama rose, but she knew better than to interfere. The cane landed on Nabil's sides and legs until it broke from the force. Baba threw the stick aside and resumed beating Nabil with his hands. Between blows, he shouted, "Beget s-secrets from f-from the youngest."

Nabil collapsed on the floor. Now Baba swung his slippers all over Nabil's body. Mama wailed. Nabil sobbed. I wished I could disappear.

"You want to ruin everything I worked for all my life. May Allah curse you!" Baba raged.

I figured Nabil needed the beating. He would learn faster this way. I knew to be grateful after suffering beatings myself. It was the only way. Baba had beaten me for dropping a charcoal, bumping into someone, tripping on a hose, or serving a dull charcoal to an antsy smoker. I learned to walk carefully and avoid talking back.

My first and greatest humiliation occurred when my uncles, aunt, and cousins came to wish Grandmother a happy new year on the first day after the holy month of Ramadan ended. That evening, the clear sky delivered shimmering lights on the low mountains visible through our family room's expansive windows.

I pretended to be a Palestinian, while Nabil and two of my younger cousins played Israeli soldiers. I chased them around the dining table, then into the family room. There, I bumped into Uncle Ramzi's hookah.

The charcoal briquettes flew off and landed on the rug. Mama dove after them. She juggled the burning charcoal to the kitchen. I froze. Adults looked dismayed. Older cousins stood distraught. They knew what was coming.

Baba rose. He slapped me so hard on the neck, I fell to the ground.

"You, blind *pimp!*" He reached under my arm and jerked me up. "You are cursed to turn steel beams into noodles."

I stood stiff. Shall I stay or go? I wondered. Which decision is going to infuriate him more?

"It's just a rug!" I said, asserting myself as budding young man.

"Hit him again!" Najat shouted. "Now, before he gets it in his head that he can overpower you."

In one swift motion, Baba slapped my mouth with the back of his hand. I felt my lips burn. I bawled. Tears streamed down my cheeks.

I surveyed the room to see who had witnessed my humiliation, but tears distorted faces and blurred the shimmering lights in the mountains. Mama returned with a wet rag to dampen the charcoal burns on the carpet.

"That will show him," Najat said.

"This is the only way!" Ramzi said.

"His lips, Ayda! Hurry!" Najat shouted. "His blood will stain the carpet."

Mama frantically sealed my lips with the rag and took me to the kitchen.

"I hate him!" I said between sobs as I choked for breath.

"They say, 'May Allah have mercy on those who die and have beaten you for your own good, not those who spoiled you.'" She pressed the filthy rag harder on my lips.

I accepted it then. When Nabil wailed, "I wish I was never born," I suspected Allah would have mercy on those who beat us.

Sadly, Nabil became the lever that Baba pulled to siphon his failure. Each time Nabil crossed the family room, Baba pulled out his cane and beat him, shouting, 'Traitor!"

With time, the beatings evolved into replacing Nabil's name with traitor.

On the seventh day of mourning—we commemorated Grandmother on the first, third, and seventh day after her death—Baba with his male guests, including Husam, sat in the living room. It was my job to respond to Mama when she signaled me from the kitchen to serve coffee and cigarettes. All she had to do was peek through the swinging door and wave her hand. When she did, I got up. One time, Husam followed.

In the kitchen, Mama instructed me to serve the coffee and cigarettes. "Insist. Don't just offer."

I turned around and bumped into Husam. He knew better than to be alone with Mama, but his edgy and comical side enabled him to dismantle barriers otherwise inappropriate. As a scissors salesman in the fabric markets, Husam amassed a reputation for being uninhibited. His pitch: "Snip the wiener of your unruly teenager." He would spin the scissors like a cowboy would a pistol. "Merchants bought from me to shut me up," he said, attributing his success to his audacity.

In the kitchen Husam said, "Rami punched like a champ, but Sami—"

"Go! Go inside!" Mama smiled, squeezed Husam's shoulders and turned him around.

"You should have married *me* for money!" He stood comically taller on his toes.

"That's enough! You're scandalous. Go! Go!"

"In Allah's name, Ayda." He turned to me. "The Hadharis' dignity is at a level below a razor blade on the tile. But you know what? If your father hadn't beaten your uncles to it, they would have committed him to the asylum to claim his share."

"I am going in," I said.

"One moment!" Husam grabbed my arm. "You know what irks me? All your uncles and your father start with ..." he wiggled his index finger and pointed up "... 'in the name of my honor' before making a commitment to anything. Today erased—"

"Please! Go inside!" Mama pleaded.

We did.

"You and Nabil ... you two are next," Husam continued. "One day you'll kill each other. I have seen your father caning both of you when you squabble. He beats you up to submit to him, not for you two to get along."

The doorbell rang. I rushed to the door.

"Sami Hadhari's residence?"

I looked through the peephole. An unarmed official stood in the elevator cabin.

"Yes." I opened the door and asked the man to wait.

I called Baba to the foyer. The man served him with court papers.

By the end of the day, we had received five notifications of lawsuits filed by my uncles and aunt. In effect we were served the declaration of the permanent severance of family ties. Baba dismissed the threats. "Let's see what their best witness will say in court!" Like Nabil would testify!

In just weeks, Nabil, once an uninhibited and vivacious comedian, withdrew into a timid boy. Gone were the days when he entertained us with his Charlie Chaplin hops over tiles to the Persian rugs. With his silence, gatherings at lunch or dinner amplified the sound of clinking silverware. Loneliness prevailed. Sporadic gunshots in the distance broke the awkward dining sounds. Nabil and I completed our schoolwork while more gunshots echoed in the background. In short months, gunshots escalated to small battles between religious and political factions.

The instability migrated to our neighborhood. The Palestinian guerilla fighters of Fatah and the Palestinian Liberation Organization, and a Syrian militia occupied a two-story building close to the Christian graveyard three hundred yards east of us. The graveyard delineated the sectarian chasm.

The more intense the gunshots, the more veins bulged in the neck of my Palestinian-Arabic schoolteacher, Mrs. Saykali. She brought the Palestinian cause to the forefront of our lessons. Her face turned red as she chanted for the annihilation of the Jews worldwide. Once, she distributed a graphic novel, the size of a cigarette pack, to all the students. The illustrations depicted a Palestinian child who floated with a halo around his head. The boy admired the view of the dead Hasidic Jews, their blood splattered on car windows, pavement, and walls. The text in the bubble read, "It is a revolution until victory."

The feeling of restlessness and the urge to contribute to the Palestinian cause took hold of my classmates, friends, and everyone in my family. Neighbors in the building, store owners in the area, and friends in school speculated that war was imminent. Everyone, it seemed, was riled up for the cause, the liberation of Palestine.

I learned more about the danger of war after Baba scheduled a social for the last Saturday in November. He ordered me to dial Sharif's number.

"It's ringing."

Baba snatched the phone from my hand.

"Put your father on the phone," Baba demanded of my best friend.

Pause.

"How are you, Abu Sharif?"

Pause.

"We have a get-together here tomorrow. I hope you forgive my short notice—"

Abu Sharif must have talked for five minutes while Baba alternated between "Pray for the prophet," "It is not that bad," and "In Allah's name, you are right!"

Pause.

"I assume Rami doesn't know."

Pause.

"May Allah be with you!" Baba ended the conversation.

"What is it that I don't know?" I asked.

Baba shoved past me.

"What is it?" I said louder.

"They are busy packing to emigrate to America!"

Near tears, I called Sharif back. We had pledged to be best friends forever.

"Why didn't you tell me?" I asked.

"Would you like to visit me?"

"When?"

"Tomorrow after school."

I told Mama and Baba about my plan to visit with Sharif the next day.

"*In sha'Allah!* Whatever!"

I took it as a yes.

The next day I shadowed Sharif in school. I mourned his departure while I stared at him during classes. After school, we walked together to his home, which was also on the *corniche*-the main road, not far from our building. Our friendship had strengthened over the years.

That afternoon I expected to enter Sharif's serene home, where windows were insulated from the street noise, the air temperature remained comfortable in spite of the seasons, and a lavender potpourri scented the air. Paintings adorned the living room, and recessed lights shined on each one.

Instead, Sharif's home looked like a storage warehouse. Boxes were piled up in the foyer and hallway. Deep in the living room, Abu Sharif and Um Sharif, as always looking glamorous, sipped a glass of red wine and listened to classical music. They stood up for *me*.

"I wish you were not leaving, Uncle Abu Sharif," I said, calling him "uncle" affectionately.

"Things look really bad, love!" He hugged my friend as he uttered the term affection for me. "We have to take care of this young man." Sharif smiled.

You are one lucky son, I thought.

"The piano is still out," Abu Sharif said. "Would you like to play something for us, Sharif?"

Would you like? Nabil and I never had a choice in any request Baba made. Grief-stricken, I sat on a chair behind the piano bench.

Before they had packed, photographs on the grand piano ushered my imagination to America. In one, Sharif and his parents stood before a giant redwood tree in California. In another, Manhattan skyscrapers filled the background.

"I will play the *Fur Elise*." Sharif brought me back to reality.

Um Sharif and Abu Sharif relished the moment. They closed their eyes as they sipped their wine. Sharif had taught me to clap only when he removed his hands from the keyboard. That afternoon I clapped when his parents did.

As usual Sharif critiqued his performance with words I figured he had read in poems.

"Let's go to my room," he said.

In Sharif's bedroom, a waist-high shelf was mounted around the perimeter, where Abu Sharif arranged books in order of height. Prominent among them were biographies from Education for the Millions Publishing Company. I had one of my own: the Prophet Muhamad's.

Sharif had dozens, with foreign and Arabic names. I recognized Beethoven's only because he had told me about him.

Abu Sharif had also built a model train engine and situated it and four boxcars on a curving track that ran along the perimeter, two feet below the ceiling. The train looked as if it emerged from a wall in one part of the room and went out another.

When it was new, Sharif had said, "Baba cut the last engine and the last boxcar at the perfect angles."

I gazed at that train each time Sharif left the room. In fact, I climbed on Sharif's bed to verify that the wall was indeed whole. When Sharif returned, I hugged him. "You are my best friend," I told him.

We talked about America for an hour, and then the time came for me to leave. I stood up. Highly uncomfortable but compelled to say it anyway, to remind Sharif of our commitment to one another: "Are we going to stay friends forever?"

"I will write. I promise."

In the foyer, Abu Sharif insisted on driving me home, for he wanted to buy a baguette from the bakery. Um Sharif saw me to the door. She gave me a long hug and kissed me affectionately. She pressed a palm to my cheek and said, "May Allah be with you, love! We will miss you dearly."

While we waited for the building's elevator, Abu Sharif described his enchantment with America. He said that ambulances, fire trucks, and policemen closed highways for car accidents. He described an animal rescue and contrasted that with a beggar's corpse found on a sidewalk in Beirut a week before.

"A day passed before the body was removed," Abu Sharif said in a solemn tone. "An animal is more valuable in America than a human here."

"Everyone is saying a war is near. Is this why you are leaving?"

"Yes, love! It is only a matter of days now."

"How do you know?"

"Killing is rampant," Abu Sharif said. "One just doesn't know when his turn is up. It is lawless. No one is investigating murders. Retaliations abound and on a massive scale."

The three of us stepped into the elevator.

Abu Sharif continued, "It is the escalation that is alarming. You see, Pierre Gemayel escaped an assassination attempt. His son, Bashir, and the Phalangists retaliated by killing twenty-seven Palestinian fighters in a bus."

"But that was months ago," I said.

"The Syrian and Palestinian militias are killing priests and Christian civilians—"

"We must leave sooner." Sharif sounded scared.

"If our flat doesn't sell soon, we will just go."

The elevator had reached the ground floor. Abu Sharif gestured for me and Sharif to exit first. "Why are the Christians vicious?" I asked.

"That they might be, but we are not exactly angelic, love. We chant for Palestine, 'It is a revolution until victory' and 'Allahu akbar' in the same breath. Now, they claim they are more patriotic than us."

We rode in silence. I was already missing my friend.

"Here, right?" Abu Sharif asked as we reached my building.

"Yes, Uncle!"

He pulled the car to the curb.

I heard gunshots in the distance. "The Christians are *pigs*," I said. "They want Lebanon to be a Christian country." I said, starting to repeat Baba's words: "You should stay and fight if the war starts—"

"No! No! No! Rami. We must not call people of any religion pigs." I saw Abu Sharif's white eyeballs in the rearview mirror fetching mine.

"Sorry."

"The thing is, love, each agreement the Christian and Muslim leaders have, they sign other secret agreements selling their loyalties to the highest foreign bidder for influence here. For a country run by men like this, nothing is worth dying for. Good night." Abu Sharif unlocked the car doors. "Ya'Allah, love." He said for me to go.

"I will see you at school on Monday," Sharif said.

"Good night!"

I went up to our home with a new point of view and a disturbing thought: if Baba loved us, why wouldn't we emigrate, too, and be safe?

Mama opened the elevator door. "Thank Allah for your return. I've been waiting for you."

"W-what happened?"

"Hookahs. Hurry! I need you to assemble three. The neighbors and Husam and his wife are coming for a visit."

Baba turned his nose up on our Palestinian neighbors. He never invited them to our socials.

"Ach-what's that smell?"

"Your father," Mama said. Baba had left the bathroom door a crack open. The foul smell hung in the air.

"Go fan the charcoal." Mama handed Nabil a sticky cardboard from a baklava box. I assembled hookahs, starting from the tobacco head to the water base.

Mama opened one kitchen cabinet and gasped. "My Allah! We are out! Call Othman! Have him deliver the Persian tobacco packages and a gas cylinder, the short kind."

I obeyed. "Othman said, 'Ya'Allah,'" I told Mama that Othman was coming.

The stairway bell rang. Mama's face flushed. "My Allah! They are here already."

On the way to open the door, Mama pounded the bathroom door with her knuckles. "Ya'Allah!" She urged Baba to hurry.

"May Allah curse you! You scared me," he said. "Ya'Allah! Ya'Allah!" He conceded.

Our only Christian neighbors, Tony and his wife, Audette, arrived on time.

"Hello!" Baba said, welcoming our guests from the bathroom. Mama and I showed them to the living room.

Boastful of their French fashion connection, Tony and Audette went out of their way to flaunt their Yves Saint Laurent logos. When Tony sat, he "accidentally" flipped his tie to show the unmistakable *YSL* logo.

Minutes later, Abu Muhamad and his wife, Um Muhamad—they were Sunnis who had moved to Beirut from Damascus—opened the door and showed themselves in.

"May peace be upon you," Abu Muhamad said. His belly bulged through his shirt. From his biceps down, his arms were tanned.

Um Muhamad had draped a robe over her nightgown. A faded gray hijab barely covered her hair. Mama received her with kisses.

On their heels, Hajjeh—an honorary title she had earned from performing pilgrimage in Saudi Arabia—and her husband, Zaki followed. She wore layers of robes under her ivory satin cloak and spandex pantyhose. Only her snow-white face, wrists, and feet showed.

Mama complimented Hajjeh on her light skin and pointy nose, her American features. "In Allah's name, your face glows," she said.

"Allah gifted me this look to enlighten the misguided," Hajjeh said.

Zaki rolled his eyes.

Just as everyone settled in, Husam and his wife, also Um Muhamad, arrived. Their loud arguing behind the elevator door gave them away before the bell did.

I ran to the door. Husam popped two loud kisses close to my earlobes. Mama stood behind me as if waiting her turn. Affectionately Husam pulled Mama from the shoulders and kissed her on the cheeks close to the lips. Baba had just emerged from the bathroom and looked on. He squinted and puffed his nostrils.

"I just found out we didn't bring anything with us. Forgive us, Sami," Husam said. "Sorry we are late."

Husam's claim for being late sounded more credible than forgetting to bring something, because our building, the Hadhari Tower, sat on the corniche.

The corniche was the busiest and noisiest road in Beirut. It connected the airport to the seaport, around six miles apart. All day and night we heard tires squeal and drivers honk musical horns. We cringed each time we heard brakes slam.

In the living room, a cloud of hookah fumes hovered three feet above the floor. Nabil and I joined the women, who sat closer to the foyer in case their husbands asked for something from the kitchen. Nabil sat next to Hajjeh. There Mama broadcasted our sins.

"Rami is skipping prayers. Look at him. He's reached puberty."

Thanks, Mama! I thought. Yes, I have pubic hair now!

"' ... And seek forgiveness of your Lord, then turn to Him whole-heartedly,'" Hajjeh said to me. "'Verily, my Lord is Merciful, Most Loving.'"

Mama continued, "Their Arabic teacher ... uh ... Mrs. Saykali ... a Palestinian refugee ... she turned the class into a recruiting center for the revolution. Instead of learning about Najib Mahfouz, they are learning about the Israelis' assassination of Ghassan Kanafani—"

"Enough!" Um Muhamad, the neighbor, said. She changed the subject to complain about the elevator stopping short of the threshold at her floor.

Audette asked if anyone was annoyed by the loud planes approaching the airport. In a solemn tone, Hajjeh took the floor with the opener, "Pray for the prophet."

We mumbled, "May Allah pray for our master Muhamad" in response.

Hajjeh frowned. "Listen, Ayda!" she said. "The Jews killed Jesus and they tried killing Muhamad— Allah prayed for and saluted him—but Allah saved him. They are not just our enemies. They are Allah's enemies. The Arabic teacher knows it. You should, too!" Then she turned to Um Muhamad. "Do you really think the elevator responds to your fingers? Thank Allah, for he is behind everything, and Audette ..." Hajjeh stared in space, avoiding eye contact with Audette. "Had it not been for Allah, not one plane would take off or land. Allah blows a breath under the wings." She waved her index finger at Nabil and me. "You must pray for your afterlife before you do anything for this finite existence."

Reactions to Hajjeh's proclamations varied. Audette sat expressionless. Um Muhamad compulsively thanked Allah for his might. Mama nodded. Nabil, on the other hand, surrendered to Hajjeh's repertoire. She held his soul in her hands. At each proclamation, he sighed as if he had witnessed a magic act. As for me, when she looked my way, I found myself obliging with hollow nods.

In the living room, Husam and Baba started a backgammon match. Baba sat below our only piece of art, a large, gold-framed canvas of Ka'aba—the black cube in the center of Mecca—depicting pilgrims surrounding it. He faced everyone, and Husam faced only him. Abu Muhamad and Zaki took his side. Tony remained neutral.

The doorbell rang. Mama answered.

"Rami!" Baba pointed his eyes in Mama's direction. I went after her.

In the vestibule, Othman handed Mama the tobacco. Gracious and friendly with all, Mama nervously smiled.

Baba shouted from the living room. "Who is it? Who is it? Don't leave your mother alone there!"

I returned and whispered, "Othman! He can hear you."

Baba never credited Othman for saving me during the squabble at the graveyard steps.

"Hurry back. If he asks, tell him I am busy." I turned around. Baba continued, "I tell you something! Othman's brother shot a policeman down here, in the median. He is a champ! Othman? Hunh! He is a coward. Did you see him?" He referred to Othman's dark skin. He then quoted a line from a poem he once helped me memorize for school. "Mutanabi said it best, 'Never buy a black slave without a cane, defiled and disobedient he will remain.'"

Tony cringed. So did Audette. Abu Muhamad and Zaki laughed.

I returned to the foyer, fearing Othman had heard Baba.

"How is your chin?" Othman asked. "From the blows on your face. The graveyard."

"I am fine now." I turned to Mama. "Othman saved me from Nazih. You should have seen him. He took his shoes off and—"

"May Allah grant you longevity! The boys told me," Mama said.

"Where is Professor Hadhari?" Othman asked. "Go, love! Tell him the balance is over one hundred and ten dollars."

"Go get him," Mama told me.

As soon as I approached him, Baba shouted, "Why did you leave your mother?"

"There is a balance of—"

"Ya'Allah! Ya'Allah!" He got up and walked to the foyer. I went along.

"Welcome! Welcome! Welcome!" Baba said enthusiastically, instantly transformed into a gracious host welcoming Othman three times.

"How are you, my fr-riend?"

"May Allah grant you longevity, Professor Hadhari! Please don't mind me! It's just that—"

"Oh, my Allah! Here! Anything else?" Baba paid him and returned to the living room before Othman could answer.

"May Allah give you strength!" Othman called out after Baba.

I stayed behind. Othman put his hand on my shoulder. "I see you and your friend reciting the Qur'an to each other on the way to school. May Allah watch over you!"

"Thank you, Mr. Othman!" I said, overwhelmed by the compliment.

"May peace be upon you!" Mama gently closed the door behind.

Before we entered the living room, Mama renounced Baba's disrespect for Othman. "Our master Muhamad— Allah prayed for and saluted him—said, 'There is no difference between an Arab and a Persian except in devoutness.'"

As soon as Mama and I sat down, Baba said, "'Surely among your wives and your children are some that are really your enemies, so beware of them.'"

No one disputed the verse.

Mama had been ridiculed in public before. She slapped her thighs and stood up to leave, but Hajjeh decided to save the evening. She pressed upon Mama to stay put.

"Do you know how many times the words Israel and Jew are mentioned in the Qur'an?" she asked.

Zaki took a loud and deep breath. "'In sha'Allah,' I don't know. Come on, say it. 'In sha'Allah!' while you're at it, I am sure Audette and Tony will enjoy an overview about their fate. 'In sha'Allah!'"

Who counts Israel and Jew in the Qur'an? I wondered.

Hajjeh savored every second. "Anyone?" She draped the thick satin white robe over her ankle and then she lifted the right slipper with her big toe and wiggled it. She exposed her crusted heels, which had cracked from her weight.

Zaki shouted, "Ya'Allah! Go ahead! Say it, goddamn it! I mean, in sha'Allah!"

Hajjeh mumbled, "May Allah forgive you!"

Zaki winked at Tony. "Israel and Jew! Hmm ... How about Christians? Not in the trivia?"

Hajjeh ignored him. "Over one hundred times directly and indirectly. Allah called them 'sows' and 'apes' in the 'Al-Ma'eda' chapter." She readied herself to take on probing questions, but Zaki discounted her point.

"That was for those who continued to serve the false deities. You always take things out of context," Zaki wrinkled his face.

"Throw the dice, Sami!" Husam said, gesturing at the game board.

She continued, "May Allah curse the Jews for what they did to Jesus and Muhamad." Hajjeh looked up, attempting to reach Allah. She drew attention to the fissures in the plaster and bubbles and flakes in the ceiling paint.

Harmonically, all but Tony and Audette said, "Amen!"

"Do you know how many times the word *Christians* is mentioned?" she asked. She curled a leg under her buttocks and sat higher.

"How many, Hajjeh?" Nabil asked eagerly.

"Allah said——" Hajjeh started to say.

"For you to shut up. You take everything ...*everything* out of context. *That* is blasphemous. I just wish you came bundled with a switch for the dowry I paid, but Allah didn't 'In sha'Allah' that, now did he?" Zaki turned to Tony. "I just don't know how to turn her off. That's it! Allah curse the hour I married you!" He stood up, wiggled his fingers, and flung his wrist. "Let's go."

Tony softly tugged Zaki's sleeve. "Please sit, Brother! Calm down."

Zaki said, *"D'accord, love!"* He said in French OK.

"Did I tell you what happened to me the other day?" Tony asked everybody.

The conversation transitioned from religion to current events. It seemed to me that all the men always agreed with each other. Nonetheless, they started with "But" and "You are wrong," "I disagree with you," and "Have you lost your mind?"

"The Palestinian fighters pulled me over and asked for my ID. Who the hell do they think they are? Some patriotic Lebanese we are! We shouldn't allow them—"

"Tony! Tony!" Husam said, humor in his eyes. "My friend! I admire your patriotism. More people should be like you, but you are still here. Celebrate that they didn't kill you."

"Enough with the nonsense! The Palestinians want to liberate Palestine from Beirut. This isn't right!" Tony said.

"What Allah wills is what will happen. Allah said, 'So when our command came, we turned that town upside down, and we rained upon it stones of clay, layer upon layer.'" Abu Muhamad enunciated every syllable.

"From your mouth to the Almighty, exalted is He!" Um Muhamad said as she settled in her chair.

Baba's face was flushed. "They roam our neighborhood at night. It's like they are amassing an attack from here. Gunshots are drawing nearer. Abu Sharif, Rami's friend's father, he is emigrating."

Baba turned to Tony. "Go talk to fleeing patriots like him. ...
That coward! *We* will protect our land and property." Baba slammed
a chip in the backgammon board. "Your move," he told Husam.

"May the blood of their children run up to their kneecaps."
Hajjeh called out in prayer.

"Amen!" all but Mama, Tony, and Audette responded.

"Let's not say 'amen' to children being slaughtered," Mama said.

Baba chewed on his dentures. His eyes turned red. How dare
Mama contradict him!

That was the moment that triggered the exodus. Abu Muhamad
removed the hookah nozzle from his lips and looped it around the
stem. "*Ya'Allah!* Let's go! Um Muhamad." Everyone followed suit.

"Stop, everybody!" Husam said. "I forgot to tell you, but first
congratulate me!"

"I am tired, Husam! In Jesus' name, what?" Tony said.

"Next Monday I start a new job at the port."

A round of loud wishes for prosperity broke out.

Baba called out an enthusiastic prayer, "Oh! May Allah bless you,
love. The importers are robbing us. Don't leave us behind." Baba
wanted a piece of every shipment.

Husam shook his head as if he had said it one hundred times before. "You know I don't filch—"

"*Pray for the prophet!*" Baba said. "Husam! Calm down!"

"Rami, why don't you meet Husam at the port? Look at the ships
and see how all that works," said Mama, creating a diversion.

"*Ya'Allah!* OK!" Husam leaned and kissed me on the cheeks.
"Next Saturday after school?"

"In sha'Allah," I said, elated.

CHAPTER 5

BLACK SATURDAY
DECEMBER 6, 1975

At 2:10 in the afternoon on the Saturday after Baba's social, I waved down a *service car*—a shared taxi—outside the school gates. Nabil waited on the sidewalk as I called out the destination to the driver.

"Port!"

The driver signaled me in with a subtle head tilt. A man already sat in the backseat.

"Through Ras El-Nabeh to drop him off." I pointed at my brother.

"Ya'Allah! Get in." Service car drivers detested passengers with extra requests. I dreaded the rides.

"Ya'Allah!" I urged Nabil to hustle into the car.

I squeezed by the smelly passenger, who reluctantly gave way on the shredded vinyl seat. Nabil slammed the door shut. The window, held up by a screwdriver jammed into the slot, dropped.

"May Allah curse this fare! Ya'Allah! Who cares! We're all going to die!" The driver puffed his cigarette into the windshield.

A little too dramatic, I thought.

Loud Qur'an recitations from the cassette player deafened me. Al-Fatiha, Al –Falak, and Annas chapters were inscribed on miniature

rugs that hung from the wide, convex rearview mirror. Only by looking at the side of the road was I able to recognize the route.

Seconds later we crossed the Barbeer Bridge. In a quarter mile, I
tapped on the driver's shoulder. "There." He pulled to the curb.

Exactly at this time, Mama always stopped whatever she was doing and waited on the balcony for Nabil and me. Nabil got out. I
looked up. Mama shouted from the balcony. The noisy street overpowered her voice. I tapped on my earlobe and shrugged.

She extended herself over the rail and formed a bullhorn with her
hands. The driver yelled, "Close the door!"

Between the door and the frame of the car, I pointed in the direction of the port. Now Mama waved frantically.

The driver shouted, "Close the goddamn door! I need to find my
blessings!"

The passenger joined in, "Ya'Allah! Hurry! *Ya'Allah*, boy!"

Before Nabil got in the entrance, I shouted, "Nabil, remind her
that I am going to see Husam at the port."

I thought Husam would be impressed with my punctuality because like him, everyone except Abu Sharif was forgetful and late.

We arrived at the port. "Ya'Allah!" the driver prompted me to get
out.

At the gate, everyone was hustling somewhere. Men looked
crazed. I wondered if ships arriving warranted such bustling. After a
few inquiries, one impoverished Palestinian worker—they are readily
identifiable by their *kufas*, patterned scarves such as the one worn by
the Palestinian leader Yassir Arafat—told me where I could find Husam. I crossed over railroad tracks and walked by abandoned trucks
until I reached the far end of the pier. The doors of the blue container, that the Palestinian had described, faced the sea. I walked around.
The swinging doors were shut. A faint sound of a crackling transistor
radio came from somewhere nearby. I tapped on the door. No response. I tapped again, louder.

"It is me, Rami!" I announced to the box.

I heard scratching and voices mumbling inside. Husam slowly swung one side open, quickly scanned the container yard, and yanked me in. "Quickly!" he said.

He locked the doors. Dim candlelight glowed in a far corner. I squinted. Two men in kufas sat there. One held a radio.

"How did you get here? Why are you here?" Husam asked as if he expected Izrael, the angel of death, instead. His eyes looked all white, and he shook.

"You told me—"

"Yes. No. Yes ..."

"Did you forget?"

The larger of the two men asked, "Who is he?"

"My nephew."

"You can't be here!" the man said. "Oh, my Allah! What am I going to do?"

"Why are you inside a container?" I asked, confused.

"Did you see anything on the way here?" Husam asked.

"No," I told him. "What is going on?"

The larger worker peeled the radio from his ear.

"The Christian Maronites ... eh, their militias ... the Phalangists and Tigers, we don't know ... they are slaughtering Muslims."

"What did we do?"

"We need to get you out of here!" Husam said. "Oh, my Allah!"

"Word has it that the Palestinians killed four Phalangists this morning," the smaller worker said. "B-but, *how* did you get here?"

"Service car."

"Which way? Which road?" Husam asked.

"Through Martyr Square."

"Didn't anyone tell you anything?"

"No! I—"

"May Allah help us get through this day!"

We heard sporadic, distant gunfire.

Husam prayed, "Oh Merciful!" invoking one of Allah's ninety-nine names.

"They are getting closer!" The smaller man stood up and paced. He stopped and looked up at the roof of the container. "Allah, guide me today. What do we do?"

"I keep hearing public busses revving. Get him to the bus stop right now!" The large worker looked at me, his eyes filled with concern. "Blend with the public!"

"He is just a boy. They won't hurt him," the smaller one said.

"That's it. Thank you, Allah! Thank you!" Husam said. "Give me your ID." He nervously waved for it as I reached around.

"Whoever asks, today you are *not* a Muslim. Do you understand?"

"What?" I grimaced.

"Are you a Muslim?"

"But, Allah—"

"No! No! No! Love, d-don't! Just don't. Blend with the crowd. You understand?"

"'One thousand times a coward; Not once may Allah have mercy on his soul'!" the larger man recited. "Count on Allah!"

I nodded, remaining calm in spite of their fear.

"Do you have money for the fare?" Husam pulled out coins from his pocket.

"I do."

"The bus station is at the entrance of the port."

"OK!"

"Tell your mother to tell Um Muhamad that I'll be fine. Allah is looking after me ... uh ... us!"

I stepped out of the container. As luck would have it, the red-striped beige public bus emerged from the far left outside the port. Husam shouted, "Run. May Allah be with you!"

I waved. He shut the door.

I sprinted to the bus stop, certain I would catch it. I waved and shouted, but the bus maintained its speed. The passengers gazed at me as it rolled by.

A few yards later, the driver slowed down. A cloud of dust swirled behind. I darted to it. The center door whooshed open.

Everyone in the bus yelled. The collector behind the glass cabin, the women, men, and even children shouted at me. "Ya'Allah! Come on! Ya'Allah!"

The bus driver closed the door behind me before I cleared the first step. I hopped on the second step below the collector's window. I pushed twenty-five *piasters* through the round hole. The bus took off, violently.

"Keep it, boy." I stood startled. He continued, "We are off the grid. We are going by the seaside."

"But that would take me away from home—"

"The executions are in the Normandy area!" a pudgy woman wearing a hijab shouted, her voice shrill.

"That's around here," a man confirmed as he bent to look out the window.

A father held his young son tight. "They are slaughtering us." The boy burst into tears. The father kissed the top of his head. "Love, Ahmad! Baba is here!"

An older woman seated by the collector looked grim. She said, "Jesus, help us!"

What's with everybody? I wondered, my fear rising from the other passengers' panic.

I climbed one more step. Most of the seats were taken. Two nervous men stood. A woman didn't even pretend to move for me to go in. I wrapped my fingers on the chrome bars mounted to the backs of the seats.

In less than five hundred yards, the bus driver slowed. I looked through the front window to see a camouflage-green Phalange truck blocking the road.

Everyone shouted. "Don't stop! Go through them!"

"Stop the bus!" a man at the blockade yelled.

"Run them down!" others demanded frantically.

The collector declared, "We are at Saifi, the Phalange headquarters."

A GMC truck chased the bus on the left side. The Phalange party decal was imprinted on the door. The truck driver closed in on us. From the flatbed, three masked militiamen shouted profanities and fired rounds in the air. They barked, "Pull over now, donkey, *Now!*"

They didn't wait for the command to be obeyed. The truck sped up and cut the bus off.

The bus driver slammed on the brakes. He swerved sharply to the right and bounced the front end of the bus onto the sidewalk. I lost my balance and pushed a woman down.

"May Allah curse your father!" She got up and punched me.

"I am *sorry!*"

"Go! Go! Go! Don't stop! They are going to kill us," the man with his young son screamed at the driver.

The driver looked as if he lived in a world of his own—perhaps deaf to the sounds and blind to the threats that everyone else saw. Suddenly he shouted, "Pray for the prophet, everybody!"

Some passengers mumbled.

One masked man walked around to the front door on the right side of the bus. The driver whooshed the door open. The other two pounded on the door in the middle, by the collector's window, where I stood.

The militiamen flaunted large crosses hung from fancy gold necklaces. One of the two next to me hustled to the back.

The man in the front held a walkie-talkie in one hand and an M16 in the other. "Give me your ID! *Now!*"

His comrades demanded the same. Then a gunshot was fired. We ducked. Passengers screamed. I peeked through the loops under the handles. One of the militiamen shot the driver in the head. His head rested on the side window, on which his blood was splattered. His left cheek slid down until it rested on the horn lever. The horn blared.

The shooter slammed the back of the driver's head with the butt of the M16 to silence the horn. Its handle broke. Two more rounds fired. I jumped back in horror. My ears rang, and my heart pounded. An explosion of pleas followed. Then more rounds were fired.

The killer shouted, "*Shut up!* Get your IDs out!"

The man behind poked me with the muzzle of his rifle.

"May I ask what this is about, sir?" I ventured.

"Shut up, pig! ID!"

"I-I don't have one. B-But, here is my wallet, sir."

"Are you a Muslim?"

"I—"

"Stay!"

The Phalangists prodded and poked everyone with handguns and rifles. "Those who I told to leave, leave *now!*"

The Christian woman, the collector, and about seven others scrambled to the doors. The rest of us remained on the bus at gunpoint.

Outside the bus, the elderly woman shouted, "We're all God's children! Let them go!"

The militiaman next to me laughed. "Go home, Grandma! One more word out of you, and I'll introduce you to the driver, *in hell!*"

The masked man beside me glared and shouted, "Let's go, pig!"

An older man to my left tried to get up but to no avail. He was entangled in the fabric of his long kufa. He tried again. The thug next to me tapped him on the shoulder.

"Stay, love! Stay! You are perfect here."

He turned and winked at the fighter behind me. "Yes! Just like that."

"Thank you, son!" the man said.

"You get the whole bus for yourself!" the thug said with a grin. He fired a shot into the man's head. The shell bounced off of little Ahmad's cheek. He shrieked. His father hugged him. People in and outside the bus screamed. Their hysteria was deafening.

Ahmad's father lifted him up, and the child wrapped his legs around his father's waist. People shoved me harder and frantically shouted, "Oh Merciful!"

My heart was in my throat, and I thought I might throw up. I imagined Mama grieving for me. I tried to move quickly, but could only walk one inch at a time. Two mothers holding infants shoved past me up the narrow aisle. I guessed that they thought if we hurried, we would get points for cooperating, a chance to live. I pushed harder to exit the bus.

While the Phalangists shouted orders for us to line up, a voice broadcasted a command over a walkie-talkie: "OK, now move all your people to the perimeter. *Vite!*" The voice said in French quickly!

I tried to think rationally. I figured the man in the kufa was Palestinian. Perhaps the bus driver, too. I will be fine.

On the sidewalk now, six militiamen pushed and prodded about thirty of us across the wide street into the Normandy neighborhood. In two hundred yards, our line made a turn into a hilly courtyard the size of a soccer field. GMC trucks blocked all intersections leading to it. Some people wailed while others begged on their knees for their lives. Bodies lay strewn about the grassy field.

At that sight, I gasped. My breath caught in my throat.

The Phalangists screamed: "Shut up, pigs." A soldier fired four rounds directly into our group.

Two men in front collapsed to the ground.

On the other side of the courtyard, men and women of all ages and classes had been lined up to face an eight-foot-high concrete wall. All clasped their hands behind their neck, and their elbows touched the wall. They swayed and wept as if they had been there for some time, waiting ...

I turned away to see two little boys whose arms were wrapped around their father's thighs. They faced the courtyard. Their father yelled, "You will not get away with this!" A Phalangist shot him point-blank. His two sons fell on him, shrieking. One militiaman approached and fired a round in each boy's head. Their little bodies fell across their dead father. They did not look like Palestinians. At that moment, I realized I was going to die.

I released sobs only I could hear. My jaw trembled, and my lips quivered. A few people wailed. Others shouted prayers. Very few cursed the Phalangists and the Christians.

A masked man slugged me with the butt of his M16. "*Ya'Allah! Move! Donkeys!*"

And like a dog, I submitted.

In front of me were women dressed in fur coats, short and long skirts, scarves, high heels, sneakers, and slippers. The younger men wore leather coats, skin-tight bell-bottom pants, and some had cowboy boots. Older men, some with canes, walked at the pace of the herd. Two wore three-piece suits. They dressed like Abu Sharif; I figured they were bankers, too.

In the short walk, the Phalangists exploited the spoils. They fondled a woman. The couples, who saw, embraced. The killers snatched an older woman's hijab. Other women knotted theirs. One severed a lady's hands, triggering an outburst. People screamed.

The handless woman wailed at the sight of her hands on the grass and blood squirting from her arms in the rhythm of her heart beat. A Phalangist removed the bracelets from her forearms. She collapsed. Frightened people tossed their jewelry atop the dead woman. The

Phalangists laughed hysterically.

A thug planted his rifle's muzzle in a busty woman's cleavage. Her husband took one in the head for removing the barrel. Two teenaged girls screamed and kicked as masked men dragged them by their hair into an alleyway. Their parents pleaded in vain. All along the way to the wall, Phalangists cursed Prophet Muhamad and called Muslims donkeys and pimps.

Those of us from the bus merged with the others at the wall and huddled closer. I squeezed into the center of the crowd.

A militiaman shouted, "Hands behind your necks, pigs! Face the wall."

I turned slowly to comply, taking fleeting looks behind me. I saw men urinate in their pants, grandmothers faint, older women keen, and some stand there, defiant. After turning, I heard children sobbing and women wailing. Mothers begged for their children to be spared.

I vomited. Allah is watching over me. I am a good Muslim. I will live.

A rugged-looking laborer shouted over the chaos. "May Allah curse your fathers and your prophets! May Allah burn Pierre Gemayel, Shamoun, and all the Christian Maronites in blazing hell!"

Finally! A hero! I decided that when he jumped a Phalangist, I would take on the one next to me and yank out his heart with my hand.

Kill before getting killed! Die a hero!

But the words of Husam's coworker rang in my head. "One thousand times a coward. Not once may Allah have mercy on his soul."

I stole glances. A masked Phalangist heard the curses. He wore large shades, a tank top, and a large silver crucifix pendant. He smiled demonically, braced his gear, and ran to the cleanest GMC truck. He ducked in and chatted with someone. It must have been the man in charge.

The man in the truck had one foot down on the median and one inside the vehicle. He spoke into a walkie-talkie. Then he stepped out. I recognized him: Bashir Gemayel! Pierre's son! Abu Sharif had mentioned him along with Shamoun.

From that point forward, it became Bashir's show. He was the commander. "Turn around," he shouted. Like a peacock spreading his feathers, he strutted toward us. He conferred with two aides. The man in the shades pointed at the laborer, my hero.

Bashir grinned. He formed a curve with his arms and gave them instructions. His comrades ran toward us and lined us in a large sem-icircle. Bashir approached and looked pensive.

Effeminate in his bearing and with a slight French accent, he shouted, "I am going to kill you all."

People screamed. Shots fired. We got quiet. He continued, "You *had* to provoke us. Today you pay! You want the Palestinians. Don't you? Well, join them in hell!"

The kufa-wearing man stood on my right. I edged away from him. I feared his presence would attract our executioners. On my left stood little Ahmad next to his father.

I trembled. I felt a sudden urge to urinate. My legs shook out of control. I cried a muffled, "Mama." I am not going to hell. I am not going to hell! I've been good. Forgive me, Allah! Please forgive me, Allah! I love you, Mama! Baba, I am sorry. Nabil, I will miss you.

Bashir ordered his comrades to stand ten yards back from us. The commander turned away from us as they leveled their weapons to their hips. Bashir mumbled a few words to the man in the shades. The man approached and pulled the one who had cursed him and his father. Two other men whispered in Bashir's ear. He nodded. The two aides gathered some thirty adults and children and forced them to kneel.

Bashir scanned our eyes and addressed the kneeling, terrified Mus-lims. "Take this view to your graves." He fired a round into the la-borer's head. His body jerked, and blood splattered on those behind him. He slumped to the ground.

From left to right, Bashir walked in rhythm with his shots. One bullet per man, woman, and child. Some took two seconds to fall on their face or to sway left or right. A few fell back. He reloaded his gun twice to finish the job.

When done, Bashir calmly said, "This is what happens to the barbarians!"

Singlehandedly, Bashir executed the Palestinians first. I thought we might be spared. We had learned our lesson—do not support the revolution and the Palestinians.

Bashir continued, "Lebanon is a sovereign country. Do you get it now?"

In a moment of relief, we began to disperse. I hustled forward, assuming the killings were over.

"Get back! Now!" The lieutenants fired rounds in the air.

I stood still by the corpse of the Jesus-cursing Palestinian. His head dangled off my right foot, where his neck rested. His blood seeped into my shoe. I wished I could move, but I was paralyzed with fear. Ahmad and his father were still at my side. I heard an older woman pray.

Bashir shouted, "Put your children in front of you. Ya'Allah!" He walked away.

A man emerged from the line. He looked familiar. "You will not get away with this, you pig! The Palestinian fighters will go after every Gemayel worldwide! May every one of you burn in eternal hell. Go ahead, shoot me! You are a *pimp* and the son of a pimp!"

A Phalangist got enraged. He strode to the brave man, pinned the muzzle of his handgun in his forehead, and fired. The man crumpled. Bashir didn't twitch.

A sudden wave of sobs and wails filled the area. Terror gripped me. My body shuddered out of control. I sobbed out loud.

Bashir walked up to the brave man's body. He raised his boot and crushed the man's face. Then he kneeled and removed the man's wallet. He looked up at us and said, "Your hero's name is Farook Hussein."

My Allah! Othman's brother.

Bashir continued, "Burn in hell, pimp!" He spat on the body.

Bashir threw the ID on Farook's chest. He pulled out his dagger, bent over, and stabbed Farook in the chest through the card. He left the dagger and walked away to his comrades.

A warm stream of urine trickled down my legs.

Ten yards in front of me, Bashir turned around and barked, "Put your children in front of you. *Now!*"

Parents wept. They pleaded. None complied.

"Have it your way! *Fire!*"

I crossed my arms and coiled my body. Our executioners fired from the hip. At the sound of the first round, I tensed my body and clenched my teeth. Ahmad's father, on my left, fell. Allah, Glorious is He and He is Exalted, messaged me to fall with him. I felt a burn in my thigh. More people collapsed. Some moaned and groaned. Others kicked while on their back. Ahmad stayed up.

I am good to you, Allah. I will pray five times a day. I will fast more than thirty days. Please save me.

Instinct told me to play dead. I closed my eyes just enough to see through my lashes. While the soldiers reloaded, I slithered under Ahmad's father. For a few seconds, the world stood still. Then I heard boots.

A lieutenant yelled, "Sir, we've got to go! We've got to go!"

"*D'accord.*" Bashir said and fired two rounds at Ahmad.

The boy fell on top of his father. His head bounced off mine. Blood streamed down his neck. Tears burned my eyes. I wanted to press on Ahmad's wound, but Allah told me, "Live! Play dead!"

I heard wailing. Survivors cursed Jesus and Mary. They called Bashir and his father street dogs. Some men begged for their lives.

They pleaded, "We have nothing to do with the Palestinians. They beat us up and take our turns in gas stations and bakeries. Kill 'em all! They are barbarians."

Bashir got antsy. "Finish them off!"

In my head, I recited a verse from the Qur'an: "Think not of those who have been slain in the cause of Allah as dead. Nay, they are living, in the presence of their Lord, and are granted gifts from Him." I succumbed to my fate. My hand was wet with blood. An idea struck me. I slowly scooped blood that streamed under me and smeared it on my face and hair.

Seconds later, another storm of bullets erupted. It lasted for a few seconds. Not one Muslim remained standing. Ahmad twitched. More moans and groans. The pounding of boots running receded, and trucks peeled out. I heard the clicking sounds of weapons. Perhaps they were reloading.

I cracked open my left eye, the one closer to the ground. Ahmad crawled on top of his father. His head shook and jaws trembled. Tears mixed with blood down his neck. He kept shaking his father to wake him. "Baba! *Baba!*"

With my arm under his father, I squeezed the little child's ankle to force him down.

"*Baba!*"

"*Shh,*" I whispered.

Ahmad resolved to wake up his father.

"Ahmad! Right?" I whispered.

"Am I going to die?"

"No! But you have to stop moving. OK?" I whispered through tight lips.

Ahmad sucked on his thumb.

I closed my eyes. "Act dead."

"Make sure everyone is dead," a man yelled.

Oh, my Allah! I loosened my muscles, slackened my jaw, and held my breath. Boots pounded closer and faster.

The butchers cursed Prophet Muhamad and Islam. They opened fire one more time.

"Pick up as many bodies as you can," Bashir said. "We will toss them in the sea."

Thank Allah! They picked up bodies from the side nearest to the water. Suddenly sirens blew, signaling the arrival of ambulances and police. Tires squealed. The Phalangists bolted.

People keened. Some prayed for Jesus and Mary.

What about Allah and Muhamad?

I squinted. Young men and women in Red Cross uniforms shouted to one another. I stayed down, frightened that the cross-wearing workers came to finish us off. Civilians approached. I took comfort in the familiar noise of the city.

I turned to Ahmad. His eyes were wide open. "Ahmad, love, move a little now," I whispered. I scanned the area. "They are gone. We can get up now. It's over. Ya'Allah, love. We made it." I tried to pull my arm out from under his father's body. Ahmad's stare was lifeless.

The civil-defense volunteers lifted the child's limp body. I summoned all my energy to release a muffled groan. A Red Cross volunteer heard me.

CHAPTER 6

THE DEFENDERS: POLICEMEN & CONVICTS

"M-Mama-aa!" I slowly opened my eyes. Through the blinds, streaks of sunlight beamed on Mama, who held my hand.

"Oh, my Allah! *Love!*" She jumped up. "It's a *miracle*. Allahu akbar. Allahu akbar!"

My throat felt dry. Wires and tubes branched out of my arms and under my robe. A mask muffled my voice. "W-where am I?"

Mama looked pale. "The American University Hospital."

Oh, my Allah! Baba must be furious spending a lot of money here. Fear gripped me. "W-where are the Christians? Are Christians here?"

Mama let my hand go and dashed out. "Doctors! Any doctor! My son is awake! Hurry!"

A doctor and three nurses darted into the room. The nurses surrounded the bed. The doctor removed my mask and unplugged wires. He smiled kindly. "I am Dr. Ibrahim Saba. How do you feel?"

All the while Mama compulsively mumbled, "love," over and over.

My voice cracked. "Am I going to live?"

He nodded. "You are a *miracle*."

I am a coward! I tried to straighten up. I couldn't.

"Don't move!" Dr. Saba carefully pressed me down. "You were shot three times!"

"The Christians are evil. They are killing—"

A nurse patted my leg. "You are a lucky young man, Rami!"

Dr. Saba continued, "We removed a bullet from your right arm and one from your right shoulder. The third bullet went through your right thigh."

I flinched, hearing gun battles outside. Explosions rattled the windows. "Mama, what's happening?"

"The country is on fire!"

"Where is Ahmad?"

"Who?"

"A little boy. His name was Ahmad. Is he here?" My eyes got teary.

One nurse said, "Love, the Red Cross vans brought only two survivors from your area. Besides you, one woman survived." She tilted her head at the curtain that split the room. "She is in a coma."

I felt the urge to urinate. I did.

"How long have I been here?"

Mama said, "Two days, love. May Allah grant you longevity."

"Why are you wearing a hijab?"

"Allah saved you. I owe him."

"We sh-should kill Christians."

"Allahu akbar!" a man shouted in agreement at the doorway. We turned.

The grocer Othman!

Dr. Saba looked unimpressed. He turned to Mama. "We can discharge him."

"So soon?"

"Let's count on Allah," he said.

"Yes, Doctor," Mama said dubiously.

My arm, shoulder, and leg throbbed. "I hurt everywhere," I told Dr. Saba.

"This will take care of it, love." The younger nurse administered more fluids into a tube.

Dr. Saba and the nurses left as Othman entered the room. At my left, Mama wrapped her fingers around the chrome rail of the bed. Othman did the same on my right.

"Thank Allah for your safety!" he said.

"Thank you!" I labored a smile.

Complying with tradition, Mama had bought a box of chocolate to offer my visitors. After the usual awkward round of "Please take one," "No," and "I insist," Othman took a piece and put it in his pocket.

He looked tongue-tied. Then he exhaled over my face.

"Did you—? Did you ... you know ... see my brother?"

"He was a hero!"

"Oh, my Allah! Where is he?" Othman quickly came to his senses. "'*Was* he?" He choked on the word.

I described in detail his brother's heroism.

The grocer fell silent.

"I wanted to fight back," I said, feeling eager to console him.

Mama collapsed into an orange chair. She crossed her arms, sobbed, and rocked.

I continued, "I thought the Christians only wanted to kill Palestinians."

Othman's face turned into a web of veins, his eyes sparked fiery red, and his knuckles were white. He pounded the rail once and then took off. An explosion of falling metal objects echoed in the hallway outside my room.

Mama took off her hijab and wiped her tears. "In all religions, it is blasphemous to kill in the name of the prophets and Allah!"

"I don't care! When I get better, I will make Christians pay."

I woke up the next morning to the sound of Mama arguing with the nurses outside the room. She returned wearing a deep frown. Then she looked at me with sorrow and pressed a button that dangled from a long white cord over my shoulder. "The hospital wants us to leave."

"Where is Baba?"

"He is very excited to see you."

"Where is he?"

"He is tending to the building."

"Did he visit me?" I always felt that I was the last thing on Baba's mind. Today was no different.

"The country is ablaze. Our fighters are pillaging buildings."

"At the corniche?"

"Everywhere!"

"Is Nabil with Baba?"

"Where else?"

"Who is taking us home?"

"Husam. He asked for you right after he returned home from the port."

"He made it home?"

"A Christian man took him and two others in for the night. I asked him to come back and pick you up."

"I want Baba."

Two new nurses barged in. The younger one pushed a wheelchair. The other handed Mama a cane and then turned to me. "You will need this for six weeks, love." She hung it on the closet door handle, and then began rummaging for my clothing and belongings. "Let's get you changed."

"I don't want to go!"

"Love, we don't have enough beds." The older nurse turned to Mama. "Make sure he keeps his shoulder brace on and change the gauze every two days."

A few minutes later, I sat in the wheelchair and rolled through the hallway to the elevator.

Someone shouted a muffled, "Stop!"

The nurse pushing me froze.

Dr. Saba walked around and faced me. He put his hand on my left shoulder. "I hope you feel better very soon."

"Thank you, Doctor."

He took a deep breath. "Rami, not all Christians are savages like those who did this to you."

"When I get out of here, my mission will be to find them and annihilate them."

"I am a Greek Orthodox, Rami. Will you spare me?"

"Get out of my way! Now!" I yelled.

Over my head, Mama said, "Dr. Saba, please forgive him." She took over the wheelchair and pushed me to the elevator. A male orderly chased after us, to bring back the chair.

In the cramped elevator, visitors smoked, stank, and wept. Mama proudly announced to the riders that I had survived Black Saturday. They shrugged indifferently. At the ground level, they elbowed past us.

Mama and I scanned the jammed lobby. I expected to see Husam jumping in joy. Instead, a mother with two children squabbled with the receptionist, insisting her husband's name was on the "Wounded" roster. An older couple huddled on a black leather sofa and wept.

Mama rolled me out the exit. Across the street, hordes looked on as howling ambulances screeched to a stop at the emergency-room entrance.

"What is Black Saturday, Mama?"

"The day Allah awarded you a new life. That's what they are calling it."

"Is it true that only two survived?"

"They say over two hundred people are dead."

"More like four hundred!" the orderly said.

"Oh Merciful!" Mama gasped.

The orderly continued, "The PLO, may Allah shield and empower them, will purify this land by helping us kill all the heretics."

"Where are the ambulances bringing casualties from?" I asked.

"The battles stretched to the hotel and market districts," Mama told me.

"Did Sharif leave to America?"

"I don't know."

"Is our neighborhood safe?"

"Nestled between two battlefields."

"Are we safe?"

"'If Allah helps you, none shall overcome you.' You are living proof."

Husam emerged from the crowd. "Love, Rami!" He spread his arms and ran toward me, then took over the wheelchair from Mama. "The car is up there."

He pointed toward Hamrah district, a block away. Overzealous beggars showered me with prayers for my salvation from bombs and heretics. Husam plowed through them. Mama and the hospital worker followed along the sidewalk.

I saw the world around me hadn't seemed to change. Service car drivers honked at pedestrians needlessly. Hookah smokers gathered at storefronts and alleyways. Grocers sprinkled water on the dusty sidewalks. Delivery cyclists whizzed in and out of traffic. Older men huddled around a backgammon match. Some men and women wearing suits and dresses walked as if headed to a cocktail party. Those who had dressed like them in the courtyard had been the first to denounce Islam before getting murdered. They pleaded for their lives and proclaimed their allegiance to Jesus the loudest.

Resentment clutched my pain. I had seen Jesus' soldiers on Black Saturday. I had heard of the Jews massacring Palestinians. My retaliation would be ferocious and divine. Allah said it in the Qur'an: "'And fight in the cause of Allah against those who fight against you.'" Allah had spared my life for a good reason. Mama had done the right thing by committing to wear a hijab.

"There! There it is!" Husam pointed over my head.

Once at the Opel, my wheelchair turned. The orderly grabbed my cane and threw it in the back seat. Husam and Mama lifted me into the passenger seat. In turn, the orderly took possession of the wheelchair and rolled it away.

Mama knew better than to arrive home sitting next to Husam. Had Baba been waiting for us on the balcony and seen her in the passenger seat, she would be doomed to weeks of scorn.

In the car, Husam looked in all the mirrors and through the windows before leaving his parking space. Traffic lights had become useless from gun blasts or power outages. The farther from the hospital we got, the more Jeeps occupied the streets full of militiamen, their rifles jutting through open windows.

In the Verdun area, a convoy of cars screamed through an intersection as we approached. Men fired their guns from the windows, and others dangled their feet from the tailgate of Range Rovers while motorcyclists ordered pedestrians to clear the way.

Husam proudly said, "It must be Arafat or one of his leaders. May Allah shield them."

A howling Jeep swiped the Opel's side mirror. Husam yanked the car to the right.

I started. "Who are these people?"

"These are our men," Husam answered.

"They look like the Palestinian guerilla fighters."

"They are called the Joint Forces. The Sae'eka of Syria, Fatah of Palestine, the Communist Party, the Progressive Socialist Party of the Druze, Amal of the Shia, and all other Sunni groups are fighting together. Glory to Allah for this union!"

Another Jeep rolled by with a big gun in the center of its bed.

"That's a *Dushka!*" Husam pointed at the gun. "Made in Russia. ... Pierces through tanks. You don't want to be on the other end of that." He grinned.

I didn't think it was funny.

He looked in the rearview mirror. "They must be going to the hotel and market districts. Did you hear the news today?" he asked Mama in the rearview mirror.

"No."

"In sha'Allah, we will wipe out the Phalangists for good."

"In sha'Allah!" I said.

"The Joint Forces pushed back the enemies of Allah at the Sodeco intersection," he continued.

"The Sodeco intersection is a battlefield? That's only four hundred yards from our building!" I said, astonished.

Mama gently patted my left shoulder, reassuring me of my safety.

Husam mumbled to himself strategies to enter our neighborhood safely. Then he turned on the radio.

Mama reached between the two seats. "Tune to El-Akhawi."

"Who is that?" I asked.

Husam smiled and searched for the station.

"He is a radio broadcast—"

"*Shh* ..." Husam said, listening to the report.

"... the fighting at the Sodeco intersection simmered down to low-caliber weaponry in battles. It is closed and unsafe. Museum-Barbeer Bridge crossing is open but unsafe. Back to you, Brother Imad!"

Husam looked tense. He turned off the radio.

"Open but unsafe? What does this mean?" I asked.

"Snipers," Husam answered. "We have to go through the Lower Basta Mosque and climb up the narrow streets." He turned to Mama. "Did they excavate the median for cars to cross to your building?"

"Yes! I will show you."

After a mile of dodging lawless drivers and speeding Jeeps, we reached the Lower Basta Mosque, where we had performed Grandmother's funeral service. There, Husam turned right and climbed to the Upper Basta area.

At the Upper Basta police station, Husam made a left turn to descend to the corniche. I checked out the police station.

"Where is everybody?" I asked.

"The police or the criminals?" Mama asked sarcastically.

"They are fighting Allah's enemies," Husam said.

"Convicts, too?"

"They were released," Husam said. "The government declared that they couldn't protect prisoners from shelling or their vengeful surviving victims."

Mama quickly added, "They joined the militias."

I saw no pedestrians along the one-way street that once was jammed with cars parked in both directions and on both sides. At the bottom of the hill, a car inched up the street in the opposite direction.

Almost one-third of the way down the hill and carefully clearing charred cars abandoned haphazardly on the street, we reached a wider space where the car coming in the opposite direction sped up to squeeze past.

Just as Husam's and the other driver's windows met, the driver barked for Husam to lower his window. I saw a bearded, disheveled younger man in the back seat.

"What is your business here?" the driver asked.

Husam looked frightened.

Mama rolled down her window. "What's yours?"

"Listen, Hajjeh! There is a lot of looting—"

Hajjeh! Like Zaki's wife! I thought. Must be the hijab that earned her that title!

Mama pointed at me. "Say hello to a hero, a Black Saturday survivor."

Without even glancing at me, the man said, "May Allah be with you! Go!"

Husam asked him, "How do we cross the corniche?"

"There is only one opening," the driver said.

"Is it safe?" Husam asked.

The man in the back seat said, "There is a sniper at Ashmoon building. Turn right down there at Omar Ben Khattab Street. No way but right or you will be shot."

Mama asked for more instructions. The driver rocked the car back and forth, releasing and engaging the clutch. "Turn right at Omar Ben Khattab. You'll see a large barricade of sand barrels and bags on your left. That is for the Ashmoon Building sniper. Stay on the left. Turn only on the Amlieh Mosque Street to the corniche. At the corniche, turn left, but quickly go to the right side of the road. The Pepsi Building sniper is vicious. Stay right, or you will be exposed. You will see a sandy opening in the median."

"May Allah shield you!" Mama blessed them.

"May Allah be with you, Hajjeh!"

As soon as we turned right at Omar Ben Khattab Street, a feeling of detachment from civilization set in. Husam almost swiped the charred cars on the left to evade the sniper. I could hear intense gun battles and shelling in the distance, but we were now unhindered by noisy horns and traffic jams.

"You said Baba and Nabil are at home?" I asked.

"And Abu Muhamad's family, Hajjeh's family, and—"

"Tony and Audette?" I asked.

"I begged them to stay, but they left."

"Spies!" I muttered.

Husam leaned across me and lowered my window. He turned off the engine and rolled downhill to the Amlieh Mosque turn. The tires rumbled over debris. "We are in the 'combat zone,'" he whispered.

I glued myself to the back of the seat. Husam and Mama looked around as if they commanded the bridge of a submarine in hostile territory.

Badly damaged cars sat abandoned on both sides of Omar Ben Khattab Street. Various sizes of shrapnel had torn holes through the cars' bodies, and stores' roll-down metal doors. Some doors bulged. A spooked cat sprinted across the street and disappeared under a car. I looked out and up. Windows were shattered, and odd-shaped shards still remained in some of the frames. A sign of life: an older man swept the sidewalk at the building's entrance.

I turned to watch him. Inside the doorway, militiamen huddled. They wore forest-green camouflage uniforms and carried AK-47s. Ammunition belts wrapped across their shoulders. Hand grenades hung from their belts.

As we continued the two-hundred-yard drive to the Amlieh Mosque turn, more men sat crammed in building entrances. One fighter in every group carried a rocket-propelled grenade launcher, the deadly RPGs.

Mama broke the tense silence. "Here! Turn here!"

Husam shifted to second gear and released the clutch, restarting the car. The hulks of more cars were along the roadside, two of them charred. In the narrow one-way street and across from the mosque door, an American car was parked in the middle.

"What is this?" Husam complained.

The car sat low from an apparent overload. On the luggage rack someone had tied down mattresses, with chairs and suitcases stacked atop. The trunk and the four doors were wide open.

Husam approached the car slowly. I looked toward the building. A few steps up in the entranceway sat three boys and a girl.

"Ya'Allah! Ya'Allah!" A disheveled man ran out to close the car doors. A woman, most likely the mother, trotted out with large plastic bags in both hands.

Husam said, "Hello, Neighbor!"

"What are you doing here? You need to get out," the man said.

"They live near here." Husam said, leaning his head toward Mama.

The man looked at her. "Hajjeh, leave this hellhole for your child's sake." He glanced at me.

"Whatever Allah has in the book for us!" Mama said.

Husam rolled his car forward. "Say Allah!" He waved goodbye to the man and his family.

At the bottom of the Amlieh Street, we found ourselves in the open corniche.

"He said stay right immediately after you turn," Mama nervously reminded Husam; her head now between the two front seats.

"Yes, yes. I know."

More debris was scattered on both sides of the corniche. A Jeep carrying four men hurtled out of an alleyway. A truck bounced off the median making a dust trail. Another Jeep followed. Men flashed victory signs through their windows.

"There!" Mama pointed at the spot where the vehicles had penetrated the median.

At the opening of the median, we stopped to allow a slow convoy of two loaded cars to pass. Household goods were stacked six feet high above their roofs. Two families with children looked distraught. The mufflers of their cars scraped the ground as they zigzagged their way in the sandy, three yards-wide opening.

Husam pulled into the alleyway alongside our building and set the brake. He blew the horn rhythmically as if to celebrate my return from a pilgrimage. I looked out. There Um Muhamad, her three girls, and three boys jammed the kitchen window. Above them, Hajjeh looked on.

Husam and Mama walked around to my side. They got under me as I hobbled to the entrance, awkwardly leaning on my new cane. Um Muhamad and Hajjeh sprinkled rice and shouted prayers.

I asked Mama, "Where are the men?"

"They must be coming downstairs."

I slowly approached the unusually dark building entrance. There I heard slippers flapping on the steps. Baba swung from the edge of the stairway rail and came into full view. Abu Muhamad, Zaki, and Nabil chased behind.

"Welcome, hero!" Zaki shouted to me.

"Salah Eddine Al-Ayyubi! That's who you are! That's who you *are!*" Abu Muhamad raised one eyebrow and wiggled his index finger at me.

I am nothing like the liberator of Jerusalem. I played dead, I thought.

Baba went down the four steps from the entrance and reached out to embrace me. I winced.

"Be careful. His right side was wounded," Mama alerted everyone.

Husam released me to Baba, who braced me from the waist and insisted on taking me up the stairs unassisted.

"Why don't we take the elevator?" I asked.

"May Allah break their hands! There is no power," Baba said.

"B-but, I can't—"

Baba was unwilling to compromise. "Enough! You are a man! Hold the rail, and I'll lift on this side. Ya'Allah! Nabil, take the cane from your brother."

I stopped to rest at each floor. Either Abu Muhamad called out encouragement, or Baba shouted for me to toughen up and keep charging. At the doorway of the penthouse, we turned left to the west wing and into the living room. At first it puzzled me, but as soon as I sat down, I got an overview of our new way of life.

Baba orated rules. "Never go in the east wing at night. If you must, go only in the dark. The sniper put six holes in the kitchen cabinets. You understand?"

"OK!" I said.

"The east-wing door." He pointed. "This door must be shut at night."

"What about if I need to get water or—"

"You close the west-wing door and then open the east-wing door. When you need to take a bath, ask your mother. She will heat water for you on the one-eyed propane gas burner."

I glanced over at Mama and Nabil. They sat next to each other and plastered on wide grins. At least we had a way to heat water.

"Are you listening?" Baba asked.

I nodded.

"The balcony is off limits."

"But it faces west!" I said.

"OK, fine. But don't go on the balcony at all. No going on the roof. Don't use the shower anymore. It consumes more water than necessary. Mix cold water with the hot water in the red bucket. Use the ladle to shower."

I drifted and nodded. Baba covered all aspects of surviving sniper fire, rationing water, and securing light switches.

Around eight in the evening, Baba said, "Time to go to bed."

Despite it being so early, I looked forward to climbing into my own bed.

In our room, Nabil rested the brass candleholder on the squeaky wooden table between our beds. In the candle glow, he pointed at the ceiling and whispered, "You see this?"

I saw a new concrete patch.

"It is from a sixty-millimeter mortar shell."

"One landed on the roof? When?"

"It's nothing."

"Were you here?"

"Just dust on my face," Nabil said, flaunting his bravery.

"We will get 'em!" I vowed.

I rested my head on the pillow and stared at the patch in the ceiling. The demonic cacophony of war played on. Gun battles and distant explosions of various intensities and calibers erupted and traveled straight to our penthouse. Nabil rolled onto his side, and soon I could hear his deep, even breathing. I wished I could sleep, but I feared I attracted the evil spirits. I took more painkillers.

Sounds and images from Black Saturday came back to me.

Before Black Saturday, I had a recurring nightmare: a huge beast wearing a black cape chased me atop narrow concrete walls. I ran in slow motion. My feet didn't touch the concrete. The beast closed the gap. But before he caught me, I would awake breathless.

But now I snapped upright from a new horror. It was after midnight. The beast returned–a Phalangist. Each time gun battles intensified and then suddenly stopped, I believed the Phalangists had penetrated our defense lines and would be charging up the stairs to our penthouse. The visions of the Christian killers attacking my family horrified me. The murderers' silhouettes flashed before my eyes. Their attack was imminent. To survive, I curled up and wrapped myself with sheets, not one finger or toe visible, to look like a pillow.

A few nights later, right after I blew out the candle, the explosions drew nearer and louder.

"To the foyer!" Mama screamed. "Get up, Rami! Nabil! *Now*."

Nabil and Mama stood wrapped in bed sheets. They looked terrified. Baba walked in slowly. "Get some blankets," he said. "We will sleep here tonight."

Mama spread blankets on the floor. I opted to sleep next to her. That night she discovered the terror I experienced in my sleep. The next morning she told Baba about my midnight episode.

"He will grow out of it," he scoffed. "He is a man! Stop talking about it."

Later in the day, Mama asked me to join her and visit with Hajjeh on the fourth floor. I obliged. There Mama explained my night terrors.

Hajjeh mumbled a short verse. "He is seeing *jinn*!" Holy ghosts.

"Oh Merciful!" Mama gasped.

"No worries! Come here, love! Sit! Right here."

Hajjeh situated me between her legs, facing away. She commenced an exorcism ritual.

For days before I went to bed, Hajjeh repeated the ritual. She carefully pressed her right hand on my head, slowly whispered Qur'an verses, gently swung my head left to right, and lightly rubbed olive oil on my forehead.

"Recite 'Annas' and 'El-Falak' chapters three times each before you sleep." She prescribed a *hijab*–a small notebook with inscriptions of Satan-repelling verses. Mama inserted the hijab in a small pillowcase and fastened it to my undershirt with a safety pin. Results varied. Upon calling Allah to expel the Satan, the very mention invoked images of the cross-worshipping murderers.

"I feel great. Thank you, Hajjeh," I lied each time she asked.

I yearned to see Sharif but quickly lost hope. Mama said that people were leaving the country in droves. In my mind they were all cowards who abandoned us, the holy and patriotic Muslims. We fended off the Christians in the combat zone, where snipers shot and shells exploded. We held steadfast against the enemies of Islam. I accepted my new reality and rejected the idea of having friends outside the neighborhood.

CHAPTER 7

TERRIFIED BY NIGHT. MIGHTY BY DAY
JANUARY, 1976

We took to the living room in the west wing of our penthouse. Mama, Baba, and Nabil sat below the plastic-paneled windows. I groaned as I sat in a chair. Nabil flashed me a look of sympathy. I leveled the cane on my knees, and like him I read the Qur'an. Mama chain-smoked. Baba lay on sofa cushions on the floor. He pressed the radio to his ear, annoyed by the pops of plastic sheets bulging in and out of the window frames and the hissing of the pressure cooker on the gas burner. Distant and sporadic explosions and gun battles rattled the windows that had not yet been broken. A horn blew hysterically. The honking overpowered the explosions in the markets district in downtown, less than a half-mile north of us.

"May Allah curse his father!" Baba screwed up his face.

I labored to stand with the cane and looked down at the street. "That's Abu Sharif!"

"Sit down!" Mama pointed at my chair. "You can't just stick your head out."

"It is Sharif! I know it is!" I said, elated to see him.

Mama didn't share my excitement. "Nabil, hurry downstairs and ask them up."

"They won't come," Nabil told her. "Not with the elevator dead."

"Go!"

Nabil mumbled a closing verse, bookmarked the page, and set the Qur'an at Baba's feet.

"Pick it up!" Baba yelled. "May Allah curse you!"

Nabil looked up at the ceiling and apologized to Allah for defiling the Qur'an. He went to the door.

"Insist! You understand?" Mama reminded him.

"How will you get out of the building? Born a loser always a loser!" Baba said scornfully. "Take the keys! Lock the entrance door behind you. If they come up, lock it behind them."

I guessed Abu Sharif would politely decline. But when Mama resolved to be hospitable, only death or a miracle would free guests from her clutches. I stood at the balcony door, hoping to see the results of Nabil's efforts. I opened it a crack. Cold air seeped in.

Mama said, "Don't think you have a halo over your head. Snipers killed a grandmother hanging laundry—"

"I—"

"Listen to me! Allah gave you a chance. Don't believe you can stick your hand in the hornet's nest and—"

"I will pay Allah back!"

"That's good!" she responded, and walked toward the kitchen.

I appeased my mother with my outward gratefulness to Allah. She had no idea that I wanted to be Islam's ultimate warrior.

The power suddenly came on. At the sound of the stereo, Baba shut off his radio. Mama ran in and started the washing machine. She returned with the iron and ironing board.

"Those Christian bastards! They have their finger on the switch," Baba said.

Sharif's and Nabil's voices echoed through the elevator shaft. My heart fluttered. Mama and I went to the vestibule. She opened the door before the bell rang.

Sharif and Nabil carried a box each. Nabil shoved past me with one. He set it down on the floor.

"Where are your parents?" Mama asked Sharif while he stood inside the elevator.

Looking flustered, Sharif didn't seem to know whether to hand the box to me or Mama. Nabil squeezed by me and took it. As soon as Sharif's hands were freed up, I hugged him with my left arm, and we kissed.

"Why is your shoulder in a brace? Why do you have a cane?"

"What did you bring?" I asked.

"The biography books and the train! We are leaving to America this evening—"

"Haven't you heard?" Mama asked.

Sharif shook his head in confusion.

"Your friend, my hero, is a Black Saturday survivor."

Sharif's eyes widened. "Oh, my Allah! Thank Allah for your safety!" He backed away. "I-I have t-to go. My parents are waiting in the car."

When Sharif said that, I wanted to throw the train from the balcony. Loneliness took hold of me. I felt envious yet disgusted by their intent to flee.

"Enough of that! Let's go to the balcony and call your parents up." Mama tugged Sharif out of the elevator.

Not only did Mama entrap her invitees, she did whatever it took to close the deal. I walked behind her, Sharif, and Nabil.

"Can you believe it? Abu Sharif is leaving this evening?" Mama pulled the curtains up and slid the French door open.

"For good?" Baba asked, unmoved.

"Yes, sir! Emigrating!" Sharif said.

"Where in America?" I asked.

"New York."

From the balcony we saw smoke rise between empty buildings in the Sodeco intersection, a quarter mile north of us, and beyond. We leaned over the rail. Between explosions, Mama yelled, "Abu Sharif!"

Nabil and I observed while Sharif stood silently clasping the rail. Like him, I was resigned to Mama's steel-willed, ill-timed hospitality.

Um Sharif looked up from the passenger window and waved. Abu Sharif got out of the car. He shouted, "In sha'Allah, we have to pack! In Allah's name send—"

A whistle shrilled. Nabil ducked. Less than ten feet from where Abu Sharif stood, a mushroom-shaped cloud puffed gray-beige smoke. A deafening explosion instantly followed. Sharif and Mama squatted, clutching the rail. I jerked back to the wall. My ears rang. Windows shattered, and shrapnel rained on our balcony. Dust rose to our level.

"*Get inside now!*" Baba yelled. "May Allah curse them! We lost the windows!" His voice faded in and out.

Sharif and I went to the rail and looked down. The car had disappeared in the swirling dust. He wedged his face between the rods. "*Baba!*" he shrieked.

I stayed put, but my legs shook. Nabil crawled on his belly into the living room.

"*Sharif! Get back!*" Mama screamed.

"*Now!*" Baba yelled from inside.

I returned to the rail. Through the dense smoke, Abu Sharif's body lay face down and motionless. Sharif stood and looked down. Inside the car, Um Sharif's panicked screams bounced off the buildings. The passenger door opened slightly. Um Sharif must have struggled to get out.

"*Baba! Mama!*" Sharif turned around. His eyes darted all over the balcony as if to find a means to jump to the street. He returned to the rail and leaned farther out. "*Baba!*" he wailed for the duration of his breath.

Abu Sharif didn't twitch. A puddle of blood formed under him.

Another whistle tore through the air, followed by another thunderous explosion. More glass shattered. This time, people screamed from inside their flats. Baba dashed out to the balcony. He picked me up with one arm and Sharif with the other and hauled us into the living room. There he threw me in a chair and let Sharif go. Nabil had the Qur'an pressed to his chest. Baba ran out again. Sharif and I followed, but I stood in the doorway looking out. Baba crawled to the rails. He squeezed his cheek between two rods and peered down.

"Rami!" Nabil tugged my shirt. "Is Ammo Abu Sharif dead?"

I nodded. I feared a crack in my voice would prime my sobs and confirm Sharif's fears.

Sharif bolted outside. "*Baba! Mama!*" He shook the rail. Baba locked his wrists around Sharif's waist and tugged. Sharif braced harder. With one arm around Sharif's waist and a hand unhinging Sharif's fingers, Baba decoupled him from the rail. He carried him all the way to the foyer. We followed. Baba let him down.

"May Allah curse their fathers! Those Zionists! The *heretics*!" Spit flew through his dentures.

"Oh Merciful! Oh Merciful!" Mama sobbed.

A godly intervention requires earthly action. It is I who will answer his prayers.

Sharif ran out to the balcony again. I limped behind. Baba, Mama, and Nabil followed. We leaned over the rail. Abu Sharif's car had caught fire. Blue, orange, purple, and red flames blazed from the four windows. Thick black smoke billowed from the tires.

Sharif shook the rail and shrieked. The veins in his neck bulged.

The Christians had to have heard him. I shook violently, and my teeth chattered. Sharif looked like he was going to jump.

Baba pressed him down from the shoulders. "Pray for the prophet. Calm down, love," he pleaded.

"To the entrance! *Now!*" Mama screamed. "Let's go! Go! Go!"

I hid from Sharif in the bathroom. Mama demanded I return. I did. She held Sharif in her arms.

"Oh Merciful," she said while embracing and rocking him.

"Go get the rosary water!" she told Nabil.

I wished she'd asked me.

Suddenly Um Muhamad screamed from the stairway. "Hadharis! Get down! Take shelter! May Allah curse the Christians. Get down!"

The neighbors' footfalls, screams, and panicky calls for speed reverberated, echoing louder than the smaller-gauge shells as we took shelter. Abu Muhamad, Zaki, and the Palestinian tenant on the second floor ordered their wives to bring sheets, hookahs, cigarettes, and backgammon boards. Mothers called their children by name and demanded a response.

In the foyer, Mama took control. "Nabil, get blankets and pillows! Get up, Rami! Walk down very slowly! Hold on to the rail. You understand? Sharif, let's go, love! Sami, Ya'Allah! Ya'Allah! We are going to be down through the night. May Allah drape a shield over us!"

"You, go on!" Baba yelled. I looked into the dining room and saw him chewing a bite of hallum cheese. He reached for a green olive from the bowl on the table. "I will catch up."

We followed Mama down. I hobbled behind Sharif.

In the stairways each family took refuge on a landing from the third floor down. Having descended last, we settled above everyone else.

Mama sat between Sharif and Nabil at the landing on blankets she spread out. They leaned on the steel elevator door. The wind whistled through the threshold. She got up and tucked a towel to block the cold air.

Nabil regressed to infancy. When bombs exploded nearer, he clenched Mama's dress while she hugged and rocked Sharif. Sharif sobbed. Each time she wiped his tears, Mama prayed. I stayed put at the highest step between the third and fourth floors.

I wanted to look and not be seen. I padded the top step, but being above everyone only made me the most vulnerable.

The stairways were a wind tunnel. Unobstructed winter air blasted in through shattered windows. The stairs and concrete rail felt as if they ran on coils connected to a freezer. I sat on my hands to keep them warm until they grew numb from my weight. My cover slipped off whenever I moved. To shield myself from the frigid air and pin the sheet down, I made a tent by pressing my toes into the corners between the step and the bottom of the concrete rail.

I fought becoming sick from the foul smell of burning flesh and tires from Abu Sharif's car. The black smoke rose to us through the underground garage. I covered my nose with the sheet to filter as much as I could as the unmuffled sound of gunfire reverberated off the concrete walls.

Battles raged on. Weapons of various calibers were fired. Mortar shells detonated on the roof, in the streets, and in the alleyway. The more frequent and closer the explosions drew, the faster and louder we all prayed for the blood of the Christian children to run up to their parents' knees.

Zaki broke the pattern of prayers with a declaration. "This was deliberate!" he insisted. "Abu Sharif was targeted! Hit twice! It's not an accident. We are being watched. There are spies in the neighborhood."

"Pray for the prophet, Zaki!" Abu Muhamad impressed upon Zaki to let up.

Abu Muhamad asked Sharif, "Is ... ahem—I am sorry, was your father ... ahem ... the martyr, in any militia?"

I glanced at Sharif. He looked perplexed.

"Enough!" Mama said. "Leave him alone. Drink, love! Drink!" With shaking hands she pressed the glass of water to Sharif's lips.

Around midday, Baba came down. He stood atop the landing empowering himself with his landlord status. He wore his ragged maroon bathrobe tied around his waist with a blue nylon rope. To warm his feet, he wore my calf-high white sports socks and Mama's furry pink slippers. On one side his hair laid flat from sleeping. "May Allah have mercy on their souls!"

Sharif burst into tears. I crossed my arms and rocked back and forth in my spot. Nabil grabbed Mama's dress tighter in his fists. Zaki, Hajjeh, Abu Muhamad, Um Muhamad, and even the children recited the Fatiha chapter in respect. Toddlers rubbed their faces with their palms to signify completion. I did, too, in case Sharif noticed.

Mama consoled Sharif. "Allah says, '... though it is repugnant to you. But it may be that you dislike a thing while it is good for you... .'"

Instead of praying, I faced a new reality. Had it not been for me, none of this would have happened. I dreaded the moment when Sharif would realize that his parents had died to give me a farewell gift. The image of his face as he carried the box in the elevator car was transformed into the portrait of an orphan.

In the evening Zaki made an announcement. "The phones are dead! Not even static!" Just as he uttered the last word, we lost power again. Now cold and complete darkness enveloped us. Abu Muhamad, Mama, and Zaki scrambled to collect candles. Zaki asked that we do not flick the lighters, so that we could distinguish them from the flash of a bomb.

I prayed for bursts of wind to blow the candles out because I took refuge in darkness. I feared my eyes would meet Sharif's. Each time he shuddered, I turned away. I imagined begging for Sharif's forgiveness. I visualized putting my hand on his shoulder. Then I changed my mind. What if he lashed out at me?

I kept him in my peripheral vision. When Sharif declined incessant offers to eat or drink hot tea, so did I. When he succumbed to naps, I took mine. But the luxury of sleeping jolted my conscience. I daydreamed how I would execute Christians while shouting, "This is for Sharif!" I would pontificate in front of reporters and bring the Christian women to lick the bottom of my blood-soaked combat boots. My victims' survivors—their parents, relatives, and their townships—would be terrorized at the utterance of my nickname, the Annihilator.

Around dawn the next day, I was awakened by Abu Muhamad's panicked demand for silence.

The announcer on the radio said, "Lebanon is on fire! Explosions are heard at the Sodeco in the Ras El-Nabeh area. It is unclear how many are dead or injured. Battles are raging on various fronts. This morning the fighting moved to Tayouneh. Schools are closed indefinitely. Beirut International Airport is shut down. We ask all citizens to stay indoors. On the political front, elections will be canceled on orders from the Speaker of the House. A meeting held between Arafat and the Joint Forces leadership at—"

One by one we visited the bathrooms and returned to our places as the shelling and gun battles continued. Sharif broke down into sobs. Mama hugged him. He continued to decline invitations to eat, as did I. I wanted to be as compassionate as possible. More important, I wished to remain invisible.

In my uncontrolled thoughts, I attended my funeral. Mama wailed at the view of the hearse leaving the alleyway. She collapsed to her knees. My cousin Jamil would recite, "'This life of the present is nothing but temporary convenience: it is the Hereafter that is the home that will last.'" The men at the shoe stand would shout, "Allahu akbar." They would bury me hastily while reciting shorter chapters for an expedited service. The gravediggers would shovel dirt over me just like a dog would after defecating. Onlookers would say, "He died cheap, he died hiding, he was behind Sharif's parents' murder."

During the next two days, we alternated between the stairways and the underground depot, now both turned into shelters. Hajjeh urged us to pray on time to maximize our rewards with Allah. "While supplicating, ask for mercy on Abu Sharif's and Um Sharif's souls," she asked.

Abu Muhamad shouted, "All the men, perform ablution and meet on the second-floor landing. 'Praying in congregation is twenty-seven multiples more rewarding than praying alone.' Our master Muhamad—Allah prayed for and saluted him—said that."

Abu Muhamad had prepared a bucket of lukewarm water and put a ladle in it. I poured water in Baba's hands, and Nabil poured for me. We slipped our socks on, leaving Nabil by himself. Between prayers, almost all of us pressed a Qur'an to our chest. If I found myself dozing off, I opened the pages and read.

The sound of combat gear traveled up from the alleyway as fighters ran through it to their positions. By night I slept like a frightened child, and by day, my body was rigid with tension fantasizing about my might during combat. For two nights I fought my eyelids to stay open, determined to avoid being startled by sudden explosions.

Agonizing over a stealth attack by the Phalangists, I took comfort in the sound of gun battles. At least I knew our forces were engaged. Should the dominant sound of weapons change to M16s, or boots pound louder, or Muslim fighters call for retreat, then I would brace for my slaughter, for I would know the Phalangists were near.

On the second night, Abu Muhamad silenced us, once again, with a call to listen to a radio broadcast.

"... since yesterday morning, the Phalange, Tigers, and other Christian militias massacred over fifteen hundred Muslims in the Karantina and Maslakh areas near the seaport."

The women gasped.

"That's about a mile from here!" Abu Muhamad said.

"*Shh!*" Zaki demanded. "Turn the volume up, Abu Muhamad! In Allah's name, louder!"

"... the Lebanese army commander, Sakel Hown, placed the last Palestinian camp, Tal El-Za'atar, under siege. Meanwhile, battles rage in Nabaa and Dikwaneh—"

"May Allah shield us!"

"Nabaa, Dikwaneh, and Tal El-Za'atar are in the Christian territory," Zaki said. "Pray for the prophet, Abu Muhamad."

Our Palestinian neighbors, Kifah, Manal, and their two sons—Riyad, fifteen years old, and Basel, eleven years old—looked frightened.

"*Shh!*" Baba demanded silence.

It was noon on January 20, 1976. The radio announcer described the retaliation for the Maslakh and Karantina massacres days before. "Damour fell. We captured the heretics. Five-hundred civilians fled by sea. The number of casualties is still unknown, but speculation is we executed over one-thousand Christians. Kamil Shamoun fled by sea—"

"Allahu akbar!" Kifah was jubilant.

Damour was a seaside village about twelve miles south of our home. I wanted to be with the PLO and Joint Forces to teach the Christian dogs a lesson as someone whose demand for retaliation was authentic, not just as someone ordered to kill.

"*Shh!*" Zaki demanded.

"... the Tigers and Phalangists, Allah's enemies, were executed upon capture ..."

Zaki switched the station to find the Christians' coverage of the retaliation.

The Christian announcer continued, "... the savages lined up Christian children, women, and the elderly against walls and executed them. Young women have been raped and babies shot at close range. Over one thousand bodies lay in the streets. Hundreds more are missing. The barbarians dug up coffins and robbed the dead. Vaults were opened, and bodies and skeletons thrown across the graveyard. Muslims residing in Christian-dominated areas fled to Muslim-held areas—"

"May Allah bring victory to our men and stream the blood of the *heretics* to the sea!" Hajjeh called out a prayer.

We all breathed along, "Amen!"

Sharif stayed silent.

On the fourth day, rounds fired got louder and closer.

Gun battles intensified. The sound of shell casings bouncing off the concrete and cars in the alleyway punctuated the clamor.

"It will be over shortly," Baba said.

In the middle of a hail of gunfire, a man screamed, "Allahu akbar!" A short whistle. A loud explosion. Shattering glass.

"That's a rocket-propelled grenade!" shouted Kifah. Inside the building, echoes of the blast reverberated from landing to landing.

I exhaled a breath I wasn't aware I had held. Women gasped, and children trembled. Sharif didn't flinch.

The blast of the rocket startled me into a new cardiac rhythm. What is next? I wondered. The proximity of the launch and explosion meant the Phalangists were close. Had the time come to get up and fight?

Zaki shouted, "Quiet, everybody! Arafat!"

"... rise and carry on with our cause against the Jews and America, the big Satan, and their agents in Lebanon. I ask my Palestinian heroes in the camps to fight until the last child. We are not surrounded. We lured them. *It is a revolution until victory.*"

We all prayed, "May Allah award Arafat victory against the Zionists and the Christians."

Arafat continued, "We will not be defeated. Rise, my fellow Arabs! My Lebanese Muslim brothers! Rise! The Arab leaders aren't, so you must!"

Each time Arafat gave a speech, I gritted my teeth and clenched my jaw. I yearned to have an AK-47, dress up in fatigues, cargo pants, wear the front-facing magazines vest, hang grenades from a belt, and be respected. Kids would rush to me and adults would consult me for updates. When I die, a poster of *me* will be plastered in the streets. And under my picture: "Think not of those who have been slain in the cause of Allah as dead. Nay, they are living in the presence of their Lord, and are granted gifts from Him."

Abu Muhamad turned up the radio.

"The Phalangists, Tigers, and other militias massacred the Shias and citizens of the Dikwaneh and Nabaa areas. Over eight-hundred believers met their Maker in those areas. The forces of Satan joined the Lebanese army in Tal El-Za'atar and tightened up the siege on our brothers the Palestinians."

That afternoon, battles simmered. Now only muffled explosions could be heard.

"I am leaving." Sharif stood up.

Oh, my Allah!

How could he? Where would he go? Suddenly nothing in the world mattered. It came down to my last moments with Sharif. Maybe I should tell him that I will avenge his parents and kill as many Christians as I can.

Mama yielded to Sharif. As if an invisible shield surrounded him, everyone quietly cleared his path. Abu Muhamad wrapped the hookah hose around the stem. Kifah and Zaki put out their cigarettes. Kids retreated to their mother's side. Pillows were drawn closer, popcorn kettles, pita bundles, used napkins, empty coffee cups, and purses were pushed into corners to clear Sharif's way.

An orphaned man walking! All the males—Zaki, Abu Muhamad, and their sons—stood up and shook his hand. I hustled behind Sharif and Mama. Baba remained at his throne on the top landing overlooking his courtiers.

We climbed down to the entrance of the building.

"Sharif!" I said.

He didn't turn, or maybe he didn't hear me.

"Sh-Sharif!" I called again, a little louder.

He turned. Our eyes met. Tears rolled down my cheeks.

"I-I am ... I am—"

Sharif hugged me. "It is not your fault!"

"Yes! Yes, it is!" I burst out crying.

"Stop, love! Stop!" Mama pulled me by the shoulders and went out to the stoop, from which she scanned the alleyway. Six militiamen huddled outside the entrance to the building. Sharif walked to the end of the alleyway.

"Stop! Where do you think you are going?" a militiaman yelled.

Sharif knelt before the skeleton of the car and wept. The rims sat low, surrounded by hundreds of black metal loops. The gold car was now black, windowless. The seats were just metal frames and the steering wheel a thin circle of steel. A hundred rounds had pierced its body.

Inside, Um Sharif's body must have melted below the window level.

The militiaman turned to Mama. "How many of you are up there?"

"Four families."

"Who are the martyrs?" he asked.

"His parents!" Mama pointed at Sharif, now up on his feet and wiping his cheeks.

"Be patient! We will get these bastards. We will get 'em," the fighter assured Sharif.

Mama recoiled from the vulgar exchange.

The man recited from the Qur'an. "'If Allah helps you, none shall overcome you.'"

Sharif walked behind the car.

"You can't cross!" a bearded militiaman said. "We lost two men on the corniche today. Snipers pop up like roaches. They shoot and run to another hole."

"Get me out of here!" Sharif demanded.

"Not now!"

Sharif wiped his tears, shouted, "Allahu akbar!" and sprinted across the road.

Around him bullets grazed the asphalt. Small dust clouds puffed. He dove head-first behind shrubs in the median. The militiamen shouted, "Go, champ!"

When Sharif lodged himself in the median, his heroism ignited the militiamen.

"Run when we open fire!" the leader called to Sharif.

They ran to the middle of our side of the corniche and opened fire in the direction of the snipers. Sharif got up and raced to safety. A gun battle ensued, but Sharif was long gone.

CHAPTER 8

THE HOLY DOME
MARCH, 1976

Three weeks after Sharif left, I got tired of being a weakling while Mama obsessed over my injuries. I took off my shoulder brace and bandages and retired the cane.

After two more months of continuous bombardment, we learned to adjust to the routine of attacks and escalation. When higher-caliber rockets were fired, we knew they flew over to reach farther targets. We felt safer then and when we heard boots on the ground in the alleyway; our fighters were about. Amid unpredictable lulls, a boy roamed through the alleyways, calling out the various headlines of newspapers for sale. Zaki, a crossword puzzle fanatic, bought a paper whenever he heard the calls.

I got my turn to read after Abu Muhamad and Baba. Pictures in the papers depicted the Phalangists and the former president Shamoun's militia, the Tigers, resting their boots on dead Shia children and women. These images were imprinted in my memory in the same frame as Black Saturday. They fueled my desire for revenge.

Our fighters turned the two mosques, close to our neighborhood, into hideouts. The comforting sound of calls to prayer, now echoed from minarets deeper inside Beirut. The radio announcers dubbed the Muslim side of Beirut "West Beirut," and the Christian side "East

Beirut"-where electricity was more often available. With each call, I reconnected with Allah on new terms. I memorized scripture relevant to fighting until death.

To fulfill my new calling to uphold Islam, I herded the boys in the building together for congregational prayers five times a day. Riyad and Basel, Kifah's sons; Muhamad and Yehya, Abu Muhamad's sons (except for Wafik, a toddler); and Nabil all gathered behind me. In essence I was the children's imam. I administered ablutions and lined them up in Abu Muhamad's living room. Nabil assisted me. When I said "Allahu akbar" softly, Nabil repeated it louder. Parents thanked me for leading the children on the path to salvation. The attention I received made me look forward to the calls to prayer. Consequently, I even extended my responsibilities to include Qur'an-reading sessions.

On one dark night while we hid in the stairway and the sound of rockets echoed from some place farther away, Baba called my name.

"Get up," he said. "Let us go to the roof and watch the action!"

Sparks flew from Zaki's, Abu Muhamad's, and Kifah's eyes. "Ya'Allah!" Zaki said. "May Allah curse the backgammon, hookahs, and radio. Let's go!"

"Get up!" I nudged Nabil.

"Pray for the prophet! Sit down, Sami!" Mama begged.

"Go prepare hot tea," he told her.

Nabil and I followed the men to the roof.

We stood behind the steel rods that protruded from short concrete columns and watched Lebanon burn. I held on to a rusty rod almost poking my chest and looked out.

We observed the sound, color, and shape of war. Shells whistled overhead toward distant targets. While Nabil covered his ears, the rest of us traced the rockets' trajectory in the sky. Flashes! Explosions! The rod in my hand vibrated. Then came shells spewing red, glowing shrapnel.

"Glory to Allah," Baba said, as he marveled at the view. "It is like someone dropped a large charcoal from the sky."

"May Allah be with our warriors against the enemies of Islam," Abu Muhamad said in a solemn tone.

"Amen!" Kifah and Zaki said.

"I'm scared," Nabil blurted.

Abu Muhamad snapped, "Fear only the Almighty! No one else."

Nabil dropped his head, thoroughly chastised.

"Around us, but not on us! Glory to Allah." Baba's words rang poetically. "May Allah protect our property from the heretics," he said invoking prayers to cast a divine shield around our building.

I recalled the times, before the war, when Baba slowed down his car on the other side of the corniche. He and Grandmother recited short prayers, blew their breaths, and waved their hands, casting a shield-blessing on it. Irritated drivers blew their horns behind us.

On the roof, Baba tapped my shoulder and pointed north. "Look! Look, there! That is the Sodeco intersection. It is now a battlefield against the Phalangists."

He turned me around and pointed to my side. "That's the Museum-Barbeer Bridge passage. Another battlefield—"

"May Allah curse the Americans and the Zionists," Abu Muhamad prayed.

"The dumb Christians are fighting Israel's war against us," Zaki said.

Baba said, "It is in the book that we are surrounded by explosions and battlefields but *not* under siege. *That* is divine intervention." He turned to Nabil and me. "You'll see how, when you win your parents' blessings Allah takes notice." He raised his arms. "Thank you, Allah! May Allah have mercy on your soul, Mama!" Then he looked down at Nabil. "Allah said, '... Show kindness to parents.'"

I recalled the repulsive sight of Baba and Grandmother in the small, pink-porcelain bathroom as I paced in the hallway, waiting my turn.

Mama mocked me. "I hope one day you will take care of us, too!"

In the bathroom Baba pleaded to Grandmother, "Please give me your blessings."

Speech impaired, after her stroke, Grandmother could only stutter sounds like a goat. *Ba-a-a-h ba-a-a-a-h ...*

"Thank you, Mama. *Thank* you," Baba said satisfied that he, indeed, fulfilled his duties toward Allah showing kindness to his mother.

Now, on the roof, I observed the flashes in the mountains and counted the few seconds the sound took to rattle our building. I leaned forward to see Nabil on Baba's other side. He stared out and looked angry, as if he, too, was eager to be in on the action.

"Nabil and I should join and fight the heretics," I said.

"Never!" Baba puffed from his nostrils and shook his head. "Only the illiterate dropouts fight."

"But you always pray for them and—" Nabil began.

"Shut up! The eggshells are still on your feathers." Baba turned on me. "We are Sunnis! Not thugs! I own a building."

Baba had repeatedly elevated us, Sunnis, to a higher social standing. He had framed Shias as farmers, Druze as mountaineers, and Christians as identity-confused French wannabees. That night he spared the Palestinians simply because Kifah was present. When not praying for them, he had called the Palestinians "savages." The French speaking classy Christians were the savages. He didn't see them in action. I did. I doubted his wisdom.

I walked up to the ledge, in the open. "There is one and only one God, and Muhamad is his prophet," I said in the tone of wise old men. "The heretics' blood is halal!"

A nearby flash. A loud explosion. Red lines formed from hot shrapnel.

"Let's get back!" Baba said.

Zaki, Abu Muhamad, and Kifah hadn't said anything during the exchange with Baba, but now Kifah embraced me and whispered, "You are a hero. You do what you have to do! Allah depends upon brave men like you! May Allah shield you!"

Kifah's gesture catapulted my sense of empowerment to another level. I needed him to be the catalyst for my determination to avenge Islam. We walked down the stairs to wait out more battles.

For weeks the Phalangists held their ground in the hotel and market districts. The carnage was dubbed "The Battle of the Holiday Inn." We took shelter in the stairways only when bombing spilled over into our area.

During the third week of March and from under our building, the Palestinian commando units, along with the communist, Druze, Sunni, Shia, Sae'eka, and smaller militias, mounted a decisive attack on the Phalangists' and Tigers' stronghold in the Holiday Inn high-rise hotel. Defected Lebanese Army soldiers brought in armored vehicles. While they lined up, a commander ordered the removal of Abu Sharif's car.

Mama and the women in the building shouted prayers while they sprinkled rice from the lower balconies. The PLO fighters waved victory signs.

I stood next to Mama and felt useless. Inside, I was boiling quietly with barely contained rage. I belonged downstairs in a tank or in a Jeep or on foot. The fighters didn't realize that they were missing the ultimate warrior, me.

After a few days in battle, the Phalange and Tigers militias collapsed. The radio and newspapers carried the news: some jumped from the hotel's high balconies to avoid the wrath of the PLO fighters. Eventually we pushed back the Tigers and Phalangists to Martyrs Square. From that point forward, both sides of Beirut came to terms with a demarcation line that split the city.

Our corniche split Beirut into west and east sectors. It earned the name the "Green Line" after shrubs, weeds, and plants grew from cracks in the asphalt, sidewalks, and walls. The green line ran from the Sodeco intersection, directly under our building, to the Museum-Barbeer Bridge crossing. The radio announcers and the newspapers made it official, referring to our neighborhood, Ras El-Nabeh, as the "Combat Zone." The market and hotel districts in downtown became the "Dead Zone." The no man's land stretched from the Sodeco intersection to the seaport.

Weeks later, street dogs made the green line, combat zone, and dead zone their new habitat. On quieter nights, the mongrels barked, roved in packs and fed on human carcasses.

Trying in vain to fall asleep again, vivid images of Ahmad, Um Sharif waving from the passenger window, Abu Sharif's motionless body in a pool of blood, Sharif dashing out to the other side of the corniche, and the massacres in Maslakh and Karantina camps tortured me.

Baba had had it with the popping of plastic sheets he used to re-
place windows shattered by explosions. They bulged in and sucked
out from wind gusts that chilled the floors. He made a decision: "We
will take Tony's flat!"

"But—"

"Enough, Woman!" he shouted to Mama. "This is not up to you!"

We broke into Tony's flat on the third floor. It was devoid of the
Islamic art and the prayer beads that hung from almost every door-
knob in the penthouse. Instead crosses hung over beds, and a portrait
of our Mother Mary holding baby Jesus sat under a lamp in a corner
of the dining room. Baba ordered the removal of all the religious
symbols. Nabil and I obliged with a vengeance.

Audette and Tony had created their own paradise in the three-
bedroom flat. Tony hung ceiling fans, and electric heaters sat in each
room. I mined the flat for books. Tony collected volumes of nonfic-
tion and fiction, which he displayed in the tiny living room on a wall-
to-wall bookshelf. I felt awkward touching them. Mama said that
Tony and Audette would approve of me reading.

"Just don't open drawers," she told me.

"May they burn in hell! This is a spoil of war."

Unlike our bedroom in the penthouse, I felt safer with layers of
concrete over my head. Protecting Tony's possessions or invading his

privacy was irrelevant.

In the new residence, Nabil and I proclaimed our independence. We each took our own bedroom. Subsequently we developed new habits. He committed to memorizing the Qur'an. He faced the balcony door and moved his lips silently while tracing his index finger across the words. Perhaps he thought his words would waft up to Allah unobstructed by concrete. As for me, I went into my new room to read novels.

The room felt like a dungeon in contrast to how the sun warmed and lighted the interior of the penthouse. After touring Nabil's bedroom, I realized that I indeed inhabited the most neglected space in Tony's flat. A useless light bulb dangled from a wire in the center of the ceiling. Condensation formed on the four concrete walls' glossy beige paint. Baba had six-millimeter glass panels installed on the metal frame of our balcony doors. With time I realized that Tony neglected to seal the door frames in this apartment. Cold air swept in, making the room chilly at night, but my reading distracted me.

The books that Sharif gave me sat in a tote by my bedside. Powered by a sense of guilt, I picked up the only novel from his box, *Les Miserables*. Once I started it, I couldn't stop. I read during meals and while walking to the stairway or to the underground depot. Once, Nabil had to remind me of prayers, and I asked him to lead the congregation. Each encounter between Jean Valjean and Javert anesthetized my fears and smothered my frustration for not contributing to Islam. The feeling of committing a sin for reading a novel, not the Qur'an, inflicted guilt on me. Regardless, I continued. I finished *Les Miserables* and moved on to the biographies.

Hajjeh was right, I realized. Music, novels, dancing, and other earthly pleasures do hijack the mind. But Thomas Edison, Helen Keller, Leonardo Da Vinci, and Christopher Columbus changed the world positively. How could learning about them be wrong?

For weeks I read round the clock. I entered the warp of the world of the imagination. Chapter numbers became the enumerations by which I measured hours.

Gandhi's biography, still unappealing, sat on my bedside table. An Indian hero! Oxymoronic! Indians were inferior to us Arabs. "Don't kick them too hard to get them off you. You might hurt your foot," one of my uncles once said.

I relied on Nabil to remind me of prayer times. He kept me obedient to Allah. When the boys and I congregated to pray, Nabil claimed the imam role. I was happy for him.

My dedication to reading irritated Mama. She barged into my room to feed or save me. At times when the shelling intensified, she peeled the book from my hands and hustled me to the stairway. When she asked what I would like to eat, I chose the least messy option, spring-water tuna wrapped in a pita, to avoid having to wash my hands from oily foods or risk staining the pages. I once went to get a drink while Um Muhamad visited. Mama said, "Look at you. You are a caveman. Wash up, in Allah's name!"

"Enough! Ayda! At least he is home and safe," Um Muhamad said.

Mama sighed. "*Wa'Allah*-in Allah's name, you are right. I will take books over guns any day." Mama swore by Allah in agreement. Husam visited in spite of the danger. He played backgammon with Baba and mingled with Mama and Um Muhamad in the kitchen, the one place Baba allowed cigarette smoking, while hookahs were permissible everywhere. Husam knocked on my door and sat by my side. "Glory to Allah, you are destined for success. I can tell."

Baba happened to walk by on the way to the bathroom. He snorted at Husam's remark.

"I will bring you Muhamad's books," Husam said, committing his son's collection to me. "He doesn't need them since he went away."

Muhamad had left for Saudi Arabia after graduating with honors from the American University.

"The only worthy book he reads is our master Muhamad's biography— Allah prayed for and saluted him," Nabil shouted from the living room.

I found Nabil's comment unsettling. Slowly and somewhere along the way, I felt no guilt for finding pleasure outside the Qur'an ... until I saw Beethoven's biography. It reminded me of Sharif. Painfully it evoked my aspiration for vengeance for him. I returned to reality.

On one warm, unusually quiet Friday afternoon, Baba stood up, lifted his pants to his belly-button, and said, "Let us go to the mosque."

At that declaration, Nabil and I bookmarked and closed our texts. We performed ablution at home. To make it safely along the corniche to the mosque, we took a route now familiar to the combat-zone residents. We snaked through two vacant lots—turned landfills—ducked to enter through a hole in a concrete wall, and trotted behind a screen that blocked the snipers' line of vision.

In the mosque, we listened to the passionate sermon then prayed. After shaking hands with those adjacent to us and exchanging wishes for Allah to accept our supplications, I noticed Othman.

Something looked odd: men of all ages stood in line to shake the grocer's hand, not the cleric's. I tapped Baba to direct his attention to it. He shrugged. I figured Baba wanted to be invited for the privilege. After all, *he* owned the Hadhari Tower.

We returned home, where Mama's cooking scented the apartment. Baba slid the glass-top coffee table toward the end of the sofa, bringing one corner closer to his head, where he lay down. He placed his most cherished possession, his transistor radio, upright on the table and then settled in for his pre-lunch nap.

Mama stayed in the kitchen, where she had been preparing lunch since early that morning. We waited for her to call us to the table.

Instead we heard people shouting from the corniche.

"Please! *Please!* May Allah protect you and grant you longevity and good health. *Please!* We are not with them! We never fired a round!"

Mama, always one to calculate the risks before we hurried to the view of the moment, hurtled out of the kitchen and through the family room. One pink slipper flew off her left foot. She bumped the coffee table and swung the cast-iron balcony door open. She braced herself on the rail and quickly looked down. She turned toward the Sodeco intersection to the right.

"A man with a gun is aiming at two others. Rami! Nabil! Where are you?"

"Here, Mama," Nabil and I replied in unison.

I rolled my eyes. "You just passed us."

Baba turned to me. "She knows where you are. Her job is to kill me. She wants me to think you are in front of that muzzle. Diabetes, blood pressure, or maybe a stroke. Yes, a stroke. That is what she wants me to suffer. This way, when she sees me urinate in my pants, she will feel superior. Damn woman!"

"What is Othman doing with those young men?" Mama asked while looking down.

Baba stepped into his slippers. "Move!" He pushed her aside in spite of the wide span on the balcony.

Nabil eagerly poked his head between their shoulders. I walked to the far end of the balcony, closest to the scene, to discern the exchange.

About two hundred yards from our building, Othman aimed a machine gun at two young men. They stood in front of a sand-colored wall facing him and us. He gestured with his gun, and the two got down on their knees. They were both crying.

"I think he captured a couple of Phalangists!" I was jubilant.

Othman fired three rounds from his pistol into the sky. That got the attention of the few remaining combat-zone residents. Onlookers stepped onto their west-facing balconies. There must have been around twenty of us in all.

Some men wore undershirts and boxer shorts. One man held his hookah in one hand and the hose in the other. Some robed women looked frightened, while others appeared eager to watch the commotion unfold.

The longer Othman lingered, the more eyeballs were fixed on him. He gestured again, and the men stood up. When they did, he opened fire. Smoke puffed from his weapon. Loud pops echoed. Bullets that passed through the men or missed them formed small dust clouds on the wall behind them. The men crumpled to the ground. One landed face-down, head bouncing off the pavement. The other sank to his knees first and then collapsed, seemingly deflated under his weight. He twitched before lying motionless like his partner. Othman walked behind his car and unloaded the entire magazine into the bodies.

The spectators came alive.

Mama gasped. "Oh Merciful! Oh Muhamad! Why? *Why?*" She cupped her mouth.

Othman shouted, "Takbeerat!"

Onlookers punched the air in excitement. "Allahu akbar!" We, too, shouted, fulfilling his request to chant. "Allahu akbar! Allahu akbar!"

Othman strode to the body on his right—a compliant Sunni, he always started with the right side. He arranged the men's bodies as if they were crucified and then fired a round in each man's head. Finally he turned the corpses so their feet pointed toward the back of his car.

He lit a cigarette, took a long drag, and then went to the trunk of his car and retrieved a rope. He squatted at the heretics' feet, brought their legs together, and fastened their ankles. He stood. With the other end of the rope, he tethered the corpses to the trailer hitch on the back of his car.

Othman looked up and waved to the spectators.

"He is sermonizing," Mama said resentful.

"Get inside. *Now!*" Baba demanded of her. She didn't move. Nabil fixed his eyes on Othman.

Othman took another drag off his cigarette and ducked into the car. He inched it forward. The bodies turned from the feet and aligned with the back of the car. Their heads bounced on the asphalt. In a few yards, he stopped the car and got out. He wiggled the rope, which was now in a straight line stretching from the men's ankles to the hitch. He inspected the line, I guessed to secure the tow. The bodies dragged thirty feet behind the car. Their arms stretched behind them as they skidded from side to side. From the balconies, most women showered Othman with prayers and rice.

When the car approached our building, I saw that the infidels' shirts had been reduced to collars in the front and shreds on their backs. Their trousers rose to their thighs.

"May Allah give you strength and might!" Baba shouted to the man who had been but our grocer.

"Amen," I said. Nabil looked entranced.

Othman noticed us. Baba vigorously waved. Othman ignored him. I waved. Othman smiled up at me. When his car passed our balcony, Baba spat at the bodies from the third floor. He missed. A wide and discontinuous swath of blood connected their execution spot to the Barbeer Bridge underpass.

"May Allah forgive us and have mercy on their souls," Mama said, teary. She blanketed the men's survivors with prayers ranging from their mothers, sisters, fathers, and wives to their children.

"Have you lost your mind?" Baba scolded her. "Mercy is *forbidden* on the heretics, Woman. You know better! The Qur'an says, 'Those who disbelieve and die while they are disbelievers, on them shall be the curse of Allah and of angels and of men all together.' Your father was a Qur'an scholar! How did you turn out this way?"

"Those boys had mothers!" she said with a crack in her voice.

"How about Abu Sharif and Um Sharif? Ha? How about the thousands in Karantina and Maslakh?"

She ignored him and returned to the kitchen. We followed Baba inside. Nabil and I sat across from him in the family room.

"Women are weak. They have no place in this world. You know, our master Muhamad— Allah prayed for and saluted him—was granted a peek into hell during Israa and Meraj. Guess what he saw?"

Baba referred to that single night when Muhamad was flown on a mythological steed from Mecca to Jerusalem, where he ascended a ladder to heaven. We all knew the answer to what he had seen in hell, but Mama yelled a diversion. "Heretics!"

"*Women!*" he said loudly. "They bring disgrace to their men and families. They believe anything a man tells them to have his way with them." He yelled in the direction of the kitchen, "The devil possesses all of you to tempt man into sin." He raised his voice higher. "Wake up! The Christians rape our women and kill our children. These heretics are weak only when they are on the other side of a muzzle. Our fighters should flatten them with tanks and stomp them with their boots."

"Allah does not approve of this," Mama retorted. "This can't be right. May Allah break the Phalangists' and Tigers' hands for killing Muslims."

Baba sputtered in disbelief. "It is like I am talking to myself. She is a wall."

"What if those two men never fired even a slingshot?" she said. "What if—"

"All of them are heretics ... the polytheists, nonbelievers, idolaters—that's their guilt. 'O who believe! Fight such of the disbelievers as are near to you and let them find hardness in you, and know that Allah is with the righteous.' The only way to stop the cross-worshippers is to annihilate them. We will make Lebanon their graveyard. Let's see if their French friends will help them now!"

"May Allah kill all the Phalangists and Tigers," Mama said. That was her way conceding, if only to quiet him.

"They want Lebanon all for themselves. They have fifty-four seats in the Parliament, and we have forty-five. But *we* are the majority," Baba told her. "They want to copy the Jews and form a Christian state in the middle of the Muslim world. They take the important ministries and leave us with the worthless offices. Tourism and Education! Are you out of your mind?" He worked himself up in spite of her attempts at a truce. "They keep the Treasury, State, Foreign Policy, and Defense ministries. Our *politicians* should be shot, while we're at it. You can buy one with a whore or a car. In powerful or worthless ministries, the doers are the Christians. They pave roads in their townships with *our* money. Look at Junieh in East Beirut. Pretty, isn't it? But go to the south suburb ... it is floating on sewage."

Baba referred to the area where Shias dwelled, cut off from government services.

"That's enough!" Mama pleaded.

"They speak French when we're around. They should go to goddamned France if they love it so much! Have you seen their women in churches? They go sleeveless and in short skirts. How are men supposed to focus on respecting Allah? *How*? We go to mosques humble before Allah, Glorious is He and He is Exalted. We sit on the ground, not on fancy benches. Places of worship are for introspection, not networking!" He yelled louder, "Are you listening?"

Mama didn't answer.

He lowered his voice and looked at Nabil and me. "Ach! Why do I bother? She doesn't get it."

"I get it, I get it! I know!" Nabil said.

"You don't remember when cleric Subhi Saleh finished the Ramadan sermon on TV. Do you?" he shouted toward the kitchen. "They ran a commercial that started with a toilet flush right after he said, 'Truth of Allah Almighty!' They made mockery of Islam and of us."

Outside, shots were fired.

"Oh Merciful!" Mama shouted from the kitchen.

"Othman has a heart of steel," Baba said. "He is a hero! That is what Allah wants."

"Othman killed those heretics on his own," I said. "He needs to be helped."

"Nobody deserves this," Mama said from the kitchen.

Here we go again!

Baba shouted, "They deserved worse."

"Enough! Othman is a pimp for doing this. Do you want Rami and Nabil to die? To die on the hands of a pimp like him?"

Othman was the first man I heard my mother call a pimp. She had never called anyone a bad name before.

"Why don't you ask your son! Just ask him what *he* was guilty of that Saturday."

"Their actions must not dictate ours. We shall not turn ourselves into them, into monsters," Mama said.

Mama is naïve, I thought. I pitied women and their frail minds and bodies.

When Baba said, "ask your son," I aspired to be the monster Mama dreaded. Only a holy warrior could defeat the savages. Baba inflamed my ambition to fight even more. I turned to Nabil. "Let's go pray!"

"But we just prayed—"

"*Istikharah.*"

I sought a sign from Allah by performing the consultation prayer, just like the prophet did. Baba didn't get it, but Nabil did.

CHAPTER 10

JESUS IS A PROPHET
AUGUST – SEPTEMBER 1976

Almost every Friday Othman nabbed Christian men from somewhere—word had it from the Museum-Barbeer Bridge crossing—and
executed them on the corniche. Weeks later and during the first week
of August, explosions and battles continued to rock the neighborhood. Always we rushed to the stairways and huddled next to the
neighbors who got there first.

Once, I sat on a landing with our Palestinian neighbors, Kifah, his
wife, Manal, and their children, in spite of my father's attempts to
deter me from befriending them.

The Christian radio announcer terrified Kifah and his family:
"The Syrian army has joined forces with the Phalangists, Tigers,
Guardians of the Cedars, the Lebanese Youth Movement, and Al-
Tanzim. Intensified bombing campaigns are under way to root out
the Palestinians."

"May Allah curse the Syrians!" Kifah leaned forward on his chair
and yelled at the radio.

"Pray for the prophet, Kifah!" Abu Muhamad, a Syrian, pleaded.

"Sit down, love!" Manal told her husband.

Kifah pointed at the radio. "The ... the Syrians are fighting alongside the Christians. We are not safe anywhere."

"Pray for the prophet! No one will harm you while we are around. Besides, Assad won't allow Arafat to be a power player in his front yard. That's all," Zaki said referring to Hafez El-Assad, the Syrian president.

"Riyad! Basel!" he said to his sons. "We will join Sae'eka, *period.*"

I had no doubt Kifah would carry through with his plan. He would join the Syrian militia in West Beirut, where the Syrians fought alongside the Palestinians and Muslims. With a Syrian militia, he would be untouchable by the Syrians, Palestinians, and most certainly the fragmented Muslim militias, which now numbered at least six.

A week later, Tal El-Za'atar fell into the hands of the Syrian and Christian forces. Local newspapers reported that two thousand Palestinians had been executed and thrown into mass graves. The Christian territories became Muslim free. That night, just after midnight, someone rattled the entrance door to our building and screamed over the sound of explosions, "Hadhari, *open up!*"

Baba beamed at recognizing Othman's voice. "May peace be upon you!" he yelled, welcoming Othman cheerfully from the third-floor landing. He hustled down two steps at a time over our neighbors and their pillows while gripping the rail to keep his balance.

A few minutes later, Baba returned with Othman, who held a special AK-47, the type with a folding butt and pistol grip. He wore a vest with four pouches stuffed with more magazines, and hand grenades showed through the mesh fabric on side pockets. The thigh pockets of his cargo pants bulged. He looked powerful and glamorous.

Baba shooed away the kids, demanded that Abu Muhamad move, and ordered Mama to prepare hot tea expeditiously. She mumbled *pimp* within my earshot as she entered the flat.

Othman squatted with his back to the elevator door.

"In Allah's name! Sit in my chair! Right here! I won't allow other-wise. I insist!" Baba slid his plastic stool under Othman.

"Please! At ease! No need. All of you, please!" Othman grunted as he sat. "I am fatigued from all the fighting." He leaned the AK-47 on the etched glass panel of the elevator door.

Abu Muhamad, Zaki, and Kifah with his two sons hunkered down in a semicircle in front of Othman. Nabil, Muhamad, and the rest of the kids sat behind them, on the floor and stairs. Um Mu-hamad and Manal welcomed the opportunity to turn away from Hajjeh. I sat behind and above the others on the stairs. I hardwired my ears to every word my hero would say.

"In honor of our martyrs, let us read 'Al-Fatiha!'" Othman requested. We recited the chapter.

"Here!" He took out a magazine and popped out one bullet after another, handing every kid a shiny cartridge. "The enemy wants us all dead!"

"The Jews?" Muhamad innocently asked.

Othman grinned, exuding wisdom. "The Christians, love! What is your name?"

"Muhamad, sir!"

"The noblest of all names!" He turned to Abu Muhamad. "May Allah keep him safe and sound for you."

"May Allah keep you around us!" Abu Muhamad said.

Othman continued, "The heretics are raping our women and kill-ing children before their parents' eyes."

Hajjeh leaned forward. "'Grieve not, for Allah is with us. Then Allah sent down his peace on him, and strengthened him with hosts which you did not see ... and it is the word of Allah alone which is supreme.'"

Each time Hajjeh intoned a verse I didn't know, I felt inferior and more fearful of standing before Allah on Judgment Day. My fear stemmed from my conviction that winning heaven after natural, accidental, or unholy death was unattainable. I lived in sin, unlike how Allah asked. I cursed. Cute girls aroused me, and sometimes I skipped prayers or recited them fast to get them over with. I disobeyed Mama and at times studied the holy Qur'an without understanding what I read. "And anyone who has done an atom's weight of evil, shall see it." Allah almighty could keep track of atoms, so I knew I was bound for hell.

Nabil's voice brought me back. "Mr. Othman, do you feel an invisible force in battle? Like more power than you thought you had?" He was totally mesmerized.

Othman smiled with a subtle thrust in his neck. "Of course! Allah surrounds us with his blessings and angels."

"Have you killed Phalangists in battle?" Nabil drew nearer to Othman, nearly touching his leg now.

I climbed down and shoved myself between Kifah's sons. I pinned my eyes on Othman.

The hero took a deep breath. "It was a moonless night. I took four of my men to penetrate deeper into the graveyard."

"Allahu akbar!" Abu Muhamad said, bemused.

Othman continued, "I asked my men to wear sneakers instead of boots. We walked only on tiled graves. You know, to avoid crackling leaves and twigs. Then we heard voices. The pigs were laughing. Very carefully and slowly we searched for them. Lo and behold, the monsters had dug out a grave and turned it into a bunker."

"And you buried them in it," Baba said.

Othman held up a hand for Baba to slow down. "Pray for the prophet."

Baba mumbled, "May Allah pray for our master Muhamad."

Othman's dark eyes swept his transfixed audience. "We listened for as long as we were unnoticed."

"Brilliant! Brilliant!" Zaki said.

"They played card games. Every other word was an insult to our master Muhamad—Allah prayed for and saluted him—and Islam. May Allah turn them into the fuel of hell. They laughed and toasted each other with alcoholic beverages."

"May Allah curse the enemy and their prophets," Kifah said.

"Ask for forgiveness right now! Pray for the prophets," Hajjeh ordered Kifah. "I seek refuge with Gracious Allah! One can't swear at Jesus or Mary. Jesus is a prophet from Allah. It is in the Qur'an."

Everyone knew that, including Kifah. But he didn't even pretend to repent.

Zaki violently flicked a match and lit a cigarette.

"May Allah curse Jesus, Moses, and all non-Muslims. Are you happy now? Leave the man alone, Woman!"

"Pray for the prophet," Othman directed.

We obliged with prayer.

"Right when they finished their poker game ..." he shifted to recite a verse. "'We rained upon them stones of clay.' We dropped one grenade after the other and opened fire."

"You, the hero!" Hajjeh jubilated.

"Allahu akbar!"

"Allahu akbar!"

I felt goose bumps. Mama scowled.

"How many did you kill, Mr. Othman?" Nabil asked.

"In the bunker, twelve! In all, thirty. My goal is to reach thirty eight, as I have committed to my brother's spirit—one for each year of Farook's life. After that, it will be what Allah wills."

"Allahu akbar!" Abu Muhamad said.

Othman slapped his thighs, stood up, and strapped the AK-47 onto his shoulder. After a few emphatic rounds of appeals for him to stay, Baba and Kifah gave up. Baba saw him out. I leaned over the railing to watch.

At the bottom step, Othman stopped. He pulled gold chains from the pocket of his cargo pants. "These belonged to Elias, Murad, Joseph ... Should I go on?" He grinned.

"May Allah grant you strength to fight on his behalf," Hajjeh shouted.

Othman's work was divine in contrast to Hajjeh's. Like the clerics in mosques, she only paid lip service to Islam. Othman's firepower connected prayers with reality. He executed Allah's will on earth, here and now. Eradicating the heretics was the ultimate calling of honorable believers.

I felt a sudden onset of readiness. My calling would be on Othman's terms. Mrs. Saykali, my Arabic teacher, and Islamic studies instructor would take pride in me when they learned about my new role. Most importantly, Allah would be proud when I executed heretics or was martyred in his name. The gates of heaven would open wide.

As soon as Baba returned from the entrance, I stood up and said, "Nabil and I should join Othman."

Nabil's face glowed.

"Sit down! This war is for brave men." Baba dismissed me.

You no longer matter, I thought, glaring at him. You are irrelevant! Allah is my guide!

CHAPTER 11

BE A BRAVE MUSLIM

Nabil and I planned a rebellion. He and I would join Othman and leave everyone oblivious of our noble aspirations. We bonded around the secrecy of our mission. Mama remained highly engrossed in her sanctuary, the kitchen, while Baba busied himself with radio broadcasts, backgammon, and political debates with the neighbors.

Othman had become a legend. Zaki once told us that Othman was now dubbed "The Holy Vigilante." In his quest to avenge his brother's martyrdom, he rose to fame and prosperity. His name traveled deep into West Beirut.

Relatives of victims of almost all massacres sought to bestow blessings on him and express their support, and mothers offered their surviving sons to join in the holy retributions. People transacted business with him to flaunt needless purchases to their friends. Zaki said that when he bought from Othman, he felt as if he satisfied a pillar of Islam, tithing. Othman embodied heavenly rewards on earth. He became the gatekeeper for the ultimate redemption. Those who sinned sought him out for absolution.

Othman approached achieving the goal of avenging his brother. According to the tally marks he used to track the inventory, he needed to kill only six more Christians to fulfill his pledge.

Just before noon that Friday, I went to the kitchen and made

Mama a rare offer. "Do you need something from the grocery store?"

She cast a comical glance at Um Muhamad to verify she had heard me correctly. "No ..."

I returned to the living room and shook my head at Nabil. It would have been a perfect excuse to leave without explaining where we were really headed.

Baba, Zaki, and Abu Muhamad engaged in their usual heated discussions. Zaki boasted insight in identifying Israeli operatives in the Parliament and ministries. He proposed to sentence the Speaker of the House to be hung from the testicles in the Tarik El-Jadidah soccer field. Baba suggested that he ought to be doused with gasoline and set ablaze.

Abu Muhamad proudly named Western converts to Islam. "Jacques Cousteau! You know? The diving guy? ... The instant he surfaced from a dive in the Mediterranean, he shouted, 'Allahu akbar,' then the *shahadatayn.*" Abu Muhamad referred to an invocation upon which a non-Muslim automatically enters Islam by saying, there is no god but Allah, and Muhamad is the messenger of Allah.

"Allahu akbar!" Baba and Zaki simultaneously said.

Abu Muhamad continued, "Who wouldn't? The Atlantic and Mediterranean waters did not mix. Just like Allah declared in the Qur'an."

"Rami!" Mama shouted from the kitchen. "Go buy pita. Whether the sniper is firing or not, duck under the sand barrels. Rub your shoulder with the walls and sandbags. Are you listening? Don't be a hero."

"Yes! Yes!" I said, downplaying my elation.

"Don't go in the open."

"I got it," I shouted.

My brother beamed.

"Let's go!" I said to him within Mama's earshot.

He tied his shoes in a flash and waited outside the flat.

In the stairway, I whispered, "Othman's store first."

He nodded, eyes bright.

Just before Nabil and I reached our destination, we saw men huddled outside Othman's grocery and the shop next door. We slowly approached. I peeked into Othman's store. I didn't see him. We continued a few more steps and peered into the shop next door—once a lingerie boutique owned by a Christian. Young and elderly men, all armed, congregated or leaned against the walls.

"There he is!" Nabil tilted his head in Othman's direction. "Let's go."

Deep inside, Othman sat behind a wooden desk, looking magisterial. He talked with two bearded young men seated opposite him. It was then that I comprehended the full extent of Othman's stature in the neighborhood.

"Rami!" he shouted.

He remembers my name! I floated. I glanced at Nabil and grinned.

"Come in, love! Come in, *champ!*" Othman said.

The men turned. Those outside nodded as if to encourage me to comply.

"Honor us in," one of the bearded young men said.

Those two must have been in the graveyard ambush, I thought. Othman had called me a hero. I am like them! In the store the fighters cleared my path.

My Allah! I hope Baba does not have an open balance. That would be embarrassing!

I stopped before Othman. An assortment of jewelry—necklaces with crucifix pendants and watches—covered the desktop. Drivers' licenses and car titles were spread out to his right.

He stood up and shook my hand. His was callused, thick.

"Please, sit!" He turned to my brother. "Welcome! Nabil!" Othman turned to me. "What do you drink, love?"

"Nothing. Thank you," I said.

"Turn around, love," Othman said.

I did.

"My Muslim brothers!" he said, attracting the attention of the men. "This young man saw my brother defy the pigs. He witnessed the martyr Farook's last moments. Tell them what the martyr, may Allah have mercy on his soul, did before his martyrdom."

Everyone mumbled condolences, then the room fell silent. For a second I stuttered as the armed men pinned their eyes on me.

"Th-the martyr puffed his chest and pounded it with his fist." I made a fist and hammered my chest. "He looked Bashir Gemayel in the eyes and said, 'You are a donkey and son of a donkey. We will go after every Gemayel worldwide.' Then he said, 'Bashir, you are a pimp son of a pimp!'" I wrinkled my face, angry at the recollection.

"Allahu akbar!" The men's necks bulged.

"But that's not all," I said.

"Oh Merciful!" someone encouraged.

I explained my strategy for acting dead, the rapes, executions, and Ahmad's last words.

"After Bashir shot the Palestinians first, he said, 'This is what happens to the barbarians.' Then his squad opened fire."

"Allahu akbar!" the men shouted.

I finished my tale with Othman's bolting from my hospital room. When I stopped, I laid my eyes on Nabil. I craved instant feedback.

Nabil sat spellbound. He had never heard the story.

Men prayed aloud for Farook's soul and my survival. Nabil took pride in my recognition. He smiled.

"'... When the help of Allah comes, there will be victory ...,'" Othman said.

"Cease-fire agreements!" an elderly man scoffed.

"We won't rest until we finish them off," a man shouted.

"Allahu akbar! Allahu akbar!" they chanted.

The elderly man said, "Arafat and these so-called leaders ... Huh! They have no idea. We are a force from Allah!"

"Takbeerat!" a young bearded man responded.

"Allahu akbar!" we all shouted three times. Some pumped their fists in the air.

"They can shove cease-fire treaties up their asses. No one invited Othman to the table. But you know what! Y-you know what! We answer only to Allah!"

"Takbeerat!" one shouted. We obliged.

Othman stood, walked around the desk, and embraced me.

"*You* don't belong in the stairways! Come out and visit with me," he said.

"He will," Nabil said on my behalf.

Outside the store, I felt light. My legs moved on their own.

"He likes you!" Nabil said.

"Did you see that? He stood up for *me*! He shooed the warriors for us!"

Nabil and I crouched and, walking under the barrels to avoid the sniper, made it to the bakery. We returned to the flat with two bundles of pita. Neither Baba nor Mama seemed to notice our delay.

The visit with Othman sparked my repressed ambitions and holy aspirations. Soon my time would come.

On the morning of the last Friday in September 1976, I went to the kitchen. There Nabil and Baba sat quietly sipping tea at the table. I joined them. I glanced at my brother, and he smiled. I never looked at Nabil with an eye for observation, but I noticed that his features had changed. Hair covered his face below his sideburns and widened at the jawbones. A fuzzy mustache shaded his upper lip. He leaned in to reach the hummus with a folded pita piece, exactly like Baba did. He cleared his throat with the same pitch as well.

After tea, Nabil winked at me as if we had joined a secret society, and the wink encrypted our mission. Then he glanced toward the front door. I got up. He followed. Baba reverted to his routine. He lay on the sofa, balanced the radio on his ear, and closed his eyes. Mama received Um Muhamad. They yapped and smoked, oblivious to the world.

"Let's go!" Nabil whispered.

"Where?"

"Friday prayers!"

"Right! Of course!"

"Othman first."

"Right!"

I went to the sink to perform ablution. In the mirror, I looked exactly like Nabil. I had grown whiskers down to my lower jaw-line too. The hair on my left side was flattened from the pillow. At fourteen and fifteen years old, Nabil and I readied to envelop our neighborhood, if not all of West Beirut, with a holy shield invoked by our deeds.

"Ya'Allah! Ya'Allah!" Nabil shouted outside the bathroom. I hustled out, and we left.

Nabil walked in front of me to Othman's store. Outside, he shook hands with most and elbowed the others. All grinned. I stood at arm's length from him, and he didn't miss a chance to flaunt me as his treasured guest.

I smiled, feeling powerful but uncomfortable while Nabil conversed with those gathered on the sidewalk as if they were friends. Two bearded men ushered me inside and directed me to sit in Othman's chair behind the desk. Nabil was at their heels.

Othman himself entered the store with an AK-47 strapped on his shoulder. I quickly stood up. He flashed a rare smile as if his prayers had been answered. "Welcome! Welcome, hero!" Then he shook Nabil's hand. My brother beamed.

"In sha'Allah today you will earn your largest rewards with Allah!" Othman said to me. He slung his arm around my shoulders and guided me outside. "Let us go pray."

We walked to his red Fiat. "Hold this." Othman handed me the AK-47.

I felt electrified.

"Sit next to me."

"Which mosque?" I asked.

Othman adjusted the rearview mirror. "Today you will enter His kingdom with earthly vouchers." He winked in the mirror.

We drove to the Upper Basta Mosque three blocks away, west of the green line. Life had resumed unaffected by the snipers, the battles, or the daily shelling. Motorcycles whizzed by, taxi drivers honked, and merchants hosed down the dusty pavement.

Upon entering the mosque, men, discouraged in Islam to bow even to our master Muhamad, bent forward mumbling prayers. They cleared a path for Othman just like the Red Sea parting for Moses. Some even shouted, "Allahu akbar."

Nabil and I followed Othman to the altar, the most prestigious spot in the mosque. He asked me to lean his AK-47 in the corner, between the altar and the base of the cleric's pulpit.

The cleric climbed the steps to the pulpit and turned around.

Oh! My Allah! Jamil!

"Jamil is the cleric?" I whispered in Nabil's ear.

"And Othman's right hand!" Nabil said, chuckling. "Welcome back from the clouds."

It took me a few minutes to fuse Jamil into my new percepts. His turban and long beard helped. Our cousin shouted and enticed, motivating us to support our forces—and one in particular among us, Professor Othman.

At the end of the second part of the sermon, Jamil prayed in a solemn tone. He raised his hands, prompting the congregation to follow suit.

"I thank Allah for the blessing he bestowed upon us, and I ask for forgiveness. There is no god but Allah, and Muhamad is his messenger. O, Allah pray for Muhamad and his nation, and Abraham and his nation. In your creations you are knowledgeable and merciful. *Allah Humma!* O, Allah! Unite Muslims."

"Amen!" we said.

"Allah Humma! Strengthen our faith in you, solidify our cause, and raise our flag of Islam!"

"Amen!"

"Bestow upon us the privilege of becoming those who guide humanity!"

"Amen!"

"O, Allah! You awarded us existence, bejewel us with better conduct."

"Amen!"

"Allah Humma, don't punish us for what the fools in Islam have done!"

"Amen!"

"Allah Humma, award us your fruits of mercy, love, and honor!"

"Amen!"

"Allah Humma, grant us wisdom to refute the devil and his attempts to rob us from faith in you!"

"Amen!"

"Allah Humma, improve our health, wealth, and our earthly lives!"

"Ya Allah!"

"Allah Humma, bestow on us victorious battles against your enemies!"

"Amen!"

"Allah Humma, flood the blood of the children of Christians and

Jews up to their knees, wherever they are!"

"Ya Allah!"

"Allah Humma, shield our holy warriors!"

"Amen!"

"Grant them expansive space in your heaven!"

"Amen!"

"Put them in the company of our master Muhamad!"

"Amen!"

"I say this, and I ask Allah for forgiveness!" Jamil dropped his hands. He looked beatific. We wiped our face with our palms.

"Start the prayer!" As he stepped down from the platform, Jamil prompted a man to chant the call to line up for prayers.

Jamil had risen to the ranks of people I admired. People change, but Jamil? He had ascended to the glorious ranks in Allah's kingdom. I felt inebriated.

After the optional Sunnah prayers, Jamil turned around and flashed me a wide smile. He seemed pleased by my presence. I walked up and kissed him on the cheeks. He greeted me with a subtle gesture of an exorcism with a hand on my head—just like Hajjeh did to expel the holy ghosts—and a whispered prayer.

"You want to be a cleric?" he joked, pulling on my whiskers.

"Maybe," I said.

Nabil and I stood on Othman's right side. Jamil stood to his left. Men crowded to surround us, awaiting their turn to shake Othman's hand. When Othman decided that those before him looked unworthy, he asked me to retrieve the AK-47. We strode to the shoe rack. Jamil still glowed with a wide smile.

Outside the mosque, veiled women showered us with prayers and rice. I smiled and hugged Nabil. For the first time ever, Nabil wrapped his arm around my waist. We went down the stairs. I love my brother, I thought.

"May Allah shield you from his enemies!" a woman screamed.

Men from inside the mosque hustled to put on their shoes so they could salute Othman. Some shouted, "Amen," while hopping on one leg.

We climbed into Othman's car and sped off. Boys chased after us and men hailed us in our wake. We turned at the Basta police station and rolled down from the Upper Basta Mosque to the corniche.

During the short ride, I scanned the area for dust from bombs and listened for the sound of gunshots and explosions. I heard neither.

We turned right on the corniche and drove past our building.

"Where now?" I asked.

Suddenly Othman's features hardened. "You'll see."

I welcomed the diversion. Mama served lunch two hours after the Friday noon call to prayer, so we had ninety minutes to spare. Riding with Othman in West Beirut resembled parading among fans. We drove to the Barbeer Bridge. He took the ramp, and right after we cleared the bridge, he drove uphill and through an opening in a concrete wall. We turned around over the gravel and weeds and headed back to the opening. The front end of his red Fiat emerged like a tongue, ready to snare the catch of the day.

We got out of the car, following Othman's lead. He went to the trunk, opened it, and tossed an AK-47 at me.

"Let's go."

Visions of holy glory suddenly indulged my senses. I knew exactly what would come next. Our mission would be to capture and execute Christians crossing from East Beirut.

I summoned every memory of my anguish: the nightmares, the bus driver, the older man in a kufa, the screaming girls, and hundreds of Muslims and Palestinian refugees, Farook, Ahmad's terrified father; Ahmad trying to wake him up, wetting my pants, Abu Sharif's body in a pool of blood, Um Sharif's charred remains, and Sharif the orphan. I clenched the AK-47, Allah's earthly tool for doing his work. I was ready!

Othman leaned on the driver's door and faced east. He offered me and Nabil cigarettes. I declined. Nabil pulled one out. Othman lit Nabil's, then his own.

"When did you start smoking?" I asked.

"While you were in the clouds reading." He punched me lightly on the shoulder. "Let's kill Allah's enemies today."

"Pray for the prophet," Othman said.

Nabil and I responded, "May Allah pray for our master Muhamad."

Othman continued, "There is a cease-fire agreement. Glory to Allah! The agreements are working in our favor. Christians will cross today. In sha'Allah, we will find two in one car and finish early."

"In sha'Allah!" Nabil said.

Othman and Nabil flicked their cigarettes. I looked up. Like a mirage, an approaching car's rooftop shimmered on the asphalt. Othman reached into his Fiat and retrieved the AK-47.

A white BMW 323 came in full view. Just as it cleared the bridge, Othman trotted to the middle of the road. Nabil pulled out a nickel-plated handgun and shoved it in his belt behind his back and followed Othman. I needed a second to come to terms with the image of Nabil armed. Nabil glanced at me behind him. He flung his hand. "Come on!"

Othman fired three rounds in the air. Then he aimed at the passengers. The driver slammed on the brakes, and he and his passenger ducked. The car came to a stop just in front of Othman. He walked around it. Nabil approached from the passenger side. He cocked his handgun and aimed at the men. Othman reached in and took the keys out of the ignition. "Identification!" Othman shouted.

The men scrambled and handed Othman their ID cards.

He leaned inside the car and yanked off their necklaces.

Crime: Christians. Verdict: Guilty. Sentence: Public execution.

Othman had said, "Today you will enter His kingdom with

earthly vouchers."

I recalled the smiles and unprecedented respect the men at the store and Jamil paid to me. Now I understood—Nabil had delivered me to Othman. In turn Othman would administer the ceremonial rites, which would unfold by our building.

Today I shall avenge Sharif.

"Get out," Othman ordered, enraged in spite of their cooperation. "Walk. May Allah curse your mothers and your kind worldwide!" He slammed their backsides with the butt of the weapon. "Put your hands behind your neck!"

I savored their submission to our might. The Phalangists had done the same to me—on Black Saturday. The prospect of payback was invigorating.

"There! If they move, kill them." Othman pointed at the two men.

I clutched the butt of my weapon to my right shoulder and aimed.

"What did we do?" one asked, his voice cracking.

"Shut up!" Nabil shouted.

They complied.

"You, Christian donkeys! Get in the car!" Othman shouted.

Tears streamed down their cheeks.

"Please don't! We haven't done anything. We go to the university. Mr. Adwan, the Parliament member, knows our parents. We go to medical school."

"Adwan the sellout! Shut up!" Othman ordered the younger of the two to sit in the front passenger seat. "Get in."

"Wait until we move," Othman told Nabil.

Nabil hadn't learned how to drive, I knew. But he started Othman's car, rolled it behind us, and waited, the engine idling. Nabil has done this before! I figured that all the time I had spent reading, he camped with Othman, where he learned to smoke, drive, and most likely fire a handgun.

Othman, the older Christian, and I crowded at the driver's door. "You!" Othman slapped the older Christian on the neck. "Drive."

In a softer tone, Othman said to me, "We sit in the back! Ya'Allah!" He turned to the driver, "If you run, I will unload forty rounds in your ass."

Othman and I got in the back and the driver took his seat. Othman threw the car keys on the dashboard.

"Drive!" He barked.

"Where?" the driver asked.

"Go! Ya'Allah! I will tell you." Othman's eyes were bloodshot.

"M-may Allah grant you longevity!" the passenger said, his voice shrill trying to sound like a Muslim. "May Allah—"

Othman whipped his hand around and slapped the driver on the mouth.

"Go!" he said to the infidel.

The pig on the passenger side burst into tears. He knew what he had coming to him. The driver remained quiet.

Our journey would end at the spot where Othman had executed the first two I had seen collapse. In the short half-mile ride, I envisioned how retribution would progress, and I visualized glory and redemption. They would wail from the wrath of Muslims and beg for their lives just like others had done before them.

I recalled the ticket-taker on the public bus. "We are going by the seaside," he had said. I felt my breaths shorten and teeth grind. I wanted to lean forward and strangle them before we got there.

Three minutes later the glare from the sun on the untraveled road made the heat and brightness unbearable. I squinted. Othman nudged me hard as if to keep me awake.

"Pull over!" he shouted at the driver.

The boy took extra care, slowing down, a pitiful attempt to score points with Othman.

"Now! Stop!" Othman ordered, getting angrier with each demand.

"May Allah curse your Jesus!"

The driver stopped the car. On the far left, Nabil rolled Othman's car to a stop and parked.

"Get on the sidewalk, heretics! One slight move, and I will turn you into blood faucets." The Christians opened the doors in slow motion, got out, and waited. Othman and I followed. He handed me his AK-47. "Give me yours! This one is on automatic." He pointed to the lever on the right-hand side and took a few steps back.

I glanced at Nabil. He frowned and nodded as if to approve my next actions. Retribution finally near.

"Turn around," I shouted. "To the wall. Hands behind your neck!"

Othman wrapped an arm around my shoulders. "Today you will earn your highest reward with Allah!"

"May Allah grant you longevity!" one of the heretics said. "Please! Listen—"

"Shut up!" I shouted. My mind raced to what would come next. I would take Nabil's handgun and pop them in the head at close range after they drop dead.

"This ought to teach you, pigs, to never ever attack Muslims," I shouted.

Othman approached me. "Look around! People are getting restless. Shoot."

I pressed the butt of the AK-47 tight on my right shoulder. I tilted my head. My left thumb blocked my line of vision between the rear and front sights as I held the front handguard. I repositioned my hand under the wooden lower handguard and leveled the muzzle. I closed my left eye, squinted through the right, and clutched the weapon. Exhilarating! I wanted the moment to last. The sight of them sobbing energized me. The more they looked terrified, the taller I stood.

I aligned the rear and front sights. My left cheek twitched. Maybe

I took too long. The AK-47 got too heavy to hold still. I lowered it.

Othman blew out an impatient sigh. I savored the moment, however. I changed my target and aimed at the eldest.

The younger, shaking uncontrollably, broke into convulsions and collapsed. The older boy stood gaping.

No tears? Brave? Defiant? I'll show you.

"On your knees. Now!" I ordered him.

"Mama has only my brother and me," the older one said as his young brother sobbed. "Please kill me! Let my brother go."

"W-we love Muslims," the younger wailed.

"We saved Muslims in Der El-Qamar. We live around Muslims and Druze. We hurt no one. We are not affiliated with the Phalange or Tigers—"

"Ya'Allah! Come on!" Othman shouted at me. "Stop torturing them! End it! *Now!*"

I felt as if my heart dropped to my groin and finger turned into a twig.

"We love Muslims and Druze," the elder brother said.

"We are studying medicine to heal people with Allah's help," the younger brother sobbed.

Suddenly my world was reduced to the two young men and me. My right arm shook from the weight of the weapon.

There was no sound of war. No shots fired, no shells launched. My mother's words rumbled in my head: "These boys have mothers. This can't be right. What if these men never even fired a weapon? Do you want Rami and Nabil to die? To die on the hands of a pimp?"

Othman stomped over to me, furious. I lifted my weapon from the slight drop. "In Allah's name, shoot!"

I recited, "'If they fight you, then fight them: such is the requital for the disbelievers.'"

"The Allah I know does not approve this," Mama had told Baba.

My chin quivered uncontrollably. I squeezed my lips together.

The sentiments of sorrow came as a torrent. From the corner of my eye, I saw Othman light a cigarette and glare at me. He knew I couldn't pull the trigger, and he wasn't going to allow it.

I swung the weapon away from the Christians.

"Easy, love." Othman froze in place, fearing I would accidentally fire the weapon while my finger remained inside the trigger guard.

Nabil pulled his handgun and kept it low in our direction.

The two brothers released a sigh.

"Give it to me." Othman grabbed the weapon.

"No, I want to do it." I turned around, more determined than I had ever been.

Nabil shouted, "Shoot! May Allah curse the infidels! *Shoot!*"

The brothers' pleas intensified. "Please be merciful. Please!" They sobbed.

Merciful?

"In the name of Allah, the Gracious, the Merciful!" I squeezed my finger on the trigger but did not pull.

Merciful! Allah is merciful. Who am I to be one! What am I doing? I thought.

I lowered the weapon a little.

Othman was enraged. "*Fire*! Shout 'Allahu akbar' and fire!" He stabbed his finger at the boys. "Their brothers and cousins almost killed you. Shoot the cross-worshippers! Shoot for Farook! The time for retribution is now!"

I raised the AK-47 again.

"Be a *brave* Muslim," Othman shouted.

The simplest and most profound recollection of a narrative by our master Muhamad jolted me into sobriety: "A Muslim is one with whom people are safe from physical and verbal abuse."

I removed the AK-47 from my shoulder, fisted the magazine, and handed it upright to Othman. In a flash he transitioned from disappointment to disgust at my cowardice.

"Allahu akbar!" Nabil shouted.

Othman and I wheeled to see Nabil fire his handgun at the brothers. They held their arms up, but Nabil fired so fast that his weapon sounded like it was a machinegun. The men collapsed.

Othman gripped the muzzle of my AK-47 and yanked on it. I let go.

"Oh Merciful!" Mama screamed from the balcony three hundred yards away.

I glanced up. Baba forced Mama inside the flat as she wailed.

Othman called for takbeerat.

Onlookers shouted three times, successively louder. "Allahu akbar! Allahu akbar! *Allahu akbar!*" while Nabil glared at me.

Othman embraced Nabil. Together they marched to the bleeding bodies. Nabil kicked the boys in the head to see if there was any life left in them.

I squatted on the edge of the sidewalk. I rested my elbows on my legs and cupped my face. I had failed.

While Othman and Nabil pontificated and formed crosses with the men's arms and legs, I slipped into a new realization. Only the brave go to heaven. I had the weapon in my hand, but I failed Allah, our master Muhamad, Islam, and Othman.

I admired Othman and Nabil. They had a heart of steel to fight the enemy. The Christian bodies with which our neighborhood, bridges, and roundabouts were adorned spoke to my brother's and Othman's prowess and commitment to the cause.

I would never be like them or Khalid Ben Walid, who brought Islam to Lebanon; Antar Ben Shaddad, Prophet Muhamad's first-sung hero; or Salah Eddine Al-Ayyubi, who defeated the Crusaders in Jerusalem. I yearned to be Allah's warrior. I had my chance to add my name to the list, to start the journey, and to be noted in history. I sat at the frontier, where the gateway to heaven had opened wide, and I discovered that I was an imbecile and a weakling. When the moment to act arrived, I failed.

I looked up. Nabil appeared dignified, heroic. Othman patted him on the back and proclaimed, "I knew it! *You* are a brave warrior. You are Antar Ben Shaddad!"

Then he looked at me with barely concealed disgust. "Say Allah! It is your first time. I understand. You'll get used to it. You and I have more work to do."

He reached for my hand. "'... Fight them, that Allah may punish them at your hands, and humiliate them, and help you to victory over them ...' Here, redeem yourself." Othman threw a rope at my feet.

My skills as an enlisted Boy Scout with the Islamic Foundation well before the war now came in handy. I made a sheepshank knot on one end and a bowline knot at the other for the hitch. I tethered the dead men to the hitch. The line stretched long enough for the bodies not to slam the rear end of the car. Nabil stood astride and observed. I feared him.

"They are in hell. Allahu akbar!" I said submissively.

Nabil looked at me with disdain.

"Let's go bury these crusaders in the open!" Nabil swaggered to Othman's car. He looked as if he had grown new muscles under his armpits.

"Take their car to the store," Othman told Nabil.

"At your command!" he said.

"Ya'Allah!" Othman waved for me to ride with him.

Just a couple of yards into the takeoff, I felt a thump. Othman got out. I looked back. He clenched the rope from the center and wiggled it to ensure it was tight. He walked back to the car while looking around everywhere but at the car.

"Glory to Allah! Excellent knot!"

"Thank you."

Two teenage boys climbed the sidewalk and spat on the bodies as we drove away. Othman accelerated gently, as if not to bother the bodies.

"Are you going to drop me off?" I asked just before we reached the mouth of the alleyway by our building.

He bit his lips and took a deep breath. Then he stopped at the alleyway.

"May Allah be with you," I said, my hand on the door handle.

Othman shook his head, disappointed. "Give your father my regards."

I opted to walk around the front of the car, despite my humiliation under Othman's stare.

Upon entering the alleyway, I noticed Baba swiftly pull back into the building's entrance. I dreaded the celebration of my involvement with Othman. I was in no mood to be showered with prayers and rice. Baba would applaud and finally hug me with one arm and use the other to fend off the aggressive admirers. In my visualizations of glory after executing Christians, however, Mama would stand behind my fans, utterly disenchanted.

I picked up my pace. Behind me, Othman drove away. The hissing sound of the dragging corpses dampened my enthusiasm.

I unlocked the entrance door and climbed the five steps to the elevator entrance. Zaki and Baba emerged from the stairway. Baba grabbed the wicker cane, his ultimate beating weapon. I stood confused. I looked up higher. Um Muhamad and Mama occupied the higher steps and braced each other.

"You coward! You are an embarrassment to ..." The beating commenced. With every blow, he shouted, "How dare you embarrass me!"

Baba slapped me by swinging his hand from behind his shoulder, punched me by cocking his fist below his waist, and kicked me like Nabil did the heretics after they lay dead.

Zaki utilized his strange power of persuasion. "It's for your own good." He pinned my feet under his arm. Baba unlaced my shoes. His hands shook as he flung them and my socks aside.

The cane cut the air, and with each lash Baba alternated between, "May Allah humiliate you like you humiliated me" and "You are a disgrace."

Mama, who had once frantically intervened to save Nabil or me from Baba's wrath, stood silent. I was on my own. My opprobrium was public and punishable.

Between sobs I gasped for air and pleaded for Baba to stop.

I committed myself to give up the pursuit of holy vengeance, but all I could do was cry, "I was wrong. I am wrong. I will not do it again. Please stop."

"Get up! Get up! May Allah curse you!"

My throbbing feet were raw.

Baba heaved from the exertion. Zaki helped me, but I couldn't stand. I buckled, and Mama rushed forward, ducked under my arm, and lifted me up.

I accepted my punishment. I had earned it. I needed to suffer pain. Torture me! Burn me for what I did – or did not do. Perhaps the agony would nullify my guilt.

Um Muhamad and Hajjeh followed. Needlessly Hajjeh said, "Enough!"

"In Allah's name! Get him out of here," Baba said, disgusted.

On the way up to the flat, Mama said, "Why do you want to be like everyone else?"

Her words couldn't have been more accurate. I had come face-to-face with a sobering reality: I was not like everyone else, even when I tried my hardest.

CHAPTER 12

THE HOLY DUO
SEPTEMBER, 1976 – MAY, 1978

With time, Nabil rose in stature and believed he had triumphed. Neighbors and children cheered his arrival, while I inconspicuously celebrated his departure from home. I became invisible. Before the beating, he and I prayed together. Now I prayed alone. With nothing to do in between prayers—and to everyone's delight—I read the Qur'an on my own terms. Before, my reading was to complete a school assignment or find comfort from the holy spirits. Now I sought answers. I was on a quest to exonerate myself, to show my family that despite my cowardice, I was still devout.

One day I overhead Nabil tell Mama, "Don't guide who you love. Allah will." He explained how Allah inspired me to pursue knowledge in the Qur'an.

When I had difficulty understanding text and context, I cross-referenced verses and chapters with the *Safwat Attafasir*—the volumes of the *Purest Interpretations*. I had completed the recitations of the Qur'an and received a "Very Good" rating in school before the war broke out, but I hadn't known what I read or memorized. Now, in a few short weeks, I had acquired a new understanding—one that enraged me.

In a moment of reflection, Nabil, as he always did, barged into my room without knocking. He startled me.

"You make me proud," he said, happy that I sought enlightenment.

Who was he to judge me? "You and your kind disgrace me," I said, reacting to his inconsideration.

He gaped at me. "May Allah curse you! I want to choke you with my bare hands!"

"Get the hell out of my room!" I shouted.

He slammed the door. Mama inquired as to the source of Nabil's eruption. In the family room, I heard him call me a *heretic*. "I don't know how to be close to this *heretic*!" he shouted. "One day I will kill him!"

"Pray for the prophet! Calm down!"

Nabil stormed out of the flat.

Mama came into my room. "You ought to reach out to your brother. He looks up to you!"

His execution of the Christians horrified her. How could she not know that I no longer had any influence over him? Did she think I could somehow extinguish his rage and call back his innocence?

"Like most Muslims, he doesn't know Islam. Do you know that Judaism is closer to Islam than Christianity?" I asked her.

"If you don't tone it down, you and him are going to end up like your father and uncles."

"We believe in Allah and the holy prophet Moses, just like the Jews do. Therefore they are believers—"

"Have it your way."

"Some Christians believe Jesus is the son of Allah and he is the Lord. You see? The Jews are—"

Mama left closing the door behind her.

My relationship with Nabil continued to deteriorate, which improved his standing with Baba.

A few weeks later, I stumbled upon an opportunity to reclaim my status in the family. I found an undetonated rocket. I knew exactly what to do. I would disarm it and be a hero!

It started when Mama asked me to buy a dozen French rolls from Abu Maher at the pastry shop. At an intersection, militiamen alerted me to sniper fire. "We will get the pimp," one of them said. "Go this way!"

I entered a vacant lot. I let my eyes wander. To me, the green weeds reminded me of the American television show *Little House on the Prairie.* I indulged my senses. I touched the plants, making believe they were sunflowers and the jumbled-up dirt with unrecognizable green ground cover resembled a lush, manicured lawn. Suddenly I laid eyes on an undetonated rocket in a bed of weeds. I marveled at the sight. The dent below the head gave away the reason why it hadn't exploded. I picked it up and held it close to my chest. I returned home, praying no one would take it from me before I had the chance to disable it.

Neighborhood kids noticed my treasure. They ran circles around me until I stood the rocket upright atop a water-well concrete encasing in the alleyway. The tip of the rocket was chest high.

Muhamad and his brothers abandoned their soccer game when they saw the rocket. Yehya, Muhamad's younger brother, reached out to touch it. Muhamad shouted, "No!" Mama heard the commotion. She spied my prize from the kitchen window and blew out the loudest shriek I thought a human could possibly make. "Oh, my Allah! Take it back to where you got it!"

I never had the opportunity to disarm the bomb. When Nabil returned home that evening, Muhamad chased him into the stairways and broke the news. During dinner, Nabil elevated himself breaking the news to Baba, who put me down. "You are a fool ... a zero on the left in a numeral. Worthless!"

Mama sat silent. I retreated to my room, defenseless.

That evening someone knocked on the front door. At the sound of visitors, Nabil crossed his legs under him on the sofa and took the rosary, which was now a permanent part of his wardrobe.

At the doorway, Muhamad, now ten, and his two brothers— Yehya eight, and Wafik seven—hurtled past me, eager for Nabil. They froze before him, awaiting his acknowledgement.

Um Muhamad asked me, "How is Einstein?" And then she laughed.

"One moment!" I turned to the kitchen and called, "Mama, Um Muhamad is here!"

"Welcome! Welcome!" Mama took Um Muhamad's hand and walked to the kitchen. Behind her, Abu Muhamad obliged with an eye-contact-free greeting. "May peace be upon you!"

"May peace be upon you," I said.

"Move!" Baba shoved me aside and extended his arm to shake Abu Muhamad's hand.

Just as Abu Muhamad approached Nabil, my brother wiped his face with his palms, signaling closing of the Fatiha chapter.

Abu Muhamad ingratiated himself. "May Allah shield you!" he said to my brother. "May Allah shower you with blessings! May Allah sprinkle the earth with men like you!"

He walked with Baba to the balcony where they set up for a back-gammon match.

Despicable! I thought, and stopped listening.

Nabil tousled the eager boys' hair. They were ecstatic.

"Bring me the AK-47," Nabil asked Muhamad.

Muhamad's eyes sparkled with joy.

"I want you to disassemble it in twenty-five seconds. Can you do it, champ?" Nabil unclipped the magazine and cocked the weapon to clear a round from the chamber. "Yes! Yes! Yes! Mr. Nabil. Please watch me."

Nabil turned to Yehya and handed him the unloaded handgun. "Let's see if you can do this without hints today."

"I can do it. Watch me."

"Say In sha'Allah!"

"In sha'Allah!"

Nabil sat Wafik on his lap. "Here. I will show you how to do the first two steps."

I heard Abu Muhamad say to Baba, "May Allah shield Nabil. He is a real man!"

Nabil glanced at me in the moment I gazed at him with envy. He grinned, satisfied.

Days later in October, the Arab heads of state met in Riyadh, Saudi Arabia, to resolve the conflict. They formed the Arab Deterrent Force. Sudanese, Libyan, Saudi, and UAE soldiers totaled five-thousand soldiers. Syria sent thirty thousand.

The tanks rolled along the corniche to the Sodeco intersection. Light traffic resumed. The Druze, Sunnis, Shias, Christians, communists, and Palestinians submitted to the machinery and size of the Syrian army. Consequently, the Lebanese army set up offices in our area to assert their neutrality. Our corniche became less risky to travel, but intermittent sniper fire still echoed at some intersections.

Baba personally replaced all the windows in the penthouse and the kitchen window in our flat. While he worked, Nabil strode with Othman exploring the dead zone. Only the women, children, and I remained behind in the building.

Months later Abu Fares, a shop owner, returned to inspect his business after almost a three-year absence. He, like so many others in our neighborhood, had closed his shop after Black Saturday. One afternoon, I had just opened the entrance door when a bullet-riddled Mercedes with a roof rack driven by militiamen screeched into the alleyway.

Before I stepped inside the entrance, four armed men swung their doors open and rushed at me. Immediately I locked the door and faced them.

"Open the door," demanded a bearded militiaman who had come out of the passenger side, aiming his AK-47 at me.

I clutched the key in my fist.

"Open the door now, donkey!" Another cocked his handgun and leveled it at my face.

"What is your business?" I shouted back.

Show no fear! They will assume I am affiliated.

"We want the first floor." The driver marched in big strides toward me.

I threw the key in the entrance.

"Put him in the car. We'll teach the donkey a lesson," the fourth and shortest said, enraged.

"Can we talk about it for a minute?" I pleaded.

The other three swung their AK-47s around their shoulders. They squeezed my arms and tugged. I fought back. Each time they grabbed an arm or leg, I freed another. The fourth man charged at me and dazed me with a punch in the gut. I doubled over. They lifted me up and hustled me to the car. I gripped the car's luggage rack. They braced my ankles and started shoving me through the rear window. As loudly as I could, I screamed, "Mama!"

Mama and Um Muhamad wailed from their kitchen window.

Abu Fares came on the run. "He is just a boy," he implored them, his voice cracking. "He is powerless!"

I am a man!

They pounded my fists with the butts of their weapons on the rack.

"Let me go!" I kicked harder.

Now Mama, Hajjeh, Manal, and Um Muhamad wailed louder. Suddenly a high screech sounded from the corniche.

The militiamen turned to the sound. So did I. Six Lebanese army soldiers hopped from an open-top Jeep. They cocked their M16s and aimed at the militiamen. "Lower your weapons. *Now!*" the captain with three stars on his epaulettes demanded. His soldiers knelt and aimed carefully in our direction.

"*Now!*" the captain shouted.

My would-be kidnappers let me go. They took aim at the soldiers. I climbed out the car window. My legs wobbled. I grabbed the luggage rack to steady myself, not trusting my footing.

Mama shouted from the kitchen window, "We are on the same team. May Allah protect you! Lower your weapons—"

"I said lower your weapons. *Now!*" the captain repeated louder.

"We have no business with you!" the short militiaman called out. "Do you know who I am?"

"I said *now!*" The captain gestured with his M16.

"We will annihilate you and your army if you fire one round!"

Um Muhamad shouted prayers from the fourth floor while Abu Fares intensified his pleas. The volley of requests to lower weapons continued and the threats of retribution escalated. Behind me the entrance door rattled. One militiaman turned around.

"Love!" Mama darted toward us, her hijab around the neck.

She stood in the center of the muzzle circle. "Lower your guns. We are on the same team. Come on, love. Let us not do this. In Allah's name!" She spun around, making eye contact with everyone.

"They go first," the militia leader demanded.

"Make tea, Hajjeh!" Mama shouted into the sky. She wrapped her fingers around the barrel of the leader's AK-47 and lowered it. "Ya'Allah, love! Let us not lose handsome men like you."

Mama approached the angriest, her tone motherly and actions appeasing, as if tending to a crying baby. "'... tough on the nonbelievers and merciful amongst each other.' That's what our master Muhamad —Allah prayed for and saluted him— said. Come on, love! Put it down! In Allah's name!"

The militiamen reluctantly lowered their weapons.

I let go of the rack. Mama ducked under to keep me steady on my feet. She knew my legs were trembling.

"This is not over," the leader threatened, pointing at me.

Another militiaman behind him said, "Oh, my Allah! These are the Hadharis! Look. Look!" He pointed at the sign behind us. ALLAH IS THE LANDLORD. HADHARI TOWER. He stood as frightened as if he stared at the devil. "These people ripped their dead mother's shroud, searching for cash at the Bachoura Graveyard—"

I shouted, "That's not what happened."

"Let's go!" the leader said, looking eager to hear more from his comrades.

The Mercedes' tires screeched once again as the militiamen sped away in a swirl of dust.

The captain approached. "What happened here?"

"They wanted to take over the first floor," I said, shaken.

"Brave man! You give him the flat, then they will take the entire building. Get him some water! He is pale!" He patted my back and signaled his men back into their Jeep.

"Ya'Allah, love!" Mama said as she wrapped her arm around my waist with a gentle lift.

The captain had just called me brave.

In the entrance, Muhamad tugged my torn shirt. "Nabil would have poked out their eyes with his bayonet!" he jeered.

Um Muhamad grinned.

Mama attended to a cut on my chin and mumbled curses at the militias and the politicians.

I played down my heroism. I knew Mama would sing my praises for my courage fending off the intruders to protect the building. After evening prayers, she gave Baba a glowing account of the incident.

"You said, 'He screamed Mama'?" Baba asked, tugging at his earlobe. He turned to me and said, "You are a disgrace."

"Are you kidding? May Allah curse this hour! I almost got kidnapped! *Killed*!" I shouted.

When Nabil came home that night, Baba quickly summoned him to the sofa. "If they think he is all we've got," he said, tilting head toward me, "they will eat our heads and spit the teeth over our bodies."

He used an idiom to coerce Nabil to act. "Look, love! You are the round in my gun."

Nabil sat taller. "Whoever it is, they will not harm this building."

"What if they come back to hurt *me*?" I said.

Baba and Nabil shook their heads, short of spitting in disgust.

We sat around the glass-top coffee table, now our dinner table, with Nabil on Baba's right hand while Mama and I sat on stools.

Nabil gave me an order. "We will go to the mosque after this!"

"No!" I said in defiance.

He clucked. "You are going to hell."

"Donkey!"

"Fire will consume you. That's your destination."

"Why you ... you dumb pimp!" I stood up and prepared to slug him.

Nabil, now taller than I, got up and took a boxing stance.

"Enough!" Baba shouted. "Sit!" he commanded me.

"I am going to crush your bones," I said louder.

"*Now!*" Baba shouted.

"I will wipe the toilet with this hat," and I reached for Nabil's *kippah*-hat.

He clasped my wrist. Nabil had gotten stronger. I pretended to cooperate, to disguise my inability to free my hand.

"To your room now, donkey!" Baba pushed the coffee table and stood up, ready to shove me.

"Go to your books, girly boy!" Nabil jerked my wrist and then released me.

Mama had always shouted at me or Nabil when we squabbled.

Now she sat quietly. My brother, on the other hand, drew power from Baba and copied his words and tone.

I left, but ranting.

A few minutes later, Mama came to my room. "Here, eat, love!" She handed me a hallum cheese wrapped in pita. Each bite took long to choke down.

I overheard Nabil and Baba discuss how Othman should be brought in to help avert a raid on the building.

"Jamil is Othman's right hand now! I'll get him on it first."

"Your cousin Jamil?" Baba asked.

"Othman said that Jamil is smart and trustworthy. You know, Jamil leads the Qur'an studies after the dinner prayers. I really don't want Othman to hear that he shouted 'Mama.' It is just too embarrassing."

"Jamil is a crook!" I shouted, coming from my room.

"I will tell him you said that," Nabil said.

"While you're at it, tell him that he is a murderer, just like you!" I stood in the foyer.

"You are a liability!" Baba said. "Go! Before I smack you!"

"Jamil supplies martyrs and Othman cashes their death and gets funding. The holy duo!"

"Go to your room, Mama's boy!" Nabil mocked. "This is all way over your head. We have a name now. We are the Soldiers of Allah movement!"

"How fitting!" Baba praised.

"How many thugs strong are you?" I asked.

"Seventy-eight!"

"What about the fourteen on posters, the ones who died? Did you count them?"

Nabil tapped his fingertips to calculate.

"Fourteen gone and sixty-four future martyrs left!" I told him.

"Enough!" Baba ordered.

"Othman gave their survivors money," Nabil said proudly.

"How much?" Baba asked.

"Ten thousand dollars each."

Baba smiled. "Very nice!"

"That is nothing," I said. "Othman got $25 million."

"Where did you hear that?" Baba asked, surprised.

Nabil was irritated. "All I know is he met with Saddam Russein and he got money to fund our ammunition and pay the survivors."

"Saddam *Hus*sein." I mocked. "He gave him $25 million."

Mama returned from the kitchen.

"Bring the olives," Nabil told Mama.

Instantly she turned around.

"You need to befriend Jamil more," Baba told Nabil. "He is loaded now, isn't he? Invite him over."

"For what? To increase Nabil's worth?" I said.

"May Allah curse the hour you were born!" Baba said.

The following week, I found Jamil napping on the sofa while Nabil snoozed in a chair.

"May peace be upon you!" I shouted.

Both of them moaned and shuffled into sitting positions.

"May peace be upon you," Jamil said.

"Where is Professor Othman?" I disarmed them with the "Professor," just like they said it.

"Traveling," Jamil said.

"Monaco?" I asked.

"He has a place there," Jamil confirmed.

"How did you know that?" Nabil asked.

"It is in the papers," I answered. "Must be expensive."

"He is conducting meetings away from the Zionist operatives," Jamil explained.

"I am sorry!" I said sarcastically. "Did you say with or away?"

"Stop it!" Nabil ordered me. He got up and sat next to Jamil. "Don't mind him."

Jamil laid his hand on Nabil's thigh. "Arm yourself with patience."

"So when you die, Othman will eulogize you from Monaco?" I asked Nabil.

"May Allah grant you with guidance on His path," Jamil told me.

Baba opened the front door. As usual, Mama rushed to greet him. Jamil got up and kissed Baba on the cheeks.

After a round of greetings, Jamil continued, "Professor Othman will get back next Friday morning. Come to the mosque and greet him."

"We will all go," Baba said.

"Pray for the prophet! We never know what Allah has in store for us by then," Mama said from the kitchen.

Jamil picked up his AK-47.

"May Allah be with you! We will see on Friday," Baba said.

"How come Othman is not here fighting the Israelis in the south?" I asked my cousin as he put on his shoes. "The Jews have reached the Litani River."

He ignored me and tied his shoes.

"They took one-tenth of Lebanon," I said, unrelenting.

"May Allah grant you clarity of thought and guidance into His kingdom," Jamil said.

For the next four days, battles raged in East Beirut. The Syrian army—which had had Christian allies who helped their militias eradicate the Palestinians in Tal Za'atar camp a year before, now turned their guns on the Phalangists and Christian militias.

"Glory to Allah!" Nabil said. "The Muslim bond is stronger than any other. You will never find two Muslims turn on each other like this."

"Bashir got too big," Baba said. "He killed his own people to claim supremacy. Syria won't allow it. Allahu akbar!"

The sound of the heavy artillery sent shockwaves through our building. Windows vibrated, and shutters rattled. We knew, however, that we were temporarily safe from the Christians, who had their hands full battling the Syrian army.

The following Friday morning Baba set out for the mosque earlier than usual. He said, "Meet me at the Upper Basta Mosque."

"In sha'Allah!" I said, God willing.

"This one is not 'In sha'Allah'! *You* will be there."

I stood stone-faced.

Baba continued, "You will do as I say—"

"And bow to Othman?"

"Pimp! Get your girly ass out of my face or else!"

"He will go!" Mama sipped coffee and took a long drag from her cigarette. "May Allah be with you, my man!"

I performed ablution at home. I saw my image in the mirror and decided to shave. My bearded face resembled Nabil's and Othman's appearance—two remorseless executioners—and Jamil's, a Qur'an-spewing mouthpiece who fueled their frenzy to kill. Then I prayed at home to avoid as many people as possible. I timed my arrival after the conclusion of the sermon and right before the congregational prayer.

At the mosque, Jamil stood atop the steps wearing a pristine cassock, where he huddled with four gowned, armed men. I figured he didn't prepare a speech that Friday and stationed himself there to secure Othman's passage to the car.

I obliged with the mandatory greeting. "May peace be upon you."

Jamil mumbled something to the four men.

Enthusiastically, they replied, "May peace be upon you, brother!"

Jamil must have told them I was Nabil's brother.

I proceeded to the shoe stand. Inside, I scanned for Baba. He leaned on a column, making believe he was far classier than those who stood in line to greet Othman. I walked toward him, making my presence known only by proximity.

"May Allah curse the devil! Why did you shave? Straighten up! Look like a man, damn it."

Othman acknowledged Baba with a wide smile. From his position, as Othman walked by, Baba said, "Thank Allah for your safe return!"

Othman shook Baba's hand vigorously. Perhaps he thanked him for allowing Nabil to be in the photos that Arab leaders rewarded with more funds.

"Say hello to Professor Othman!" Baba said.

Professor!

"How are you, son?"

To hell with you. "I am fine."

"Nabil says your head is in the books."

And in the Qur'an that you don't know.

He continued, "The only language you need to learn is Arabic. The only book you need to read is the Qur'an! It has all the answers."

Baba had grown now impatient. "Tell him about the—"

"Let's go where we can talk." Othman led the circle out.

Nabil stayed behind to complete the Sunnah prayers. Baba tugged on him to skip the optional prayer and go outside with Othman and the others, but Nabil yanked his arm back, whispering, "*Takbir-* Allahu akbar" louder during the opening of his prayers, his way of pushing back.

I went outside with Baba. There, Jamil looked distraught. He waved me and Baba back inside while Othman put his shoes on.

Don't you tell me what to do! I thought.

Loud chants and prayers echoed at the bottom of the stairs. People sprinkled rice. A few men got between Baba and me. Baba hustled to catch Othman, now separated from us.

Jamil dropped his arm, stopping Baba in his tracks. "May Allah accept your prayers," he said.

"Let go! Move!" Baba shoved, but Jamil held firm.

"I told Othman about the invasion attempt on the building. He wants to see you this afternoon," Jamil said.

"B-but, he said to go outside with him."

Othman now turned to go to his car.

"Let go, damn it! Move," Baba snapped.

Suddenly, a storm of intense gunshots thundered. I ducked. Baba swung behind Jamil and hid. People screamed. Others sprinted to take cover.

A masked man darted forward. He fired more rounds aimed in one place. Then he jumped on the seat behind a motorcyclist, and they sped off. Jamil yanked on his cloak to free it from Baba's grasp. Baba stood up.

Jamil shouted, "Freeze! Dogs!" and fired rounds in the air.

Women wailed. Men shouted, "Allahu akbar!"

Nabil came outside on the run. He stopped, dumbfounded. I got up and looked around. Some people were clutching their wounds, blood flowing between their fingers. Down the stairs, Othman lay motionless. Nabil and Jamil hurtled themselves toward him. Jamil tore off his robe and threw the cassock over Othman's body. Two young armed men lay beside him.

"Help me! *Lift!*" Jamil shouted at Nabil.

Nabil and Jamil carried Othman's limp body and threw him in the backseat of Jamil's brand-new BMW 745. All the while, Nabil screamed, "Love, Othman!"

Jamil took the wheel. The car rocketed away from the curb. Smoke billowed from the rear tires. He kept his hand on the horn while Nabil fired his handgun to clear the traffic.

"Run! Run! Oh Merciful!" Baba yelled at me.

I chased after Baba.

Two boys screamed for help. Three men lay moaning on the

ground, others appeared lifeless. I slowed down to help.

"Keep going, damn you! Run!" Baba shouted. We kept running until we got home.

Later that night Nabil came home, red-eyed. His world had collapsed. "Othman is dead," he told Baba and wept.

"May Allah have mercy on his soul! 'Think not of those who have been slain in the cause of Allah as dead. Nay, they are living, in the presence of their Lord, and are granted gifts from Him.'" Baba quoted the verse inscribed below every martyr's poster. "Jamil will take care of you. You will be better off with Jamil at the top."

Nabil mourned Othman for forty days. He prayed and read the Qur'an by day and wept by night. I avoided him, fearing he would find in me an outlet for his anguish. As for me, Othman's demise watered the seed of a dormant desire: to pursue humane work. Since witnessing Othman's brother's execution and surviving the Black Saturday massacre, I had felt indebted to Islam. Othman had bridged my survival with the vengeful need for retribution. Now that he was gone, the spell was broken.

CHAPTER 13

COME ON! SHOOT ME!
AUGUST, 1978

A few assassinations later, toward the end of August 1978, word got out that the schools would reopen. At sixteen years old, I felt invigorated by the announcement. Nabil, on the other hand, found the bunkers to be his centers of growth.

Dressed in fatigues and armed with his nickel-plated automatic handgun, he stood in the middle of the family room and said, "I will not sit softly in a classroom with the likes of him." He shot me a scornful look. "I will give my life to Islam. You go and learn English and French."

I recalled Husam's prediction after Grandmother's funeral at our penthouse. "You and Nabil ... you two are next." Husam referred to the fallout between Baba and his siblings. "One day you'll kill each other," he had said. Perhaps Husam was only half right. I hoped.

On the first day back in school, I looked for Sharif in class and during recess. When I didn't find him, I asked the principal if he knew anything about my friend.

"We think he is in America! May Allah bless him! Word has it that his parents died before his eyes in Ras El-Nabeh. May Allah have mercy on their souls!"

The principal's tone evoked my vivid memories of Abu Sharif's blood and Um Sharif's charred remains. I dashed to the bathroom to seek refuge. Whereas most of my heroes, whose biographies I read with fervor, found their calling on a mountaintop, under a tree, or on the high seas, I found mine in my reflection in a bathroom mirror. At that moment I saw my future.

I decided to join the Red Cross, the very organization that saved me from bleeding to death on Black Saturday. One day, I would be a healer just like Dr. Saba, the Christian physician who cared for me at the American University hospital. I would attend to the disabled and help stop the pre-mature death caused by those who absolved themselves from questioning the means of their salvation. I would unsubscribe from the cycle of provocation and retribution, just like Gandhi, on peaceful terms. With that conviction, I left for class.

On the way home that afternoon, I walked to the Red Cross headquarters in Koraytem, a little more than a mile from school. I sought the director, Simone, a Christian. An athletic-looking man, he welcomed me in on the spot. He assigned me a mentor, Jerjes, another Christian. I accepted that Christians would surround me at the Red Cross. I didn't mind that.

It was then I realized that the only upside to living in the combat zone was that Simone called me brave. Minutes later, he awarded me a Red Cross badge and said, "Welcome to our family of volunteers."

Jerjes told me that Simone had returned to Beirut from Paris, where his family lived. "His giving spirit is unwavering."

I thought Simone was nuts for coming here willingly when he could have been safe in France, but I had to respect him.

"Let me show you around," Jerjes said.

The center consisted of a one-story building with an expansive reception area and four large rooms, one in each corner. Simone used one for his office. The second was for training, the third for providing first aid to those who could not afford a hospital, and the fourth was a massive storage space. In the courtyard protected by two large wrought-iron gates, we maintained and parked ten vans under the Lebanese and the Red Cross flags.

For two weeks I worked at the center after school until around nine at night. Jerjes and I became good friends. He attended the American University of Beirut, where he majored in business management. To that end, he briefed me on all the required tests and deadlines so I could someday apply to the university.

Being the oldest volunteer, Jerjes had honed a repertoire of first aid skills. He trained me to administer intravenous injections and draw blood during blood drives. These skills came in handy especially when the war entered unpredictable lulls.

During these periods of relative peace, we searched for children in remote villages and vaccinated them against polio, funded by a civic organization called Rotary International. On those long drives through rugged mountains closer to Marjayoun in south Lebanon, Jerjes taught me how to drive. When we rolled slowly down the main street of villages, children ran alongside the van and cheered our arrival. The elderly called me doctor. On those trips my spirit soared, and I felt worthy.

I came back to reality upon reentering my neighborhood, where rats roamed freely in broad daylight. Along with the explosions or gunfire, the area had become the foulest section of West Beirut. The corniche reeked with a stench that clogged my nostrils and penetrated my head. I held my breath around the mountains of garbage along each block. Every now and then I observed the bakery owner, Abu Ali, who kept his shop open despite the battles, torch the trash. The slow-burning fires smoked for days.

Past the Sodeco intersection, the breeze from the Mediterranean swept the sickeningly putrid foul odor of the decaying bodies into our family room.

Inside the flat, flies and mosquitoes buzzed. During the day, the flies hovered and landed on me so frequently, I gave up brushing them off. As for the mosquitoes, I shoved towels in the door cracks and fumigated with repellents to secure my room for the night.

Every night before going to bed, I made sure the entrance door of the building was locked to ward off street dogs. Then I flipped all the light and appliance switches off in case power came on to avoid exposure. I kept the kitchen faucet on, however, just in case the government supplied water. We would hear the air pops. Then we'd rush to fill bottles and buckets and the tub. In my bedroom as I lay still, the runaway mosquitoes hovered around my ears. I succumbed and allowed them to sting me just to win their silence.

When I finally slept, the street dogs barked. I forced myself out of bed and picked up two precious, filled water bottles from the kitchen. I dashed to the balcony and hurled one after the other, screaming at the mongrels, "*Die! May Allah curse you and this world!*"

They scattered.

On an unusually sizzling September night, Mama sneaked into my room.

"Get up! I laid down some pillows and blankets on the floor for you," she whispered, careful not to startle me.

"Why did you open the door! *Why?*" I snapped.

"We are sleeping on the balcony. Come on!"

"Are you kidding? It stinks out there!"

"Not tonight! Say Allah! Get up!"

I heard explosions echoing in the distance.

"The rockets could get near," I said, and rolled over.

"Say Allah! The Christians and Syrians are still at it."

I got up. I would do anything for Mama. I peeled the sticky bed sheet off my skin, picked up my pillow, and followed her to the balcony. Like Nabil and Baba, Mama had become inured to the filth in the combat zone.

When I reached the balcony, she showed me to my spot, at Nabil's feet. I maneuvered around Baba.

"You hear that?" Baba turned down the volume on his radio to tune in to the explosions. "The Syrians—May Allah award them might—are bombarding the Christian militias in East Beirut."

"When is it going to end?" Mama asked.

"When the Christians submit to the might of the right, Islam!" Baba replied.

Nabil said, "Nah! That will be when we kick out all the Israelis and reclaim Palestine. The Palestinians are giving them a nice beating in Tel Aviv all the way from here, Sabra and Shatila." He chuckled, referring to the two largest Palestinian camps in West Beirut, where the world's most notorious criminals hid in plain view.

Blah, blah, blah, I thought, and settled in my spot.

"Listen! Listen!" Baba raised the volume. Bashir spoke in French to foreign reporters. Nabil and I had been learning English and French until the schools shut down.

"That French pig! He and Anwar Sadat sold out to the Zionists." Nabil referred to the Egyptian president, who was first to sign a peace agreement with Israel. "Blessed are those who kill them! Mark my words. Their end is near."

I shrouded myself and left a thimble-size opening for one nostril to deny the bugs a landing zone. I heard sounds like paper rustling. I felt a tickle on my nose. I jumped. "Roaches!" I shrieked.

Nabil rose calmly.

"May Allah curse this life!" I said, brushing myself off.

Mama and Baba groaned. Nabil cupped his hand and swiftly trapped a roach in his palm. He turned his hand over and released it like it was a white dove. The gesture nauseated me. I took comfort knowing he performed ablutions between prayers.

I picked up my pillow and stood. "May Allah curse this shit hole!" My prayer infuriated Baba. I knew better than to attack his only accomplishment, the only thing that mattered to him in the world, the building. I went inside.

"Stop! May Allah curse you!" Baba said.

I turned around to see Nabil, now leaning forward to watch my humiliation through the balcony door.

Baba continued his tirade. "You burn candles, and you eat and sleep for free. You come and go and don't even bring a stone for a token. Look at your brother! He gives your mother money."

I stood like a statue.

Baba turned to Mama. "Where does he get his pocket money, woman?" referring to me.

"I-I don't know," she stuttered.

"I get a stipend," I lied.

"Oh?" he scoffed.

I feared Baba would punish Mama for giving me pocket money. "I make good grades. Aren't you proud of that? I am at the top of my class."

Baba turned in disgust to Nabil. "'I make good grades.' Ha! Books softened him up."

The ranking order at home couldn't be clearer. I occupied the bottom with Mama.

"Leave him alone!" She got up, came into the family room, and reached for my hand. I recoiled before she touched me.

My heart pounded. "I am leaving!"

"You better bring something with you from those cross worshippers," Nabil said.

I shook my head in disgust. "It is the Red Cross." I emphasized the *s* to boil their blood. "We give to the needy."

"How is it working for you, away from Allah! Huh?" Nabil asked.

"Everyone is talking about you," Baba added. "We all are in one place, and you are in another. You look and act oddly."

"We are your family, love," Mama said.

"Family!" I yelled. "Explain to me my overwhelming need to get away from all of you."

"To be with the cross worshippers?" Nabil said. "You infidel!"

"Those Christians drink alcohol," Baba said. "You have lost your way—"

"We save lives—"

"You wear that apron with the cross on it, don't you?" Nabil's eyes lit up.

He had touched upon the most difficult change I had to make, wearing the cross. "It saves me from getting shot!"

Nabil jumped up and came at me. "You ought to get shot for wearing it."

"Pray for the prophet!" Mama pleaded.

"Quiet!" Baba ordered her.

"Did you bring your cross into this house?" Nabil shoved past me to my room.

I got in his way and bumped him aside. "Don't you touch my stuff, you murderer!"

"Stop it! You are brothers!" Mama yelled.

Nabil grabbed my shoulder and threw me aside. I lost my balance and fell. I scrambled up and hurried after him. He flung open the bedroom door. I chased after him and gripped his arm.

"Let me be!" I shouted. "I am leaving this shit hole forever!"

"Then leave!" Nabil stormed into the family room, where he ranted and prayed for my demise. "Glory to Allah, He armed me with patience not to teach this donkey a lesson!"

Mama came into my bedroom and put her hand on my shoulder.

My hands shook as I stuffed clothing and books into my back-pack.

"Love! Why must you carry the ladder sideways?"

I was shocked that Mama was saying I made matters worse for myself. "They call themselves Muslims!" I turned toward the family room and shouted, "You don't know anything about Islam!"

"Oh Merciful!" Mama whispered. "Please stay."

"I can't."

"Wait! I will get you money." She left the room and quickly returned with bills in her hand. "Here." She passed me money. I shoved it in my pants pocket.

"How do you do it?" I asked.

"I save from groceries—"

"I mean live with those two."

"Go! May Allah be with you."

"And leave you here with those two—"

"What do you expect me to do?" she asked, miserable.

"I will break your legs if you ever return empty-handed!" Baba shouted from the living room.

I shrugged on my stuffed backpack from which a pair of shoes dangled.

Mama clamped my shoulders. "Focus on school," she said, her eyes searching my face. "Be safe. I will visit with you when I can." She planted kisses on my cheeks.

I laced my sneakers in the foyer while she showered me with prayers.

Nabil shouted over Mama. "May Allah curse you!"

I opened the flat door. Instantly Baba quoted the Qur'an. "'O ye who believe! Surely among your wives and your children are some that are really your enemies, so beware of them.'"

That quote bolted the door behind me and steeled my resolve.

As soon as I locked the entrance door of the building behind me, absolute loneliness struck. I could not tolerate Baba and Nabil anymore, but to face the world alone, starting from the combat zone, horrified me. No one in the world except Mama cared if I lived or died.

I turned right and walked slowly. Dogs barked madly in the distance. Rats scurried through the alleyway in the vents of the garage. On the corniche, I kept my head down and watched my shadow slither over rubbish and fleeing roaches. I reached an intersection, where a sniper fired. Without further thought, I walked to the middle of the intersection. I stopped, faced East Beirut, and screamed, "Shoot me!" I paused again. "Where are you, pimp! End my misery!" I yelled, spreading my arms wide.

A round popped to my left, followed by an echo of the shot.

"Is that all you've got? Come on! Shoot me!" I roared.

The sniper fired three consecutive rounds, missing me by yards.

"You blind idiot! Son of a whore!" I crossed to the other side.

In that instant the sniper opened fire on automatic. Rounds popped in the asphalt and the median behind me. I knelt on the edge of the sidewalk, buried my face in my hands, and rocked in despair.

CHAPTER 14

ABRAHAM'S NIGHTMARE
FALL, 1978 – FALL, 1982

In the two years that followed, I experienced more peace than I ever had at home, even before the war broke out. Now in my third year of high school, I rose to the top of my class, and at the Red Cross center Jerjes became my brother and the friend I once had and lost.

Mama frequently visited me at the center. She gave me pocket money, and pressured me to join Jamil's militia. "Work in the office so you can make some money," she urged. "The Libyans are throwing money at him."

Jerjes's father, Elias, also frequented the center. Soon after we were introduced, he sought ways to help me.

"If you get accepted at the university, look me up," he said. Elias was the athletic director there.

On October 1, 1981, Sadat paid with his life for having signed a peace treaty with Israel in 1978.

Outside the center, celebratory gunshots were fired. I ran out to the street. Cars honked. Riders waved their militia flags from windows. People chanted, "Allahu akbar! We killed the traitor!"

I retreated to Simone's office, where he, Jerjes, and I watched the broadcast on the black and white TV. The assassination played over and over. Sadat and dignitaries sat in the bleachers behind a concrete wall, watching the annual victory parade. Tanks and rocket-mounted trucks rolled by. Three soldiers jumped from a truck. One approached the bleachers and lobbed two grenades that landed at Sadat's feet but didn't explode. As Sadat's bodyguards stood in shock, the soldier tossed a third grenade. It exploded. Then the three assassins ran to the stands and opened fire. Sadat died instantly. His vice president, Mubarak, was shot, but lived. Other survivors crawled away, still others lay bleeding.

"That's what he gets for selling out to Israel and America," Simone said, shrugging.

If Sadat got what he deserved, I wondered what I had done to be trapped in West Beirut when the Israelis put us under siege in the summer of 1982.

After graduating high school, the Israeli government declared war on the Palestinian guerilla fighters in the Sabra and Shatila camps in West Beirut. Ariel Sharon, the Israeli defense minister, led his forces into Lebanon.

After six days of ferocious ground battles and fighter jets screaming overhead, Israeli soldiers pushed the Palestinian militias, Fatah and the Palestinian Liberation Organization; the Syrian army and militias; Amal of the Shias; the Progressive Socialist Party of the Druze; Murabitoon of the Sunnis; the communist party; and the smaller factions all the way into West Beirut. In our neighborhood, armed men stopped at the Museum-Barbeer Bridge, now the front line with the Israeli forces, not even a half a mile from my home. West Beirut was under siege.

During negotiations and when bombing raids let up, Jerjes and I ran aid missions to the Palestinian camps. Before the war broke out, I had gone there with Baba to buy cheap knockoffs of French designer clothes. Thousands of refugees lived in a warren of tin-roofed shacks that floated on sewer or rainwater in a maze of alleyways.

The poorest citizens—those who had no choice but to remain inside West Beirut—barraged our van. Their desperate cries for aid boxes tore at my heart, even when I lay in my cot. The boxes held sugar, flour, vegetable oil, and rice, and they often made the difference between life and death for the very poor.

Late one afternoon as I rested at the center, Mama rushed toward me and shouted, "Thank Allah you are safe!" She embraced me as tears streamed down her cheeks.

"What is going on, Mama?"

The volunteers at the Red Cross, my extended family, including Simone, hurried to surround us.

"Your brother has been hit." Mama scanned my colleagues' faces. "The Israelis dropped firebombs. Nabil is burnt."

Some gasped. Others gave me a sympathy nudge and drifted away.

"When? How bad?" I held her hand and led her out to the yard. Simone and Jerjes followed.

"Second-degree burns all over his right side. You have to come home with me."

My emotions were a jumble of anger and pity for Nabil.

Mama saw my hesitation. "Ya'Allah," she said.

"Jerjes," Simone said, "drive them to the hospital." In essence, he indirectly ordered me to go.

"He is at home," Mama said. "There are no beds in the hospitals. They only bandaged him up."

"Let's go home, Mama." I wrapped my arm around her shoulder and walked her to the van.

Simone asked Jerjes to put two aid boxes in our van. He intended for me to give them to my family. Jerjes nodded and trotted ahead of us.

I drove. Mama sat next to me while Jerjes rode in the back.

"Your father is very upset," Mama said. "You know Nabil means the world to him."

"Then why are you dragging me into this?" I asked.

"He is your brother—"

"Ha!" I scoffed. I wanted nothing to do with him.

"We are your *family!*"

"Some family we are!"

"In Allah's name—"

"In Allah's name, Mama!" I scoffed. "I have news for you. Here is how we spend our time ... ok! We feed, treat, haul, and bury the victims of those fighting in Allah's name. You know ... those who are most spiritual ... the pray-on-Friday-Saturday-and-Sunday bunch."

Mama fell silent, and Jerjes shifted in his seat. I knew he was extremely uncomfortable. After ten minutes driving through empty roads, we entered the combat zone. There I saw weapons piled next to the trash mounds.

"What is this about?"

Mama said, "The Israeli jets dropped leaflets last night to warn if they come in our homes and find weapons, they will kill us."

I pulled into the alleyway alongside our building. "Who is left here?"

"Just Kifah and his wife."

"Where are their sons?"

"Fighting. Riyad was also burned. He might not live."

Kifah feared the Syrians after they fought alongside the Phalangists and eradicated the Palestinians in the Tal El-Za'atar camp in 1978. He forced Riyad to join the Syrian militia, Sae'eka.

I looked in the rearview mirror. Jerjes's eyes were wide with fear.

"Go ahead, Mama. We will be right up."

After she stepped out, I parked the van tight to the alleyway wall, to prevent a thief's access to the fuel tank. Jerjes and I each carried an aid box. Simone unknowingly awarded me a passport to enter the flat again—Baba probably wouldn't have allowed me inside without him.

Jerjes and I entered the building. A TV echoed through the stairways. We climbed the steps, maneuvering around sofa cushions and stools. Jerjes rested his load on the rail. "Jesus! Your family lives in the stairways? I've got to get out of here!"

"As soon as we drop these off!"

"I meant this country."

I lowered my voice. "Hey, listen, don't mind my family. They're—"

"Welcome! Welcome!" Loud slippers flapped on the tile steps. Baba shouted. "You honor us!"

Mama must have told him about the aid boxes. He came into view at the top of the landing. His smile spread across his face from ear to ear.

"This is Jerjes!" I preempted Baba's wrath on Christians with the name—*Jerjes* being a giveaway.

"The best of all names!" Baba said warmly.

At the front door of the flat, he tugged Jerjes inside. Mama reached to hug me again after I put the box down. She smothered my face with kisses as if she hadn't seen me earlier.

"May Allah curse the fighting and the war," she prayed over the loud TV, and took me into the family room.

"How come there is electricity?" I asked.

"The Israelis are messing with us, Jerjes," Baba answered me via my friend. "Right there, Jerjes." Baba pointed at the coffee table for him to set down the box.

Jerjes did.

"Sit, Jerjes." Baba patted the sofa cushion next to him.

Jerjes sat.

"Ya'Allah! Come with me. Nabil will be happy to see you," Mama said to me.

Mama—always the peacemaker, I thought, and did not move.

"How did it happen?" I asked.

"Fighting in the Horsh," Baba said.

The Horsh was a densely wooded park a mile south of our home. "The Israelis dropped napalm bombs to clear the trees and locate the antiaircraft weapons. Fighters were doused."

"Fighting?" Jerjes leaned forward seeking eye contact with me.

Nabil was my dirty secret.

"He is a militiaman with—"

"A *warrior,* damn it!" Baba said. "A *holy* warrior. You didn't tell Jerjes about the *hero* in this family?"

"May Allah crush the Israelis bones!" Mama tugged on my hand, trying to pull me toward Nabil's bedroom.

"Go meet my son, Jerjes," Baba said.

"It will be my honor, sir." He stood and followed me.

Mama cracked Nabil's door open carefully. He lay on his bed, covered with a thin white sheet. Bottles of painkillers and boxes of medicine covered the bedside table to his left. He groaned.

I knelt before his bed. Mama and Jerjes stood behind me.

"Thank Allah you are alive!" I said, moderating my sympathy. More affection, and he would have uttered, "Weakling" before "Hello."

"Allah told him to cover his face. All his right side is burnt," Mama whispered.

Nabil's voice was barely audible. "Ah. Is ... is this Jer-Jerjes?"

"Yes."

"M-may Allah b-burn the Christians in hell for harboring the Jews," Nabil said. "You defile my room and this house by bringing him here!"

"Shut up!" Mama shouted at Nabil.

Jerjes's face turned fire red. He looked at the door.

Nabil slowly picked up a bottle of pills and threw it at Jerjes, who caught it and gave it to Mama.

"He is an idiot! Let's go!" I pushed Jerjes in front of me.

"I fight for you, and you ... you are one of them!" Nabil rasped. "If you ever bring a Christian again, I will kill you both—"

"I will poke your burns before you lay a finger on him!" I shouted.

"Enough!" Mama shouted. She slammed Nabil's door behind us.

"Let's get out of here," I told Jerjes. My hands shook.

"*Shh!*" Baba demanded. "Come here! Turn up the television, damn it!"

Bashir Gemayel, the man who had ordered the Phalangists to open fire on me on Black Saturday, was giving a speech. His supporters carried him on their shoulders.

Jerjes tugged my shirt. "I want to go," he whispered.

"Not more than I do. One second."

I walked in and raised the volume while Mama sat down next to Baba.

"Years of war are enough," Bashir was saying. "Today, Lebanese Muslims who reject occupation are cautiously looking for the way to freedom. However, they do not yet possess the means or the organization to actively overcome their oppression. Liberty, security, and justice for all Lebanese within a democratic government that guarantees basic freedoms for all citizens, and—"

"He will be the best thing ever for this country," Mama said.

"*What?* This guy almost killed me!" I was enraged.

"Well, listen to him," she said. "Someone needs to end the war."

"He is a monster. ... a mass murderer!"

"Shut up or get out. I want to hear him not you," Baba said.

I turned to leave. Jerjes craned his head over my shoulder and said, "May Allah bless Nabil with a fast recovery!"

"May Allah shield you," Mama said, keeping her eyes on the screen.

Jerjes stepped outside the apartment door. I hesitated in the foyer, then picked up a shoe and hurled it at Nabil's bedroom door with all

I had. The loud bang must have startled him.

"Ach!" Nabil shouted.

"What was that?" Mama and Baba asked simultaneously.

I quickly ducked to open the aid box that I had left in the foyer.

"The aid box slipped from my hands," I said.

"May Allah curse you!" Nabil yelled.

"Is it all there?" Baba asked.

"A full box. Thank Allah!" I retrieved the shoe and left.

Outside, Jerjes asked, "What was that noise?"

"Let us just go."

We hurried down the stairs.

"Did I defile your home?" Jerjes asked over the sound of our boots.

"OK! Stop."

Jerjes turned around. "I am sorry if—"

"People like you purify homes like mine."

Three days later, the Americans, French, Israelis, Syrians, Palestinians, the Arab League, joint forces, and the Lebanese government agreed to allow Israel into West Beirut peacefully. On the heels of that understanding, on the evening of September 14, 1982, an explosion rocked the city.

While passing time watching TV alongside my peers at the Red Cross center, breaking news cut into *Sah El-Nom*, a Syrian comedy show. Bashir Gemayel had been assassinated during a speech in his party's headquarters in East Beirut. Our Christian volunteers wept while the Muslims reveled. At first I indulged both sentiments, but then I feared retribution. Bashir ushered the Israelis into Lebanon; they had installed him as president. It unsettled a regional power. Someone would have to pay.

The retaliation was swift and beyond imagining. On the afternoon of the fourth day of the Israelis' passage into West Beirut, Simone blasted out of his office.

"Get up! Everybody! Get your gear on! Pack the vans with first-aid supplies and stretchers!" He scanned the room to size up the volunteers. About thirty of us gathered around him. "We are going to Sabra and Shatila right now!" The Palestinian camps were only three miles southeast of the center.

Mona, a Lebanese Muslim born to Palestinian refugees in Beirut, approached me. "I'll ride with you and Jerjes."

"Hurry!" I said.

We put on our gear and dashed out to the vans. I slid the side door open. Mona, Jerjes, and I frantically loaded stretchers and supplies. Jerjes jumped in the driver's seat while Mona and I hopped in the back.

Simone waited on the street in his white Red Cross-marked Peugeot 504. As soon as the vans lined up behind him, he blew the siren and peeled out. We followed.

Over the sirens howling from the ten vans and our sudden swerves and turns, Mona and I organized IV bags, gauze packets, and bandages. A mile out, she squeezed between the two front seats and sat where she could look out the windshield.

"I wonder what is going on." She leaned forward as if the answer lay around each corner.

"It must be big! We never deployed like this," Jerjes said, then cursed at the pedestrians in our way.

"Don't be scared." I put my hand on Mona's shoulder. She gave me a disapproving look. I recoiled.

At the Tayouneh roundabout, Simone's voice came over the walkie-talkie. "I need the five vans behind me to follow to Sabra. All others, head to Shatila."

We made a hard right to the Sabra camp. Upon entering the camp, Jerjes slowed down. "Oh, Jesus, shield me!" he muttered under his breath. "In the name of Mother Mary—"

"Oh Merciful!" Mona gasped.

I shuffled around to peek out a window, but the painted Red Cross logo obstructed my view. Jerjes stopped the van. He opened his door and vomited from his seat. I slowly slid my door open. The stench of decaying bodies overcame me. Jerjes had parked next to a pile of bloated corpses.

As if through the eyes of the Red Cross volunteers on Black Saturday, I viewed the carnage, searching for signs of life. Nothing moved. On top of the heap, a woman lay with her stomach cut open, her fetus dangling by the umbilical cord. Piled next to her were four headless children. Flies swarmed over them. Dogs roamed, sniffing the corpses. I imagined the last moments of these poor souls. They must have pleaded for their lives. Some might have accepted Jesus as their savior to save their lives but still got killed.

Suddenly I vomited. Mona approached me. She was sobbing. "Are you OK?" she asked.

I wiped my mouth with my sleeve. "Where is Jerjes?"

She pointed to the right.

Twenty yards away, in the courtyard of the camp's only three-story building, he stood with Simone, huddled with suited politicians and policemen. Simone wore a mask. Jerjes broke away and walked toward us.

"Do you think they are gone?" I asked.

"Who?" Mona asked, puzzled.

"Who did this?" I asked Jerjes.

Jerjes was within earshot. "The Christian Lebanese Forces and Phalangists," he said grimly, and looked down. "Word has it that when the Israelis got control of the entrances to the city and camps, they ushered the killers here and secured the perimeter. They even fired illuminating flares to enable them to work around the clock ... in shifts."

Jerjes confirmed my suspicions. Unable to think straight, I glared at him and then at Simone, both Christians like the killers. Perhaps Nabil and Baba had it right. What was I doing with these cross-worshippers?

I shoved past Jerjes and scanned the camp. A few survivors stumbled around in shock. Women huddled and wailed, while men held them and wept. Children were inconsolable. Some onlookers stood gaping. Others searched for survivors while covering their noses with their arms. Civil Defense agencies of many affiliations arrived. Journalists roamed with cameras. People threw up over the dead.

Next to Simone in the courtyard four veiled women sat on the street. One shouted, "Where are you, you Arab leaders and Americans pigs?" She took her hijab off and waved it as she wailed. "May Allah curse the Christians for doing this! May Allah curse the Americans for supporting Israel!"

Some echoed "Amen," while others bawled.

Simone signaled to Jerjes, Mona, and me to join him. I had hoped that he would lay the blame on the Israelis.

"This is a mass-grave burial operation," he told us over the sound of women wailing. "Word has it that the killers worked in shifts for three days, so search everywhere for bodies—sewer openings, attics, cupboards, under the beds ... everywhere someone would try to hide. Wear your masks and gloves."

A haggard half-veiled woman clenched Simone's arm. He looked frightened. She shook him violently and screamed, "You, Christian dogs! You kill us, and now you save us! May Allah shred you into pieces! May the rats eat your remains. May Allah—"

"They are martyrs, hajjeh," I reminded her.

Jerjes stepped behind Mona.

I continued, "'Think not of those who have been slain in the cause of Allah as dead. Nay, they are living, in the presence of their Lord, and are granted gifts from Him.'"

"May Allah grant you longevity, Mama!" She let go of Simone. A man draped his arm across her shoulders and led her away.

Simone gave me an approving nod. I stared at him stone faced. "Rami, can I talk to you for a minute?"

"No! I have more important things to do now." I left.

The Beirut municipality had ordered a mass-grave excavation the size of an Olympic swimming pool. Mona, Jerjes, and I entered shacks, alleyways, and homes while the rusty bulldozers roared and puffed black smoke.

Scavenging dogs and the stench of decaying bodies guided us. Toddlers and babies lay in their dead mother's or father's arms. Most were bloated. Some had been executed on sofas. Others were killed in their beds or hiding in attics and cupboards. Jerjes and I lifted beds and found children shot through mattresses. Some women were left with their legs spread and panties hanging from an ankle. We lifted the bodies and hauled four at a time to the gravesite.

At sunset, nearby merchants brought generators and powered work lights. We labored around the clock. I counted 124 bodies that I helped haul to the graveside. Too exhausted to continue, we left for the center, where we cleaned up and rested. The instant I lay down, the images of the massacre filled me with rage. The magnitude of the executions and grotesque images overcame me.

After a sleepless night, we returned to the camp. Five hours into searching, hauling, and burying, Mona and I entered a tin-roof shack. The sharp odor pierced my mask. Inside, a family of six had been executed. Hundreds of flies buzzed. I wished earplugs were included in our gear. I found the corpse of a toddler stuffed into a round metal trash bin under a sink. While Jerjes and Mona hauled another body out, I fought the flies to pick up the toddler. I gently tugged to free him. His skin squeaked against the inside of the bin. His body's bloating locked him in. I wedged the bottom of the bin between my boots and pulled harder. When his little shoulder cracked, chills ran down my spine.

Mona returned, and I gestured to her. "I can't get him out. Please hold the bin down."

She squatted and held the bin. She looked away.

"Ready?" I asked.

She nodded vigorously. I clamped the child's forearms and tugged harder. The right arm came off in my hand. I lost my balance and staggered back two steps. Mona fell on her rear end and shrieked. Blood dripped from the severed arm. I flung it down. Mona bolted out, sobbing, and I was at her heels.

Outside, Jerjes was unloading a stretcher from the van.

"I can't do this anymore," I told him.

"Ya Allah!" Mona sobbed.

"What's the matter? What happened?" Jerjes asked.

"A child's arm. It came off in his hand," Mona bawled.

"I will be back shortly." I grabbed the stretcher from Jerjes, threw it in the van, and climbed into the driver's seat.

"What are you doing?" Jerjes asked.

I pulled off my gloves and mask and threw them in the back. Jerjes's cigarettes and packs of chewing gum were on the dashboard. I held up the packages.

"Do you want these?" I asked. Jerjes stared, saying nothing. I threw them back on the dashboard and took off. I had to get away.

I parked just outside the camp. In a few minutes fatigue set in. My eyelids weighed heavy, but my head throbbed. I felt hungry, but had no craving. I took a stick of gum from the wrapper. Either my jaw muscles were too weak or the gum was too hard to chew. I spat it out. Then I took the pack and pitched it out the window.

I reached for the cigarettes. Jerjes had tucked the lighter in the pack. I lit up and coughed harshly. How does Mama inhale and not cough? Suddenly I wondered: how does Mama do it? How could she live with Nabil, a killer, and Baba, his supporter? I had to do whatever was necessary to protect her.

About four cigarettes later, I started the van and went back to where I had left Mona and Jerjes. They sat shoulder to shoulder on a broken concrete slab in the open courtyard. I parked and approached.

"I'm going home," I said.

Mona stood up. Her face was pale. "Let's go." She turned to Jerjes.

"We have to keep working," he told her.

"You must be eager to cover the crimes," I said.

"What is that supposed to mean?" Jerjes stood up.

"The most vicious and barbaric massacres are committed by you, the Christians—and the Jews, for that matter."

Mona stepped between Jerjes and me.

My hands were fists. "You're enjoying this, aren't you? Have you been keeping a tally? Jesus loves you more now for every corpse, doesn't he?"

Jerjes glared at me. "I've seen what Muhamad's soldiers can do. They are no better."

"Stop!" Mona cried out.

He continued, "It is too bad you were hiding in the stairway with your charming family—"

"Stop it! What is wrong with you two?" Mona shouted.

"Have you met his brother?" Jerjes asked Mona, keeping his eyes on me.

"Y-you!" I lunged at him, but surprisingly Mona pushed me back and held on to me. I retreated.

"Are you going to tell your brother where to find me?" Jerjes taunted.

"Shut up!" I shouted. "You are lucky Mona is here, you—"

"What? Say it! Cross worshipper? Say it!" Jerjes's face turned crimson from fear and anger. We were in West Beirut, my territory. The look of panic on his face simulated mine a hundred times before. I yielded.

"In Allah's name, stop!" Mona shouted.

"Let me go," I lowered my hand.

"Promise to go to the van," Mona said.

"I want to go home."

Mona slowly released me. She grabbed my hand and Jerjes's. I yanked mine away and stomped off to the van.

"Rami!" she shouted. "We serve people! We soothe their pain regardless of religion or social standing. Rami!"

I ignored her. I slid the door of the van open and crashed in the back. I buried my face in my hands. Jerjes and Mona slowly and quietly climbed in the front. After a few moments of awkward silence Jerjes said, "An arm came off in his hand?"

"Yes." Mona's voice cracked.

"That was ... that is traumatizing," Jerjes said.

"How could one human do this to another?" Mona's voice quavered.

Jerjes turned to me. "I am sorry—"

"We worked inside a massive crime scene, but no one was investigating," I said through my teeth. "The killers spent days raping women and executing people. They feared no retribution."

"It is as bad as the vacuum-bomb site," Jerjes said.

He was referring to a building where an Israeli vacuum bomb targeted Arafat, the chairman of the Palestinian Liberation Organization, a month before. There, Jerjes and I saw a child's eyeballs hanging from their sockets.

"This is worse," I said. "This was face-to-face killing. The toddler reminded me of Ahmad. He was a boy who died on top of me on Black Saturday."

"Oh! My Allah! Someone has to investigate and the monsters have to answer for this," Mona said, tears rolling down her cheeks.

"Investigate what? The entire country? Everybody is killing everybody. Some use fighter jets, others use knives. What's the difference?"

Jerjes asked.

"We live among war criminals," I said. "And no one is getting arrested." I paused. "I hate my brother for what he does. He thinks that fighting and suffering is the highest calling of Islam."

"I've been around Christians who are the same," Jerjes said. We became Abraham's nightmare—"

"More like Satan's fantasy." Mona wiped her tears with her forearm. She turned to me. "Is your brother a militiaman?"

Before I could answer, Jerjes deliberately changed the subject. "All the victims get are onlookers and photographers desecrating their remains." He lit a cigarette.

"Can I have one?" I asked.

He gave me his and reached for another. Then, he observed my smoking. "When did you start smoking?"

"A few minutes ago. Can we go now?"

Jerjes put the car in gear, and we took off right at sunset.

"They should *all* die," Mona grated. "May Allah kill the Jews and Christians worldwide. I mean, the *killers!* Sorry!" She patted Jerjes on the shoulder.

"It is OK! I've heard it all before, you know! My father got tired of hearing his old friends' daily prayers for the blood of Muslim children to run up to their parents' knees."

Jerjes felt absolutely safe to divulge his proximity to such prayers. Mona and I fell silent.

He continued, "We are all damaged goods. We mourn when we are victims and rejoice at our enemies' misery. We pray for the victory of our fighters and the demise of the enemies. We don't do anything in between. No one talks to anyone. We just shoot or cry."

"By playing both parts, we are winning the pity of the dumb Western countries and rich Arab leaders," I said.

"What parts?" Mona asked.

"Victims and perpetrators," Jerjes answered for me. He scanned the dashboard. "Hey, where is the gum?" He turned the cabin light on.

"I tossed it out."

Jerjes adjusted the rearview mirror to find me. Our eyes met. I grinned and looked away.

"Kill the headlights," I told Jerjes when we turned from the Barbeer Bridge onto the corniche.

"Why?" Mona asked.

"Snipers," I said.

"Oh, my Allah!"

"We'll be fine."

We drove slowly up to my building. The tires crushed debris as we stopped in front of the alleyway. Jerjes pulled the handbrakes. I got out, took off the blood-stained apron, and tossed it in the back.

"I need a break. I will tell Simone I quit. What are *you* going to do?" I asked Jerjes.

"I want to go to America."

"I am sorry, Jerjes," I said in the most sincere tone I could muster.

He got out and walked around the van. He reached in and hugged me. I patted his back.

"When—not if—you get accepted at the American University and I am not around, you call my father." He returned to the van. "You understand?" Jerjes pointed at me, waiting on my nod of agreement.

"I will," I said, and turned to Mona. "Take care of yourself." I tapped on her hand on the window frame.

"You, too!" She put her hand on mine. "What are your plans?"

"I don't know. All I have is big dreams."

"How do we get out of here alive?" Jerjes asked, looking out.

"Keep the lights off until you turn there." I pointed at the Upper Basta turn before the Sodeco intersection.

I stood watching until Jerjes made the turn, exactly where Nabil had shot Christians just like him.

CHAPTER 15

THREE HUNDRED SEVENTY DOLLARS
SEPTEMBER, 1982

After a few days of refusing to talk to me except for curt greetings, Baba broke down. As he, Mama, and I sat around the dinner tray over the coffee table, he said, "You couldn't cook your eggs in the wind. Ha?"

He wore a white gown and crossed his legs. I sat on a low stool facing him, next to Mama. A kerosene lantern atop the TV set and a candle in the kitchen provided the only illumination in the apartment. Nabil lay in bed, still nursing his burns.

After the Syrian army and the Palestinian guerilla fighters, were forced to flee and the Palestinian civilians were wiped out, security concerns vanished. The neighbors, except for Tony and Audette, returned to their homes. Mama had found solace in Um Muhamad's and Hajjeh's company. Manal, however, had become a recluse since her son Riyad died after the battles with the Israelis.

"The cross-wearing do-gooders," Baba said, looking at me, "they got sick of you, didn't they?"

I stopped chewing. I wished he would stick to one of his rants about my uncles and the inheritance.

"Enough, my man," Mama pleaded with Baba.

She was my best ally, but she was just a woman, and that was that.

"Answer!" Baba insisted. The white of his eyes glowed in the candlelight.

"No. The time had come to help *you*, not strangers," I said.

"Oh!" He seemed ready to bargain with me so I could remain at home. "Well then, the car is in Tripoli."

"What car?" I asked.

"You have to earn your way around here."

"What are we talking about?"

"Tomorrow you go in a service car up through the mountains and bring the car back on the seaside roads through the Barbara checkpoint."

"*Barbara!*" I said in disbelief.

That checkpoint had the reputation for racketeering, abductions, and outright attacks on Muslims. It was situated in the Christian territory between Tripoli and West Beirut, two Muslim strongholds. Muslim importers who transported goods between the two cities paid extortion fees to get through rather than drive over seven hours on tortuous mountain roads.

"Nabil should be able to get it through the mountains when he feels better," I said.

Baba picked up his glass of water. "They might have his name on a blacklist somewhere." He sipped, slammed the empty glass on the tray and then turned on me. "All this time in the streets. I thought you become a man, but—"

"Why didn't you ship it somewhere safer?" I asked.

"It is four hundred dollars more everywhere else. Are you going to ask questions or do it?"

"But it is the Barbara! Geagea is ruthless. He is an assassin."

Samir Geagea led a group of militiamen and executed a former president's grandchild before her parents' eyes, then killed the parents to claim supremacy for Bashir over the Christian region. The former president, Suleiman Franjieh, was spared. Geagea had acted on

Bashir's commands then.

"Calm down! The Americans, Italians, and French forces brought order!" he said.

Under the watchful eyes of the multinational forces, the Syrian and Palestinian fighters boarded ships and departed West Beirut. They had come to Lebanon to support Bashir Gemayel's brother, Aziz, who just got elected a president. Baba's assurance rang empty. He was putting me in too much danger.

"Multinational forces? Are you joking? They have no idea who Geagea or Barbara is from their aircraft carriers and screaming jets."

"OK! What do you want to do?"

I knew exactly what the ultimatum was. Get the car or move out. I took a deep breath. "OK!"

Baba rambled on about handling the car on turns to keep the tires square and shifting gears early to save gas. I tuned him out.

"Get my wallet," Baba ordered Mama.

She did.

"Here!" He handed me thirty dollars. "Ten for the fare and twenty for gas."

I stared into space.

"Be a man!" he demanded.

I looked at him in disgust.

"You will leave before sunrise!" he said.

I snatched the money from his hand.

"Get someone else to do it," Mama begged.

"Take your Red Cross badge. Say Allah!"

So now the cross is convenient! I thought.

"Let us pray the dinner prayer." He pushed the coffee table aside. "You will pray for protection and forgiveness."

I followed him to the vanity, where he performed ablution. Mama washed dishes. After prayers, Baba walked out onto the balcony, where he shouted for Abu Muhamad to come down for a backgammon match.

I went to my bedroom. I stood in the darkness and wondered, am I overreacting?

Moments later Baba opened my bedroom door. He held the lantern with license plates under his arm and a paper in his hand. "Take this!"

I took the paper from his hand.

"This is the bill of lading to claim the car. Don't lose it." He put the dirty license plates on my bed. "Put these on the new car after you leave the port."

So the plan entailed not only impersonating a Christian but evading the extortion fee on imports at the Barbara checkpoint.

"Good night," he said. I ignored him.

He left the door open.

Silence. Then I heard Mama implore Nabil, now twenty years old, to persuade Baba to change his mind. From the age of eighteen, Nabil had assumed his father's demeanor. He raised his voice, expressing indignation while Mama sobbed.

At dawn the next day, Mama woke me up.

"Wear the hijab," she said.

I had lost the little booklet with inscriptions that Hajjeh once prescribed to exorcise me from the holy ghosts, after the nightmares from Black Saturday.

"OK! I will!" I lied.

She insisted I performed the dawn prayer. I did. Then I put on the backpack and left. She followed me to the landing. There, she prayed, getting louder as I descended.

I walked to the Cola underpass, two miles beyond the combat zone. There, service car drivers shouted their destinations. One yelled, "Tripoli." I paid the ten dollars that Baba accurately figured and rode with four other men through the mountain roads.

We travelled through countless Syrian and Joint Forces check-points on one-lane roads. At times the driver backed up a hundred yards to allow trucks to pass by. Less than eight hours later, I tapped on the driver's shoulder to pull over outside the port in Tripoli.

Around four on a cloudy afternoon, I presented the bill of lading and my ID and received the keys to the car. The port worker pointed at the 1981 White Mercedes Benz. Both fascinated and angry, I stood before the car. How could Baba afford it during war and be so miser-ly with everything else?

I opened the driver's door. The rich aroma of the tan leather seats calmed me. I marveled at the gauges. I touched the dashboard, in-spected the flawless interior, and then drove off. The gas indicator lit up. A mile out of the port, I pulled into a gas station. I added fuel with the remaining twenty dollars and drove up to the air-pump area. I replaced the white round German plates with the dirty plates I had. I tossed the foreign plates in a trash pile and drove off.

As soon as I cruised on fourth gear, my mind spun into what-if scenarios. What if the Christian militias abduct me? How will Mama find me? What if they ask me for the car registration and discovered that I had replaced the foreign plates with the older car's plates? I had no money to pay the extortion fee. What if I turned around and re-turned through the mountains, to avoid the checkpoint? No, I couldn't do that—I had no money to add fuel. Without registration, the Joint Forces or the Syrian army would justifiably confiscate the car.

I hung the Red Cross badge from the rearview mirror and drove into despair. Mist covered the windshield. Forty minutes later, I ar-rived at the Barbara checkpoint. Two lines of cars formed. Five Jeeps on the right and a GMC truck on the left created a roadblock. They had formed the barrier at a tin-roofed storefront, a makeshift com-mand and control center. An armed militiaman ordered me to the left line. I nodded and smiled.

Armed men swarmed around the line on my right. Only unruly
kids and fidgety, veiled women sat waiting. I concluded that the militiaman who pointed me to the left identified Muslims and ordered
the drivers out. I felt a little relief. Perhaps they fell for my Red Cross
badge trick.

Four cars separated me from the militiaman at the checkpoint. He
wore an M16 over his shoulder and a handgun at his waist. He
directed the car in front of me to pull aside. Gunshots rang out.
Ragged Muslim men pleaded for passage. Two other militiamen
dragged a young woman away by her hair. I looked with the corner of
my eyes. They lifted her off her feet and took her to a roofless hut
between the street and the rocky shoreline, fifty yards west.

My line moved. I rolled forward. I was third. My heart thumped.
The misty rain turned into a gentle drizzle. I turned on the windshield wipers once.

The Christian militiaman approved the passage of the third car.
Now I was second.

My survival depended on my ability to con The Killers at the
Gateway to Muslim Hell.

I panicked. I am an idiot. What have I done!

In the car in front of me, a young girl with golden hair in the
backseat turned around and smiled at me. She waved. Next to her, a
veiled woman yanked her down. Without requesting credentials, the
militiaman threw his hand to the right, ordering the driver to pull
over. The driver didn't move.

I lowered the window in a show of respect. If I take on drizzle like
him, the militiaman might appreciate my courtesy. What am I thinking? I had seen these murderers. They were possessed by the devil.

The man in front of me put both his arms out pleading for passage. The Christian thug stepped back and removed his M16. The
drizzle turned into intense rain. The muzzle of the M16 now pressed

against the driver's forehead. I heard the children cry in the backseat. The veiled woman wailed. The driver pulled over to the right. I was next.

The gangster signaled me to approach. I put the car in first gear. A gush of heavy rain poured down and sideways. I turned on the wipers, unhooked the Red Cross badge from the mirror, and I approached ever so gently. I leaned to the window. The leather seats took on rain. I stopped at his side. I placed my fingers over my name. I smiled and presented the badge.

"Go! Go!" He flicked his wrist.

Unknowingly, a Sabra and Shatila murderer extended my life with a flick of a wrist. I put the car in first gear and rolled up the window. I looked in the rearview mirror. The militiaman ordered all the cars behind me to stop. He ran to the store and took shelter with his gang.

I switched to second gear, and it dawned me: I had made it!

I wiped away the hot beads of sweat and cold raindrops that misted my face. Then a knot formed in my stomach. I hadn't eaten anything since Baba cut my dinner short the night before. At first I felt my stomach growl. But in that instant felt rage. My breaths got shorter. I am a pathetic weakling, I thought—twenty-one years old and still craving my father's acceptance and approval.

I knew my value had sunk low in his eyes, but to put a number on it, three hundred and seventy dollars, and possibly have me killed in the bargain, severed the last emotional link I had with him. I abolished the idea of having a father and mourned the loss in my mind and heart. I shed tears. I grieved alone.

Just after sunset, I arrived at the combat zone. I pulled into the alleyway, where apparently Baba paced. He looked jubilant to see the car. Before I had the chance, he flung the door open and yanked me out.

"Why is the leather seat spotty? Oh, never mind!" He hugged and kissed me on the cheeks.

I had craved this affection all my life, but that day I had defined the relationship in new terms. I stood stolid.

"Thank Allah for bringing this car safely," he cheered and thanked Allah. "You are a hero!"

His praise rang hollow. I pushed him away, saying my goodbye without uttering a word.

"You *pimp!* How dare you shun me!" Baba looked up to see who witnessed the rejection.

Mama rested her chin on the bottom frame of the kitchen window and sobbed.

CHAPTER 16

THE GIRL IN BLUE BIKINI
MARCH – JUNE, 1983

My father thought he was punishing me with the silent treatment, but I cherished the peace. With four more months of high school before graduation, I applied to the American University of Beirut, three years overdue to start college because my school had closed during the war. Mama paid for the application and achievement tests. I hoped for the best. Prophet Muhamad said in a narrative: "With optimism come rewards." He proved right. The world opened its arms for me.

Unfortunately, joy came on the footsteps of the Americans' demise in West Beirut. Around noon on April 18, 1983, while taking a physics exam in high school, a thunderous explosion shook the building. The windows rattled. Most of my classmates, who lived far from the combat zone, were terrified. The teacher shouted, "Damn you! Get back to work! It is not like you haven't heard explosions before."

During recess, the principal, a Christian Palestinian refugee, took a bullhorn and stood at a window overlooking the playground.

"We bombed the American Embassy in Ein Murayseh," he shouted. "Death to America! Death to Israel!"

Students chanted after him. His victorious tone had reignited them.

While the sheltered anarchists broke in takbeerat "Allahu akbar," I thought about the Red Cross volunteers frantically searching for survivors. I also dreaded the celebration at home.

Shots rang out that afternoon while I sat on my bed studying. *Ta-ta-tatata!* Moments later inside the building Takbeerat echoed. I braced myself for another round of with-Allah-on-our-side-we-will-always-be-victorious rhetoric.

"Ya'Allah! Ya'Allah! Get up," Baba feverishly knocked on my bedroom door. I went to the door. Mama clanked dishes in the kitchen. Baba held the radio while Nabil entered the apartment, followed by Jamil, two bearded men wearing gowns, and four others.

Nabil passively introduced me. "My brother," he said, but looked inside the flat. It would be hypocritical for him to ignore me and then call his comrades "brothers."

I acted enthusiastic lest I project sympathy with the big Satan, America, or the victims.

"May peace be upon you, brother!" the bearded men said one by one.

I am not your brother! "May peace be upon you, brothers," I said.

"Come here, love!" Jamil opened his arms to receive me. I walked up. We kissed.

"Sit," Baba ordered me into the family room.

Nabil and his comrades leaned their weapons by the TV.

Jamil kept his close. "'If Allah helps you, none shall overcome you.'"

"Allahu akbar!" the rest shouted.

"What do you like to drink?" Mama asked from the kitchen doorway.

"Make tea!" Nabil said.

"*Shh ...*" Baba pressed the radio to his ear and then lowered it. "The Americans declared they will continue their mission in Lebanon—"

"We will bury the Zionist supporters here." Jamil picked up his weapon and slammed the butt on the floor. "Right here in West Beirut!"

"Allahu akbar!" they shouted.

"Now they know not to ever ... ever defile our soil," Jamil said louder.

While they binged on holy talk, I feared America's retribution. What if they cut funding to the American University and it shuts down?

I quietly retreated to my room. Minutes later I heard faint wails from the street. I sought Mama. "What is going on?" I scanned the family room. All shrugged in confusion.

"Allah knows!" a bearded man said.

Mama stood in the kitchen doorway. "Oh Merciful. Omar Sayed is dead."

"Who is that?" Jamil asked.

Baba said, "The Sayeds are Shias from the south—"

"How, Mama?" I asked. I had seen Omar pass through the alleyway. He was so shy, he hardly looked up.

"Inside the embassy," she said. "He worked in the cafeteria."

"Ya Allah. What was he doing working with the Americans?" One of the bearded men shook his head.

"I don't think the Americans will ship laborers and cooks from America," I said with a hint of sarcasm.

Nabil stared at me. "'O ye who believe! Take not disbelievers for superiors or friends ...'"

"Let us read 'Al-Fatiha' to bless the soul of the martyr—our brother Omar," Jamil ordered, and raised his hands. The men closed their eyes and uttered the short chapter to eulogize Omar.

I glared at them. I had hoped one of them saw it like I did. I thought, "'And who so kills a believer intentionally, his reward shall be hell wherein he shall abide.'"

One after the other, they wiped their face, signaling completion. Mama served tea.

The next day Mama, Um Muhamad, and Hajjeh left to pay their respects. Mama continued to visit with Omar's mother well into springtime.

In May, the American University released the status of applications. I left school and went straight to the admissions office. The campus was nestled on the hills of Ras Beirut, a seaside, upper-class suburb two miles southwest of our home. The main entrance of the campus was located on Bliss Street. Movie theaters, restaurants, and fancy high-rises lined the cobblestone avenue.

Guards at the gate enforced the entry of only students and staff. I pleaded for passage. After several minutes' imploring, with a few students witnessing my humiliation, the guards gave in.

In the admissions office and after verifying my credentials, a veiled student employee handed me an envelope. I ripped it open.

"Thank you! Thank you!" I cried.

She smiled.

I looked up. "Thank you, Allah! You are good to me!" Then I said, "I am going to name my firstborn girl ... Um, what is your name?"

"Jamila." She giggled. "Registration is in a month. Don't forget to bring money," she added, joking.

"Oh! Right. I want to work part-time."

"Go to Hariri's office. He gives scholarships. Everyone is getting money to go to America and Europe. For here, it is a no-brainer. You know where to find him?"

I recalled that Mama mentioned Rafik Hariri on one of her visits to the Red Cross. I also knew that he hadn't been assassinated, yet.

"No?"

"Next to the former prime minister's residence, Salim Hoss."

I passed Hoss's residence on the way home from school daily.

"Of course. Hey, where can I find the athletic director?"

"Most likely on the bleachers in the Green Field. Oh! That's what we call the soccer field."

I carefully folded the acceptance letter and slipped it into the envelope, then darted out of the office to the main gate. I walked out and made a 180-degree turn to reenter.

"Now what?" a guard asked, disgruntled.

I unfolded the letter and waved it before him.

He grinned. "Honor us in, doctor."

Damn right! I will be a physician one day! I stuffed the letter in my backpack and took the eroded stone steps into the campus. I held my head high. I breathed in the fresh Mediterranean breeze. Birds sang. Tree branches swayed. On the grounds, preppy students roamed. Others sat on benches or on the steps of the Rockefeller Hall directly across from me.

I am like you, you, a-and you!

I hiked down the lush green bluffs, down the steep and long stairway by the Civil Engineering building. I had seen the Green Field from Corniche Bahr—the corniche that separated the fortified campus from the rocky shoreline. Word had it that below the corniche, a tunnel connected the field to the university beach, where a steel tower rose to the sky.

At the bleachers, three guards sat next to Mr. Elias. They wore dark-blue overalls. Mr. Elias wore a pair of jeans, a white university T-shirt with the cedar-tree emblem, and thick sunglasses. I approached. He lowered his shades.

"Rami!" he called out, and smiled.

Keys on a ring hung from a cloth strap around his neck. He swung them aside and stood up. I took off my backpack and climbed to his level. He opened his arms. The guards moved aside.

"How are you?" He patted my back and then clamped my shoulders at arm's length.

"Thank Allah. Excellent, sir. How are you? Is Jerjes in America now?"

"Sit down, young man."

I put my backpack aside, eager to show him the acceptance letter, but I waited.

"The Americans declined his visa. He is in Australia. Umm ... with my money." The guards laughed.

Mr. Elias took a few minutes complimenting me in front of the guards. "You were accepted in the pre-medicine program?"

"Here, sir." I presented it to him.

He read it quickly. "Love, Jerjes knew it! Congratulations, my boy!"

The guards congratulated me and left.

"OK! Now let's set you up with a job. Do you have a lifeguard certificate?"

"No, but I can get one—"

"Do you have a pen and paper?"

"Yes, sir!"

He scribbled a note to the chief of the fire department and then told me how to find the man's office. "He will take care of you. Win the certificate, and you will have the lifeguard job."

"Thank you! Thank you!" I smiled in spite of myself. Baba raised me and Nabil to arrest our joy at the time when others treated us cordially and gave to us generously. He had instructed, "Always act disenchanted. Wear a scowl while trying to win pity. Hold your gratitude. If you are grateful, they will have you for lunch before you have them for dinner." That day Mr. Elias set me free. My spirit soared. I was thankful and grateful.

"This is how you pay me back—enforce the rules one hundred percent of the time. Will you do that?"

"I think I can. What are the rules?"

"Let us get 'I think I can' out of your vocabulary and put in a 'Yes,

I will."

"Yes, sir."

"First and foremost, you will keep the villagers and peeping thugs off the beach."

"They will drown before they make it—"

"Let us not get carried away."

"Right!"

"I can't hear you!"

"Yes, I will, sir!"

"Good. Do you know why it is peaceful inside the campus?" he asked rhetorically. "Because we follow the rules! Don't make up your own. Ours work. Will you uphold the rules?"

"Yes, I will, sir!"

"Pity the country where it is lawless and the citizens make up their own. You ..." He lowered his shades and eyeballed me over the frame. "Not only will you enforce the rules, you must *follow* them!"

"Yes, I will, *sir*!"

"OK, son!" He looked out at the field, my cue to go.

I got up and grabbed my backpack.

Mr. Elias reached to shake hands and held on. "You just made my week. Next time I talk with Jerjes—"

"Please tell him that I miss him."

"You get thirty percent off at the beach cafeteria."

The perk rang meaningless. I was broke.

"Thank you, sir. I am grateful."

"I need you to work the first two weekends in June, then every day afterwards. Can you do that?"

My faith, now reduced to Friday prayers, arrested my speech.

"You can't?" Elias asked.

"Yes, I will, sir!" He let go of my hand and removed a key from the ring.

"Here!"

I stood puzzled.

"For the gate. The padlock." He inclined his head in the direction of the beach.

I held the key to the entire beach. I felt powerful.

"Come in early on your first day. Let me see ... June 11. You'll have some paperwork to complete." He squeezed my shoulder affectionately. "Jerjes will be very happy to hear that you are with me now."

Allah! You are good to me!

When I reached the bottom step of the bleachers, Mr. Elias shouted, "And don't harass girls in bikinis! It is grounds for dismissal!"

"Yes, I will, sir! I mean, yes, sir. I will *not*."

That afternoon, I sought Hariri's Foundation and the fire chief. I got the application forms for the scholarship and secured the appointment for a two-day lifeguard-certification program. Allah favors those who strive in life for a better world, I thought.

I hustled home to break the news to Mama. She would be ecstatic, but I dreaded a "Whatever-Allah-has-in-store-for-you" response.

I arrived at the building at dusk, just as the muezzin called the dusk prayers. I swung the apartment door open to find Nabil, Jamil, and Baba sitting in the family room. Quickly, I wore the look of maturity—the frown. It didn't help.

"The rose-picker and breeze-sniffer is back," Baba mocked.

"Say Allah!" I replied uncharacteristically.

They glanced at each other. "Allah!" they mumbled.

I went to my room and prayed without giving anyone the satisfaction of seeing me. I thanked Allah for my prospects. Then I headed to greet Mama in the kitchen.

On the way, I heard Jamil say, "Hariri is a traitor. They are selling out to him!"

"He thinks he can buy our faith with money," Baba said. "This war is for the Muslims worldwide. May Allah curse him!"

"Hariri is the best thing that ever happened to this country," I said as I cleared the family room.

"You pimp! What do you know? Go to your mama," Baba said.

"I am, am I not?"

In the kitchen, Mama wore her pink rubber gloves and faced the sink. I leaned in the doorway. She had dinner prepared on a tray: kashkaval and hallum cheeses, labneh, diced tomatoes, and a bowl of olives.

"One day I will get you a maid and shred these gloves with my bare hands!"

"Why must you always provoke them?" Before I had the chance to answer, she said, "Go pray the dusk prayers."

"I did! I thanked Allah for my blessing."

Mama turned to inspect my sincerity.

I pulled out a chair and sat at the table. "All you do is hide in this kitchen. It is not like you roast a lamb every day, and they are not royalty."

"You are so young. One day you will get married and will want her to serve you."

"I will want her to be happy."

"Just go inside!" She poured water from a ladle to rinse a plate.

I grabbed an olive, sliced off a bite from the hallum cheese, and went to the window. "Once I become a doctor, I will get you a maid!" I smiled, pretending to look outside, but I watched her from the corner of my eye.

Mama studied me. I smiled wider.

"Rami! Love! He is a doctor!" she crooned from the kitchen into the family room.

"*Will* be, Mama!" I quickly said. "I have to do well during my first three years."

"Who is paying?" Baba yelled from the family room.

Suddenly Mama stood stifled. "Allah is generous!" she said.

"Not you!" I yelled back.

"Who is paying? Damn it!" Baba asked louder.

"Working on a scholarship from Rafik Hariri," I shouted back.

"I knew it!" Baba called. "It took a while, but you ... you finally came through! May Allah grant you success! May Allah award Hariri longevity—"

I ignored him. Mama asked me to wait. She left the kitchen. Moments later she returned, took my hand, and curled my fingers around a one-hundred-dollar bill. "Buy a bicycle. You will need to get to your classes on time."

"And to work."

"Allah opened his gates for you. It is in the book for you."

I leaned in and gave Mama a kiss on each cheek and left to my room.

That evening neighbors converged on our flat. They brought their own lanterns and hookahs.

"Where is the doctor?" Abu Muhamad shouted from the foyer.

I came out to bask in the glory.

"Glory to Allah!" they said over and over and marveled at me one by one. Zaki, Hajjeh, Um Muhamad, Abu Muhamad, Kifah, and Manal prayed for my success. They said they knew all along that I was special. I found myself describing my success from the Red Cross blood drives, acceptance at the American University of Beirut, my connection with the fire chief, and the prospect of a lifeguard certificate. They cared about one thing only—I was destined to be a physician.

Suddenly I became privy to their deepest and most awkward secrets. During that week, neighbors tilted their head in a subtle movement for me to follow them to a private location. Women approached me first. Um Muhamad described a concoction she slipped into Abu Muhamad's tea to subdue his sex drive.

"It is not working. Help me!" she begged. "Is there a pill for it?"

Hajjeh lifted her robe above the knee and exposed her varicose veins. Zaki, who sat by her side, winced as if he had just seen the branching veins for the first time. I forced a quick glimpse.

"Can you do anything about them? They are unsightly!"

"You are doing the right thing with all that spandex," I said, striking two birds with one stone. Allah and apparently Zaki would be pleased with her cover. But what did I know?

Zaki complained that he saw clouds and a purple halo around the candle flame while reading the newspaper. "I think the devil is telling me something?" Zaki glared at Hajjeh. "She's been casting curses on me."

"Say Allah!" Abu Muhamad said. "It is cataract!"

I nodded in agreement. How would I know?

On Saturday and during training at sea, I exceeded the chief's expectations. I saved a pudgy fireman from drowning. Early Sunday afternoon, he sang my praises and handed me a laminated YMCA Lifeguard certificate. I floated.

On the way home, I bought a Peugeot road bicycle with shiny chrome fenders, lights, and a rack for books. That evening, while everyone chatted in the family room, Abu Muhamad winked several times and tilted his head toward the balcony. He got up. I followed.

"A friend wants me to ask you how to remedy a sharp bend in the penis. It just appeared overnight. It is at the—"

"Tell your 'friend' to take a four-week rest."

"In sha'Allah! May Allah shield you!"

Back in the family room, I glanced reassuringly at Um Muhamad! That was free of charge! I thought.

After everyone left, Nabil and Baba waited for Mama to serve dinner.

"They visit with us because you are a doctor now. People!" Baba scoffed at the neighbors' sudden increasing interest in social calls. He continued, "You think you can predict my longevity with a gentle strike on the knee? Maybe the hammer will do."

"The hammer is too light," I said with a straight face. "Nabil, lend me your handgun. I'll check your pulse instead." After a few seconds I offered my diagnosis. "Your heart is made of stone."

"You are the man of the family." Baba was joyous.

Nabil jettisoned himself from the sofa, grabbed his AK-47, and slammed the flat's door behind him.

Mama ran out of the kitchen. "What happened?"

"Allah called," I mocked.

Baba smirked. Mama shook her head, disappointed in my arrogance. She humbled me.

The first day at work exemplified the reality of my world: eat them for lunch before they have you for dinner. Above all, though, enforce the rules.

From the moment I emerged from the tunnel under the Corniche Bahr, which connected the Green Field with the rocky shoreline, I exercised my vision of order. I picked up the white plastic beach chairs and tables and moved them to the naturally leveled rocks, so they would be closer to the waterfront. Then I rearranged the reclining beach chairs and smaller white plastic tables on the area where the university management had poured concrete, to accommodate more beachgoers. I evaluated the minute details, such as the location of trash bins next to the children's shallow swimming pool.

I asserted myself as a fearless lifeguard and reported the slightest movement. I chatted over the walkie-talkie as if I ran the command and control center for the entire university.

A professor identified himself. "Would you be so kind as to lower the volume?"

"Of course, sir! My objective is to keep you safe and happy."

He lowered his sunglasses and inspected my sincerity. I mean it! I thought. I wore a whistle around my neck. Each time someone broke a rule, I whistled. I blew it so frequently, by the time I took it from between my lips, I almost fainted.

On Sunday, I started a routine. I did a set each of push-ups, crunches, and squats. I spread my arms, strode the perimeter, and inspected the barbed wire. I dove into the water, checked the buoys—moored together to demark the beach boundary—and sprinted back to climb the white looped ladder at the edge of the concrete slab. In my mind, the hookah smokers on the sidewalk admired me, onlookers outside the perimeter envied me, and beachgoers wanted to be me.

By ten in the morning, I lit my first cigarette. Minutes later, a girl in a bikini the color of the sea emerged from the tunnel. She looked fit. I stole glances at her as she spread a towel on a beach chair to the left of the tower base, away from the catcallers. Her golden hair was pulled back in a ponytail. She lay down and raised her face to the sun. When I vowed to Mr. Elias that I would follow the rules, I had no inkling how bottomless my unattended emotional needs were.

I became self-conscious. I put out the cigarette, fearing she would count it against me. She sat to my far right. I kept one eye on the swimmers and the other on her. I observed her every move. She walked confidently in her bikini. Her shimmering hair hung below her bikini top's strap. I tracked her graceful walk to the snack bar, on the right side of the tunnel. The construction took advantage of a natural cave formation in the rocks under the sidewalk.

As she walked around the few tables and chairs arranged before the counter, the server's teeth glowed. He smiled, which people rarely did. Holding a beer, she came back to her chair.

Alcohol! At first it tore me up that she was either a Christian or a loose Muslim girl, yet the idea of not having to deal with a mother wearing a hijab, strict father, or violent brother catalyzed my vision of being with her. I had to find a way to meet her, but I lacked the courage and experience.

After two weeks, a pattern formed. The dream girl came only on weekends. Consequently, weekdays moved excruciatingly slow.

On a Saturday, to get her attention, I confronted an intruder. The village boy had crossed the buoy lines in the choppy sea. I blew my whistle. He ignored my calls. I went out of my way to pass by her. I summoned the guards on my walkie-talkie. When the swimmer arrived at the ladder, gasping for air, I ordered him off the university's beach. I was in charge. The guards stood behind me.

The boy begged to rest, but I forced him back into the waves. When he reached the rocky shore outside the perimeter, the swells hurled him against the rocks. He bled from his head, arms, and back. I was ashamed of myself.

I returned to my post, walking past the girl. She looked up, and I smiled. She coldly looked away. I wanted to say, I am doing my job! I kept walking.

The next morning, I left home earlier than usual. I cruised the area outside the perimeter. Trash littered the area and tires lay in smaller pools formed between the rocks. The impoverished villagers in ragged shorts squatted on cardboard sheets. I sought to befriend as many as I could and persuade them not to risk their lives again.

"These girls are like my sisters," I explained to the largest and hairiest of the group. I learned his name was Ghazi. "Your catcalls are stabbing into my honor."

"*Wa'Allah*-In Allah's name, you are right!" he said.

"If any of you gets in trouble around here, shout my name, OK? I will take care of you. We are brothers."

They exchanged glances with each other, and we cut a deal. No peeping, and I would be their ally.

From then on, I walked up to the barbed wire and struck up conversations with them. They boasted about knowing me—the lifeguard of the American University. The rowdy men dispensed with, I could now focus on the girl in the blue bikini.

I scooted my lifeguard chair behind her usual spot before she arrived. When Elias visited the cafeteria that day, I hustled to defend the move.

"I need a wider view of the beach. You know! Police the sunbathers as well."

"OK ..." He rolled his eyes, just like Jerjes did when he thought, whatever!

"Thank you!" I said needlessly.

From my new vantage point, I studied the girl's habits. Every hour or so, she shifted in her chair and finger-combed errant golden hair from her face and secured her ponytail. She rubbed herself with tanning oil. She rolled balm on her lips. She looked glamorous. I was mesmerized.

After three weeks of obsessing over her, I resigned myself to being invisible. To make matters worse, she began wearing oversized white-frame sunglasses. They tortured me. I couldn't tell if she even stole glances at me.

I wanted to make a move, but Mr. Elias's warning played on. "... and don't harass girls in bikinis. It is grounds for dismissal!" I needed the money and a place to retreat outside the combat zone. I feared risking all. I had to figure something out.

CHAPTER 17

MAY JESUS BE WITH YOU
JULY, 1983

After more than a month of torment, I decided that the time had arrived. I rehearsed pickup lines all the way from home to the beach gate. ...

"Hi, I am the lifeguard."

"I know! Last week I wanted to shove the whistle up your ass."

"My name is Rami! I am the lifeguard. Let me know if you need something—"

"More like a death guard! You almost got a young man killed on the rocks a few weeks ago."

"Hi, I am Rami. How come you only come here on weekends?"

"Are you watching me? Pervert! I am going to report you."

I unlocked the beach gate. Just after I swung it open, a woman said, "Keep an eye on our son today."

A boy of about twelve walked in front of her and her husband.

"Good morning," I slowed to their pace through the tunnel.

"What is your name, love?" I asked, ducking to make eye contact.

"Caesar!"

A Christian.

"If you need me, shout 'Rami.' Now what is my name?"

"Rami!"

We emerged from the tunnel. The waves splashed thirty feet on shore.

After I settled in my post, the girl in the blue bikini arrived. She put down her beach bag and sat at the edge of a chair. I watched as she put on her shades and rubbed suntan lotion all over her toned body. After orienting her chair toward the water and retrieving a book from her bag, she parked it under the white plastic coffee table next to the chair. As soon as she opened her book, I got antsy. The choppy sea demanded alertness to the swimmers, but I fixated on her. I decided to go for it, to introduce myself. My heart fluttered.

I climbed down from the post and walked with a little swagger. About thirty feet before reaching her, I heard a scream.

"*Rami!*"

Caesar flailed frantically in the water as waves shot him high. I burst into a sprint, my eyes pinned on him. He disappeared behind the swells. I yanked off the whistle, threw it on the rocks, tossed my walkie-talkie, and flung off my flip-flops. Another swell sent the boy high in the air. He fanned his arms above the water.

"Get out of my way!" I shouted to onlookers in my path.

On my right, Caesar's father rushed past me and jumped into the waves. I leapt over the ladder in the concrete slab and dove in. I took strong, quick strokes, my head above water.

"Hold on, Caesar!"

I locked my eyes on his position, just as I had learned in training. Now his father was behind me. After a towering swell, the boy didn't emerge.

"He is under!" the father screamed at me.

Ten yards to go. I swam faster. I gasped for air and dove two yards in front of his last position. The water was murky. I swam in a small circle and ran out of breath quickly. Nothing! I shot up to the surface. I took a deep breath. I coiled and dove again. I swam deeper in the direction of the current. A blurry image of Caesar appeared five yards deeper. I kicked hard, now out of breath. The deeper I swam, the tighter my chest felt. I could not last. I reached and yanked him into me. Then I kicked upwards. We bounced on the surface. I gasped for air.

"Give him to me," the father ordered.

"Go to the ladder! *Now!*" I shouted.

Over the crashing waves, the mother wailed, "Love! Caesar! Jesus! Save us!"

The boy was unconscious. I threaded my hands through his arms, tethering him to me, and swam backwards. High, rolling waves whipped us forward, and low ones sucked us down almost to the bottom.

"I've got you! I've got you!" I said each time I exhaled.

I looked behind me. Ten feet to the ladder. His father stood on the bottom step, one arm wrapped around a loop, and with the other he reached out to us.

"Now!" I kicked as hard as I could before a large wave lifted me and Caesar. The father bent and extended his arm. I turned Caesar around and raised him up. His father clenched him. I went under.

I swam to the surface. Caesar and his father cleared the ladder. With one kick, I gripped it, scrambled up, and then sprinted after the boy and father. A crowd encircled them.

"Back up!" I said, violently shoving my way through. The father leaned over Caesar on the ground, shaking him.

"Take him to the hospital!" someone shouted.

The father picked Caesar up to whisk him away.

"Put him down!" I ordered.

The father gaped at me.

"*Now, damn it! Now!*" I reached to take the unconscious boy.

The father set him down gently. I knelt over him and pressed my ear to Caesar's nose. He wasn't breathing. His lips were blue. I straightened up, interlaced my fingers, and pumped his chest. I counted out loud and continued the compression as his parents screamed, "Jesus!"

I stopped counting.

Come on, love! *Pump*. Please, Allah! *Pump*. I can do this! *Pump*. Allah, he has a mother! *Pump*. Breathe! *Pump*.

"Breathe! Come on! *Breathe*!" I pleaded.

The boy twitched. Softly I pumped one more time. He choked. I quickly rolled him onto his side and gently thumped his back. Water spewed from his mouth, and then he looked at me.

"Rami. Am I alive?" His voice cracked.

"You are a miracle," I said, repeating Dr. Saba's words over my bed after Black Saturday.

His mother collapsed to her knees. She kissed Caesar all over. I stood up and proclaimed, "Caesar is a champ!"

Beachgoers cheered. Those outside the perimeter shouted, "Allahu akbar! Allahu akbar! Allahu akbar!" I felt goose bumps. Suddenly "Allahu akbar" celebrated saving a Christian.

"Robert Deeb," the father said. "I-I don't know how to ever pay you back."

"No need! It is what I do—"

"If you ever need anything. *Anything!* Anything you can think of, like ... eh ... a job, call me." He carried Caesar and said, "Please walk with me. I want to give you my phone number."

With the mother following, we reached the family's blanket and chairs. "Here!" Mr. Deeb handed me a business card.

"Your office is in East Beirut?" I asked, looking at it.

"Our ships sail from the port there, but we have an office here as well."

"I am a Muslim. Is that a problem?"

"Of course *not*! You are my hero, Rami!" He wrapped his arms around Caesar and me. He playfully squeezed us to his sides. "What is your last name?"

"Hadhari. Why?"

"You are not the only Rami I know!" He smiled, then sobered. "Are you related to the Hadharis who ... uh ... never mind."

Yes, I am the proud son of the one responsible for the permanent disgrace of our family at the graveyard steps.

"Thank you," I said. "I must get back to it."

"May Jesus look after you!" the mother said. "Call my husband! It is his company. We must repay you!"

Professors and students approached to praise me for my courage. The security guards thumped me on the back. Elias summoned me to his office. "The dean will hear of the rescue," he said.

I returned to my post. I looked out at the waves and felt a sense of redemption. In my mind, I nullified my guilt for abetting Othman when I tied the two Christian corpses to his car. Instantly a feeling of dread followed. I had been thirty yards farther from Caesar because I had ventured toward the girl. I had placed my lust above saving lives.

I climbed down and pushed my station forward to its original location, closer to the water. I sat and gazed out, blocking everyone and everything behind me.

"Your walkie-talkie," a female voice said in English.

I looked down.

Oh, my Allah! She is gorgeous. Why must I experience a seismic event to get what I want?

I smiled. "Thank you."

"You were miraculous. When he opened his eyes, he called your name! How—?"

"I met him this morning!"

"How divine! You gave him your name, and you saved his life."

"It was what Allah willed!"

"Perhaps! Are you going to stay up there?"

I climbed down.

"Are you a Christian?" I asked.

"Palestinian-Christian, but my great grandmother was a Muslim. My grandmother fell in love with a Christian man. No one could stop her."

"Are you stubborn like your grandmother?"

"Does it bother you that I am a Christian?"

"My best friend is a Christian. His name is Jerjes—"

"Add Sophia to your list!" She grinned.

"I get a discount at the cafeteria. Can I buy you a beer?"

"OK!" She smiled.

I love how you say "OK" with your American accent.

"Laziza. Right?"

I had seen her order the popular Lebanese beer, but suddenly it felt odd.

"Right ..." She looked uncomfortable.

"I watch everybody. I-it's my job! I'll meet you at your chair." I picked up my backpack, hustled to the flagpole, and raised the red flag. I conveniently banned swimming for the rest of the day.

I would run, but I would look foolish. I walked to the snack bar while glancing back and forth between the choppy water and Sophia. I feared someone would ignore the flag and drown, rendering me once again invisible.

"Two Laziza bottles, please!" I said, barely looking at the server behind the counter.

The manager shouted from inside the kitchen, "It's on the house, hero." He came around with two boat-shaped plates. "Tufik!" He introduced himself and lowered one plate of carrots soaked in lemon juice and one filled with mixed nuts.

I knew Tufik and most of the staff. They were Shias, which limited our interactions to shallow greetings.

"Rami! Thank you!" I said, and hurried away with the tray.

As she always had done, Sophia lay in her reclining chair. I set the tray on the table and then lowered the volume on my walkie-talkie. I pulled a chair to sit next to her.

"Do you drink?" Sophia pointed at the bottles.

"Today is special."

The battle with my demons ensued. I liked her a lot. Was it lust? Pure? I had grown remorseless about skipping Friday prayers. Almost all my Muslim peers skipped prayers, but never on Fridays. Now I intend to drink alcohol.

"You OK?"

"I am on top of the world," I said.

She laughed and toasted my bottle. "I like your spirit."

I hesitated, holding the bottle to my lips.

"Join us!" she said, grinning. "We are the devil worshippers!" She opened her eyes wide and wiggled her fingers in front of my face, acting diabolical.

I forced a smile. Our master Muhamad's narrative couldn't have been clearer. "May Allah curse the one who drinks it, the one who conveys it, the one to whom it is conveyed, the one who serves it, the one who benefits from the price paid for it, the one who buys it, and the one for whom it is bought."

"Maybe I shouldn't," I said.

"The Qur'an says alcohol contains some good and some evil." Sophia shocked me with her proclamation.

"You know the Qur'an?"

"I told you I have a Muslim bloodline." She grinned and reached for my bottle. "Too much of anything is bad for you." She started to pour it out.

"No! Don't!" I reached for her hand.

"I don't want you to drink—"

"Don't waste it," I said.

"Why?"

"'Approach not prayer when you are not in full possession of your senses ...,'" I quoted. "It is only *haram*-forbidden to drink before praying."

"My great grandmother wouldn't have liked it that I made you drink."

"Is she—"

"Gone."

"Sorry!"

"She always wanted me to befriend a Muslim man!"

"Look no further!" I joked.

"I won't!" She smiled.

I took a sip and winced from the taste. I can do this, I thought, grabbing a slice of carrot. I wiped my tongue with it.

"Please don't die on my account."

I took another swallow and then wiped my lips with my forearm. "Disgusting. How can you stand it?"

"Give it to me!" She laughed.

Sophia grabbed the bottle and poured it out. In the meantime, I took full advantage of our nearness and admired her in a manner that she wouldn't interpret as lustful. A voice pounded my conscience, a narrative. "'If one of you were to be stabbed in the head with a piece of iron, it would be better for him than if he were to touch a woman whom it is not permissible for him to touch.'"

"You have that look again," she said.

Sophia was sensitive to my expressions. I would never expose her to my whirling thoughts. Islam meant *salam*-peace ... *sallem*-surrender and obey Allah. The meaning of purity enveloped Islam. Islam was founded on peace and love. I drowned in love and indulged in peaceful times, but now feared I had crossed over to the devil. The devil symbolized all impurities. He thrived in prosperity and earthly joys. Joy! Nabil and Baba would chastise me for sitting with a girl in a bikini. Moreover, I drank alcohol. My Allah! If Hajjeh found out, she would shun me and demand I recite the *hijab-*

the prescription of verses that expelled the holy ghosts. Had I abandoned my values and beliefs to sit with this yellow-haired girl? When Allah showed our master Muhamad the population of dwellers in hell, women were the overwhelming majority.

"Rami. What is the matter?" Sophia took my hand. She looked utterly concerned.

I think I love you! "It is nothing."

"Show me your university ID," she said.

I retrieved it. She gazed at the picture. "What is with the frown and afro?" She smiled and shook her head.

"What is an *afro*?"

She leaned forward and tousled my hair.

"You are almost twenty-one years old. It says here that this is your first year." She handed me the card.

"The war. Schools were closed for two years in West Beirut. Show me yours."

"Daddy enrolled us in a school in Boston when the war broke out. I just finished high school at the International College. I start with you, next semester." She raised her shades to her forehead and searched for her wallet in the beach bag. "Here!" She handed me her ID, then retrieved a pen and a small notebook and scribbled.

Sophia Nader. She was seventeen!

I wished I could keep the photo. What am I thinking?

"I will major in pre-medicine," I said.

"How divine! I will, too. That is so exciting! Here are my numbers." The numbers were useless to me.

"Two?" I put the note in the backpack.

"We have a place in the mountains as well. I love it there. Snow covers the entire mountain in the winter and well into the spring. We spend the last two weeks of every summer up there."

"Aren't you going to give me your number?"

"Our phone died eight years ago. Besides, "All I need is this!" I wiggled the walkie-talkie.

Sophia insisted I tell her about my family. I revealed only the softer side, my affection for my mother.

"Isn't it time to close the beach for the day?"

"Oh! My Allah!" I snapped up as if waking from a dream. I feared Mr. Elias had caught me. "Will you come back tomorrow?" I stood up.

"Monday! *Hmm* ... maybe."

Maybe!

The next morning I looked for Sophia between my workout routines, after inspecting the floating buoys and while walking the beach's perimeter. I took to my chair and alternated between watching the swimmers in the bright sun and anticipating Sophia's emergence from the dark tunnel.

Without her, the beach seemed desolate. In one day, I let her cut open my cocoon. She ushered me into a new world, one which I once thought was the sure way to hell.

How could love be a sin? I wondered.

Back at my post, I felt bored. I strolled along the beach and held long and meaningless conversations with the villagers. Ghazi asked if I could buy him and his friend a sandwich. I returned with two hamburgers and fries.

"Thank Allah!" was Ghazi's way of thanking me.

"Love, *I* bought the sandwiches. Thank *me*!" I joked.

Ghazi's face turned expressionless. He took an enormous bite of his sandwich and talked with a full mouth. "So? Did you?" He smiled wide and winked at me. "You know! Do her?"

"It is not like that!" I said angrily.

"Marry her," another one said. "She is pretty."

"I wish! May peace be upon you," I said, and excused myself.

I went back to nothingness. I sat at the edge of the shallow pool and cooled my feet. A gust of wind drove stinging splashes on my sizzling skin. Whether she knew it or not, Sophia tormented me.

Each morning, I prayed she would show up one more time. I returned to my chair and looked out at the world that, once again, had become irrelevant.

May Allah curse me! What if she had brought me up to her family? Her parents might have told her to cut the Muslim loser loose. By Friday evening, I knew I wasn't special to her. She had remained true to her schedule, weekends only.

On Saturday, I rode my bicycle through the car entrance on the north end of the university. I rolled downhill on the paved and windy pathways until I reached the beach gate. Sophia was leaning on the gate. She wore the oversized white shirt, denim shorts, and brown sandals. Her beach bag hung by its strap off her shoulder. I came alive. I picked up my pace, and she dropped the bag. I stopped right in front of her and I dropped my bicycle in the dirt.

"Are you going to hug me or what?" She opened her arms and smiled. "I have been thinking about you."

"You have no idea!" I ducked under her arms and lifted her up. I sniffed her neck and then put her down.

"Tell me!"

"I can't."

"Don't be silly! Come on! Tell me!"

"I missed seeing you."

"That's better."

"I missed your pointy nose." I passed my index finger slowly over the tip of her nose.

She smiled brightly, and her white teeth glistened. "And what else?"

"I missed how you say 'OK.'"

"You like how I say 'OK'?"

"No, I love how you say 'OK.' I love how you walk, talk, eat, drink, swim, read, look, laugh, sleep—"

"Sleep?"

"You took a nap or two before I met you."

She pointed behind me with her eyes. I turned to see about a dozen students watching us and laughing.

"Oh! My Allah!" I opened the gates.

"I love how you say okay-yay!" a prankster mocked me in the tunnel.

"No! No! It's like *this*." A hairy guy slid his finger over his friend's nose. "I lo-ove how you say okay-yay-yay."

Sophia laughed, but I wanted to wring their necks. "Jerks!"

"Aren't you feisty!" She wrapped her arm around my waist and squeezed me affectionately. I melted.

I obsessed about Sophia's companionship. On Sunday morning and outside the beach gate, I asked, "Can't you come out during the week as well?" I tried not to beg.

"Only if you carry me through the tunnel." She fluttered her eyelashes playfully.

I swept her off her feet. She giggled all the way to the other end. I put her down. My legs wobbled and arms shook. She stood on tiptoes and kissed my cheek.

I craved and expected more, but then I saw Sophia kiss another boy on the cheek that afternoon. I felt sick at heart. How could she? I had proven myself to be heroic. She had witnessed the rescue. That morning, she said I was kind, humble, and funny. She even hinted at introducing me to her father. I had myself convinced that I was special.

After we opened the gate, I tried to tighten our bond by showing I was different from the callow boys on the beach. I seduced her with graphic descriptions, down to the fetus that hung from his mother's belly in the Sabra camp.

"You have seen terrible things," she said, her eyes teary. "You are very special."

She remarked about my talking with the villagers. "I've seen you with those poor men. You are humble."

"Have you been to the villages in the south?" I asked.

"No, but I have been to Florence, Zurich, and of course Boston."

"Have you been to Damascus?"

"Once. The diesel from buses nearly suffocated Daddy."

"Does your daddy ..." I removed a five-dollar bill from my wallet, picked up the walkie-talkie, and flexed my biceps "... get discounts and carry a walkie-talkie?"

She giggled.

"I didn't think so!"

"You are funny." Sophia laughed from the bottom of her heart.

Before noon, she asked me what my favorite novel was.

"*Les Miserables*," I said, "but I mostly read biographies." I rattled off some names.

"Who is your all-time favorite character?"

"Jean Valjean."

"What about Gandhi? Beethoven? And—"

"Only a fictional character can earn my admiration."

"Say more."

I heard Baba's voice in my head: "Nothing you say is worth anything to me!" I grimaced.

"Are you OK?" She touched my shoulder. She cared about me.

"Real-life heroes are motivated by achieving status and immortality. Most of them sought to invent, discover, and explore. Jean Valjean was an unrelenting benefactor to those in need."

"My father will like you." She opened the doors of hope. "Maybe you will meet him one day, maybe soon."

"It will be my honor," I said. "Why did you say 'maybe soon'?"

"The subject of emigrating always comes up during dinner."

"Everyone wants to get out of this dump." I needed to change the subject. "Hey, it is lunchtime. Or should I say 'beer hour'?"

"Perfect!" She smiled.

How much I love to put a smile on your face!

At the register, the cashier said, "Man! She's got a nice ass! Oh, what I would do to put my hands on it!"

"Shut up, Hasan!" Tufik, the manager, yelled.

I basked in my good fortune but wanted to choke the likes of Hasan for their penetrating eyes.

I took the two beers, and then there it was: the prelude to the kiss. Three boys, surely from her high school, surrounded Sophia at her beach chair.

They laughed. One patted her thigh. She leaned and kissed him on the cheek. Sophia could just as well have gutted me. In Allah's name, I drank beer for you. I dismantled my entire value system of holding Allah's word above all for you. I reinterpreted my Islamic teachings to justify being with you.

I walked up and stared at them. I set the beers on the table. "I have to go to my post."

"OK."

OK? That's it?

Their laughter faded in and out with the sound of waves crashing. At one point, I thought one of the rich bratty boys laughed louder to enrage me. I turned my attention to the swimmers to keep my sanity. Each time Sophia laughed, I died a thousand times. Once, she caught me looking. She waved vigorously with a wide smile. I pretended I didn't see.

At closing time, she approached. "I missed talking with you today. I waved for you to come over to meet my friends from class—"

"I can't socialize. I have to save lives."

"I know, I know. Tomorrow?"

"OK!"

That night I went straight to my room and sat alone with my pain.

The next morning, I met Sophia at the beach gate. Shortly after, I started my routine and Sophia played drill sergeant. She pressed her foot on my back during push-ups. "Faster!" she demanded. Then she counted my crunches. I increased the number beyond her demands to flaunt my prowess until I couldn't get up.

"I've seen your kind before. You build your body to impress the girls."

Her sense of humor breached my defenses. I laughed. Maybe I need to lighten up, I told myself. I got up and rubbed my hands together to clean the dust off. She mimicked my every move. She took my whistle and walked in front of me.

"Look at me. Who am I?" She stretched her arms out and moved forward, her legs and arms straight and rigid. I admired her legs and craved an embrace. She turned around and wiggled her butt. "That is how *you* walk."

"I seriously doubt that," I said, and hugged her. May Allah forgive me, I wished I could be glued to her.

I extended my hand and led her to the water. We swam to the buoy line. I went under, and Sophia followed. She pulled me toward her and then threaded her arms through mine. I wrapped my arms around her waist. We drifted deeper. Her hair floated. Sunrays beamed through it. She pressed her lips on mine. I moved my hands up and cupped her cheeks. She released me and swam to the surface. I wished water could be our new habitat. I followed her up. On the surface, I treaded water and found myself speechless.

She smiled, flipped, and dove under. I was right behind her. We stayed longer that time. I moved my hands around her back and kissed her again. She jerked me away and went up. I ascended slowly. She grinned and wrapped her legs around my waist.

"Someone might notice," I said.

"Who cares? We are friends."

"Friends?" I pulled back, dismayed.

"OK. More than friends."

Christian girls are loose! I should have known.

"I have to get to my post." I swam away.

"Rami!"

I stopped and treaded water.

"I like you a lot." She splashed me playfully. "You get too serious too quickly."

I swam slowly toward shore. She caught up with me.

"I like you *a lot*," she said.

You fill my life with ecstasy. "OK." I exerted self-control to seem levelheaded.

"You are the best thing that's happened to me this summer," she said.

You are the best thing that's happened to me *ever*. You stripped me clean of the last of my prejudice against Christians and girls. Memorizing the Qur'an was mere practice for the major feat of committing every inch of your body and your face to memory.

"Thank you," I said mildly, and climbed into my chair.

At closing time she said, "I will see you in two weeks." She tapped the bridge of my nose and then popped a kiss on my lips.

CHAPTER 18

SEX CORRUPTS
AUGUST 1983 – FEBRUARY 1984

Militiamen fought at night, making most mornings tranquil. A
week before my first day of college and Sophia's return from her family's mountain home, Mama and I sat in the family room. We drank
our morning coffee and smoked. Baba had locked himself in the bedroom, as he inexplicably did once a month.

I considered confessing my love of Sophia to Mama, but how
could she or anyone else know how I felt? Hers and her sisters' mar-
riages were arranged. Besides, they all loved only one, the Almighty.
Loving another human detracted from worship. It also honored the
devil.

Nabil opened the flat door. His intrusion shelved my thought.

"This is what we, the *jihadists*, do while you chase girls in bikinis."
He threw a newspaper on my lap and elevated himself to the ranks of
Muhamad's holy warriors.

I glared at him. "Not bathing should be added to the list of ablution nullifiers."

"May Allah curse you!"

"Cursing, too!"

"Pray for the prophet, you two!" Mama demanded.

On the front page, a picture depicted bodies piled inside a home.

The headline read, WHAT WAS ELIAS MILAD HADDAD'S GUILT? The Druze butchered sixty-four Christians in the mountain village Ma'ser El-Chuf. Elias had been three years old.

The thought of Sophia in danger or trapped in the mountain home enraged me.

"You are a monster!" I said.

He turned to Mama. "I knew it! He sympathizes with the idolaters!"

"Stop it!" Mama said.

"The Christians and Jews take comfort in weaklings like you living among us," he said louder.

"... and Allah grieves when people of the holy books butcher each other." I got up.

"Donkey! Pimp—"

"Stop it! May Allah curse you!" Baba shouted from the room. "I am talking to you, Nabil."

Since my acceptance at the American University, Baba continued to hold me in the highest standing.

"I am going to pray and ask Allah to enlighten you to renounce impiety and the worldly pursuits, to let you in his kingdom. That is what Allah wants from me," Nabil said.

My brother, a school dropout and a war criminal, prayed for my salvation because he considered me an ally to the infidels.

"Let us go to the kitchen," Mama said to me. She summoned me to her sanctuary, where we both would escape the discord.

Why not? I dreaded the solitude of my room. I no longer cared about anything except Sophia. I missed her terribly. I sat at the kitchen table and gazed into space.

Mama noticed the extended silence. "What is her name?" she whispered.

"Who?"

"If you can't tell me, who will you tell, love?" She crossed her arms and smiled.

"Sophia." Her name put a smile on my face.

Mama gasped. "A Christian?"

"Her great grandmother was a Muslim!"

"Never ever go alone to any place with her. *Khalwa* is haram." Mama said, warning me against retreating in seclusion with Sophia.

"Why is it *always* about that?" I got up.

"Because whenever a man and woman gather alone, the *devil* is third amongst them."

"No. Fourth."

"What?"

"Allah is always around, isn't he?"

While Nabil fought battles on random front lines, I went to school, which opened in spite of the escalation of fighting in the mountains. On the first day of class, each time a student arrived late, I craned my neck, hoping to see Sophia. She didn't show up. Neither did the professors call her name from the roster. Instead teachers targeted the absentees saying, "The university never closes. Attend or drop out."

After classes, I sought Jamila, at the registration office. There, pandemonium broke out. Attending students demanded filling the open spots made available by the absentees.

I plowed through the mob and leaned over the counter. "Jamila, can you look up a student, please?" I gave Sophia's full name.

"Sophia Nader?" she asked, startled.

"Yeah. why?"

Suddenly, I feared Jamila would say, "Word has it that she saw her parents getting killed before her eyes. She is in America now." Just like Sharif.

"Her parents funded a building on campus."

I didn't realize the full extent of her family's wealth and influence until then. I loved Sophia even more for her humility.

Jamila continued, "I answered her call last week. She dropped out. She said they couldn't leave their mountain home."

May Allah curse this world!

Late one night in September, unusually powerful missiles thundered. The American destroyers had opened fire from sea. I retreated to my dark tomb, my bedroom, rather than joining the neighbors in the stairway. That setting repulsed me because even eight years later, it evoked memories of Sharif weeping at the loss of his parents.

I couldn't focus on schoolwork. I slammed the books shut. Then I pushed through the neighbors on the stairs and climbed to the roof, where I watched the flashes of the launches from the seaside and the detonations in the mountains.

Half an hour after watching the inferno, I returned to the stairways in time to hear Zaki's interpretation of the battles. "Of course the Americans are going to bomb our fighters," he said. "They are stupid. They don't get it. Christians control the Lebanese army. The Christian commander is claiming his army is getting wiped out. You know! Our army is the boots of the Americans on our soil. But guess what!"

I grew indifferent to conspiracy theories, but Abu Muhamad eagerly asked, "What?"

Zaki continued, "The commander isn't trying to save the army. He requested the Americans to open fire to save ... let me see." He looked around until his eyes settled on Muhamad. "To save *you*, Muhamad!"

Muhamad, now a teenager, wore the same look Nabil had before, when he joined Othman.

"Muhamad," Zaki said, "who does the Lebanese army commander want to save?"

"The Christians fighters, the Lebanese forces, and the Phalangists, his friends," Muhamad said in a matter-of- fact tone.

"Bravo, Muhamad." Zaki lit up a cigarette and turned to Abu Muhamad. "May Allah grant him longevity! Your boy is a smart one."

Hajjeh, true to her calling, prayed, "May Allah curse the Americans, Israelis, and the Christians—"

Since Manal had lost her son Riyad in the Horsh during the Israeli siege, she had been reclusive, but now she took Hajjeh's prayer to a new level. She curled her fingers like claws and said, "And may Allah run the blood of Israeli children down my elbows."

Now equipped with the eyes and ears of an aspiring physician, I saw their actions and heard their words from a new perspective: the shit-hole dwellers would only be satisfied by the vicious demise of their enemies, Christians and Jews. They rallied behind the prayers to bring that about. Jerjes said that the Christians around him did the same thing. One time, I blindly accepted this as the norm. Like Jerjes, I almost siphoned my humanity into the sewers of war.

"The Americans will get theirs. When Allah is on your side, you will always be victorious," Abu Muhamad said.

Abu Muhamad's words were prophetic. On the night of October 23, a van exploded inside the US Marines' barracks by the airport, killing 241 men and women. Baba, Mama, and I stood on the balcony. The moon lit the rising dark smoke from the barracks, south of our building.

"How do you like helping the Israelis now?" Abu Muhamad cheered from his balcony.

I submerged into my private hell of anxieties. I visualized myself shivering from terror while the shit-hole dwellers begged Allah to send invisible reinforcements. I feared the Americans would annihilate us, a country two-thirds the size of Connecticut. And yet they were my benefactors. American missionaries in Syria and

Lebanon had founded the American University of Beirut in 1862. I was benefiting from the Americans' and Hariri's generosity more than I ever had from the most influential patriot.

I rode to school the following morning. Upon entering the campus, I took a deep breath. The school remained open. I thanked Allah that the Americans operated differently. Had the Lebanese lost 241 men in one day, and had we the power and the reach, we would have American males hung from their testicles and set on fire.

The frame of mind that dictates our actions quashes our ability to develop the power and reach exhibited by the Americans, I thought.

I thrived at school. My final grades put me on the dean's list. My biology professor said, "You are going places, son."

I got more motivated, yet disheartened that I sourced my energy from strangers. I told Mama about my academic success and reaching the dean's list. In Arabic, *dean* meant religion. She told the neighbors about the honors. They assumed I reached a holy status. I didn't clarify.

On the last day of school, I leveraged the Naders' name to request using the phone at the registration office. I dialed the mountain-home number. Sophia answered. She screamed in joy. I suppressed my happiness before the university employees. Sophia and I agreed to meet each other on the first day of the spring semester, in February.

"Only a catastrophe could stop me," I promised Sophia.

"I love you," she said.

Nothing else mattered. Life couldn't get any better.

One afternoon, Baba said, "They killed the president of your university. Makaron Kheir ... something."

Not catastrophic enough! I felt sorry for his son, however. I often saw him play basketball by the Green Field.

"Malcolm Kerr. May Allah have mercy on his soul!"

"It is forbidden to pray for heretics."

Tell me something I don't know, Mr. Righteous ... who scammed his brothers from their sharia mandated inheritance. May Allah have mercy on Malcolm's soul! I prayed silently for the son and for Sophia's safe return. Then it occurred to me: My best friend, Jerjes; the man who exemplified humanitarianism and earned my respect, Simone; the love of my life, Sophia; the boy I saved, Caeser, and his father who expressed everlasting indebtedness to me, were all Christians. The thought that I favored Christians over Muslims irked me.

Ronald Reagan, the president of the United States, put matters back in perspective. The American president ordered the marines to withdraw a few days before the second semester began and authorized the destroyer *New Jersey* to unleash its firepower over Lebanon. Just as when the Israelis had withdrawn and handed over the reins to the Americans, a power vacuum meant a power struggle. Battles broke out everywhere.

I would go to school to see Sophia anyway.

Days later, an *intifada*-revolution erupted. This time the Shias' Amal movement and fast-rising Hizbu'Allah along with the Druze's Progressive Socialist Party, the Sunnis' Murabitoon, and the communist militia, all turned their guns on the Lebanese army for partnering with the Americans.

On the first day of school, I traveled the embattled streets where militias raced to claim territories. I knew I ranked at the bottom of the pecking order, right next to the kurds. I passed a Murabitoon checkpoint. A militiaman fired a round. "Stop!" he shouted.

I threw myself on the sidewalk. Long before, I had learned that pain from bullet wounds was delayed. I frantically checked for bleeding.

A short fighter walked up pointing his rifle at me. "ID! Now, donkey!"

"Yes, sir!" I got on my knees and dumped the contents of my

backpack on the pavement. Mr. Deeb's business card and Sophia's note fell out. I felt at ease.

"You think this is funny! Ha?" The fighter pressed the muzzle in my forehead. His hands shook.

"No! No! Please! Please don't shoot. I am Rami Hadhari." I offered my wallet. "Here!"

He turned the weapon around and hit me with the butt on my shoulder, where I had been shot on Black Saturday. My body convulsed from the pain.

"Let him go." An older militiaman approached. "Is Nabil your brother?"

"Yes! Yes!" I celebrated the connection.

"Do you have a death wish? Go home. Damn it!"

"Thank you! May Allah grant you longevity."

I picked up the bicycle and hustled to the university. I stood before the chain-locked main gate and felt brave. A disheveled pedestrian said, "They are closed. Are you nuts? Go home!"

"I know!" I interrupted him before he could call me a rose-picker or a breeze-sniffer. Nothing was more important than seeing Sophia.

But in Allah's name, where would I find her? I had no inkling where she lived and no access to a phone. When is this damned war inside a war going to end?

I got home, only to be trapped for days because of the violence. Battles broke out on the open roads, narrow streets, and alleyways. I even heard a militiaman shout, "The window!" followed by an RPG explosion. Many buildings were ravaged, and smoke bellowed.

While Nabil fought, Mama prayed for his survival, and Baba napped.

During the following week, Hajjeh got in her element and transformed eulogies of the fallen into sermons. "Those who die disbelievers will suffer greatly in their graves awaiting judgment day," she intoned. Hajjeh's words articulated my sentiment well.

My room morphed into an aboveground grave. My own day of reckoning would be when I returned to school. Had classes resumed while I was trapped inside our building? The outcome of my academic ambitions lay in the hands of the likes of Nabil and Jamil and their battles against other Muslims and Christians.

Two weeks later, the fighting had become sporadic enough that I decided to risk leaving home. I pedaled to school on side roads and alleyways. I heard gun battles. RPGs were launched randomly. I sprinted to the university. It was open. I threw the bicycle over the rack and hastily locked it. I dashed into the campus. I grabbed the railing and leaped up the stairs into the admissions office. Inside, an older lady stood behind the counter. She lowered her reading glasses and frowned.

"What happened to you?"

"The school is open?" I asked, gasping.

"Did you strike a deal with the dean to postpone classes for your highness?" She removed her glasses.

"*What?* You think this is funny? I dodged grenades to be here. How much more do I have to do to get what I want in this world?"

"You can reregister for the next semester in two months. You will lose some of the tuition since it is still early in the semester—"

"This is a disaster! I will lose my scholarship! What am I going to do? I risked my life to be here." I pleaded my case in vain. "How can you do this to me—"

"Listen!" She slammed the counter top. "We all have problems. OK?"

Not as devastating as mine. "I have nothing now. I am nothing. I am wrecked." I sobbed.

"Try losing a son," she shouted. "Goddamn it! *You* don't have problems!"

"Can I make a call, please? I have to talk with the Hariri Foundation. Please!"

She gestured toward the telephone with a head tilt.

I sniffled and held back tears. I explained the circumstances to the
Hariri Foundation representative. Nothing I said affected the out-
come. The representative dropped the guillotine on my scholarship
with legal precision, and said, "May Allah be with you!"

I collapsed on the stairs outside the office. Helplessness and hope-
lessness struck me. I was defeated. What did I do wrong? I thought I
had done my part. I modeled my heroes: Edison, Pasteur, Da Vinci,
and Ghandi. Like them, I was resilient.

I had repeatedly risked my life to attend classes. I finished my
school assignments on time. I made it onto the dean's list. I saved
people, buried victims, comforted survivors, and rescued a child. I
aspired to attend to the sick and injured. I craved granting Mama a
better life. I didn't deserve this! Had Allah punished me for saying,
"Satan is fourth"? Did kissing and hugging Sophia underwater
warrant Allah's wrath? It must have been the beer.

I should have never dreamed big. I should stop striving for a better life. Baba made the best of what he had. Jamil retooled continu-
ously. He evolved from an activist, a cleric, to a militia leader. He got
wealthy. Nabil saw it. I was dumb! It was my fault for listening to
Mama and the neighbors: "Stay. It is what Allah wants for you to do
to live and heal people."

I detested Israel, Palestine, Lebanon, Druze, communists, Kurds,
Shias, Sunnis, Christians, and Jewish fighters and their causes. Had
there been a mighty power at my disposal, I would use it to annihilate
all of them. May Allah curse them all!

I slowly regained my senses. Through a haze I saw students roam
the campus. Some laughed. Two held hands. Their joy stabbed into
my misery a thousand times. The tree branches swayed. My eyes
glazed over. The Mediterranean breeze wafted across the campus.

The breath caught in my throat. I felt weak and exhausted. There was no one to take my hand, to tell me, "Come this way. You will be all right."

I buried my head between my knees.

"Rami?"

It can't be true. My mind is still a blur.

"Rami, it is me."

I looked up.

"Oh, my Allah!"

Sophia opened her arms and smiled. "Are you going to hug me or what?"

"You have no idea!" I stood up and swept her off her feet. I smelled her neck and smothered her face with kisses. She jumped on me and wrapped her legs around my waist. I pushed her back to admire her face and embraced her again.

"Tell me how much you missed me," she said.

"I didn't only miss you. I adore you. I worship you. You are my world."

Blasphemous! Only Allah is worthy of worshipping. Repent!

She tilted her head and smiled. "What about my nose or how I say OK?"

"Oh! Yes. I missed your pointy nose and ..." I passed my index finger slowly over the tip of her nose. Her teeth shone. I set her down on her feet. "I am a loser. I have nothing. I am cursed—"

"What are you saying? What happened?"

I explained my ordeal.

Sophia's presence and encouragement rescued me from a free-fall into despair. "Love, people like you rise to the top everywhere else in the world. You remind me of Daddy. You are smart, loving, and have integrity. Good things always happen to good people, even if it takes awhile. You know what else?"

"What?"

"I love you."

"I love you, too."

For the next four hours, Sophia and I sat at a bench overlooking the Mediterranean past the Green Field and the Corniche Bahr. She leaned her head against my shoulder. We watched the sunset. I held her hand and kissed it.

"I must call Mr. Deeb and try for a job until I figure things out," I said.

"You want to call him from my home tomorrow? Your mind will be more at ease then."

"Thank you. You are the best thing that ever happened to me. I would never do anything to lose you."

Sophia gave me directions to her home and descriptions of each of her family members. Walid, her younger brother, was a computer whiz. Sophia said that her younger sister, Maha, wanted nothing more than to be like her. I looked forward to the next day but dreaded separating from Sophia and returning home.

An hour later, the evening call to prayer echoed from the minaret as soon as I entered the building. Inside, our flat was chilly. Baba sat in his chair, wearing his bathrobe, his hands almost touching the charcoals in the grill to keep warm. His transistor radio broadcasted another call to prayer. One candle glowed in the family room. Um Muhamad gabbed with Mama in the kitchen. Nabil was likely cruising around at the Corniche Bahr, drinking coffee with Jamil or firing weapons in the combat zone.

"What took you so long, doctor?" Baba asked.

"With friends."

Mama stood in the hallway between the kitchen and family room. "How was school?" she asked innocently.

I sat across from Baba, tired and hungry.

"The Hariri guy said I am on my own now."

"What? No money?" Baba yelled.

I sat stone-faced.

"Born a loser. Always a loser," he quickly ruled.

"If it hadn't been for this goddamned shit hole. I would rise to the top everywhere else in the world." I got up and headed for my room.

Baba spewed curses and prayers for my demise. In my bedroom, I wanted to punch the walls and throw books.

Mama and Um Muhamad opened the door.

Mama quoted the Qur'an. "... it may be that you dislike a thing while it is good for you ... '"

"Please!" I implored. "Not now! Please leave me alone."

Um Muhamad said, "Whatever is in the book for him." They closed the door.

I considered throwing "The Book" at the door, but I held it together.

At half past three in the afternoon the next day, I buzzed Sophia from the intercom outside her building door.

"Hold on," she said.

Moments later, Sophia beamed from the elevator, wearing a pair of jeans and a beige linen blouse. She unlocked the door hastily. "Before the concierge notices," she said.

As soon as the elevator door closed, Sophia jumped on me. I lost my balance. We bumped the walls. The cabin shook as it ascended while we kissed and bounced from side to side. When the elevator stopped, we straightened up.

Sophia opened the flat door. A rich aroma of potpourri instantly wafted over to me. "Everyone is out. They will be back in an hour."

"Oh, my God!" I felt overwhelmed. My heart raced, and body temperature soared as she held my hand and ushered me into her world.

In the foyer were two chairs on each side of a half-moon-shaped marble-topped table. A phone, a decorative notebook, and a pen were carefully arranged on top.

"Make your call. Hurry!" Sophia pointed at the phone and walked down the long hallway.

"I love you." I sat down and dialed.

Mr. Deeb shouted my name. "Rami Hadhari! My hero! How are you, son? My wife and I talk about you all the time."

I was ill trained to hear compliments, much less respond to them. I mumbled incoherently. "I am embarrassed to call you about this, and I wouldn't have if ... you know ..."

Mr. Deeb interrupted. "Hold on. Let me check my schedule." He paused. I heard papers rustle. "Can you come and see me on March 22?"

"Of course."

"One in the afternoon."

"Yes."

"Do you need me to get you a pass to cross over to East Beirut?"

"No, sir."

"*D'accord?*"

I thought he would insist.

"*Merci,* Mr. Deeb."

The appointment was a month away, but at least it was a guaranteed job.

I set the phone down gently and looked around. Sophia's home was true to her father's reputation. The amber sunset washed the walls and lighted four-foot tall oil paintings.

"Sophia," I whispered. I feared I would alert the holy ghosts.

"Come in." Sophia emerged at the end of the hallway. She had changed into denim shorts and a pink tank top. My entire spectrum of emotions converged on her gorgeous face. It was all about Sophia. I could die happy right now!

She gave me an expedited tour of her five-bedroom home. No

candles, no lanterns, no religious symbols. Floor-to-ceiling sliding glass doors stretched over sixty feet wide. The Naders could see the sunset from their living and dining rooms.

As I gazed at the view, the bottom rim of the sun flickered as it eased into the horizon. Sophia's backlit silhouette transformed her into an angel.

She turned and said, "This means we should hurry."

She took my hand and led me to her bedroom. Shelves covered an entire wall from top to bottom, where books and spotless decorative items were beautifully stowed. The bookshelves flanked a desk with a fancy leather swivel chair. Her bed was as large as my mother's and father's—put together.

We sat on the edge of the bed. Then she moved to lie on her back and held her arms out to me. I leaned over and kissed her. "I love you," I whispered.

She tried to remove my shirt. I pressed my body against hers. We kissed.

"Guess what!" I interrupted with excitement.

"What?"

"I got the job interview with Caesar's father!"

Sophia's eyes looked at my lips.

"Can you believe it?" I asked.

She reached behind my neck and pulled me down.

I spoke in her lips and pulled her up. "Come on," I said.

"Where?"

"The balcony. Come on!" She didn't move. "Before the sun goes down." I needed the cold air.

She looked confused. I lifted her up and carried her out to the spacious balcony, while she giggled and popped kisses on my cheeks.

"Look at this! Isn't it beautiful?" I spread my arms at the expanse of the Mediterranean.

Sophia lowered my arm and faced me. We kissed. "Let us go back inside, Rami."

"Just look! When I work at the shipping company, you and I will board a cargo ship and visit Europe."

"I'd rather fly." She cupped my cheeks and pressed her body against mine.

"Seriously! The silence of the sea! The splashes of the waves! The sea mist blowing in our faces!" For the first time, I saw it Sophia's way. The view was gorgeous. My soul was set free.

I drew a deep breath, closed my eyes, and envisioned her on the beach. "I can see you in your blue bikini next to me as the boat bounces on the swells."

"I will put it on for you. Come on," Sophia now tugged me inside.

We locked lips all the way to the bedroom.

"Sit." Sophia pointed at the chair. I did. She retrieved her bathing suit from her walk-in closet and tossed it over the bed. She stared at me as she took her tank top off. She smiled. I felt embarrassed and turned away but stole glances when she put on her top. Then, she removed her skirt and took off her panties. My heart pounded in my neck as if it changed positions.

"Do you like me better now?" She spun around playfully, then she swayed her hips as she walked up to me in her bathing suit.

"I loved you before. I love you now and will always love you."

She took my hand and tugged. We lay on her bed.

"When I start making money and buy a flat, will you——"

"Make love to me!" Sophia scooted closer.

I leaned over her.

"You are shaking. Breathe."

I kissed her lips and neck. She took my hand and softly landed it on her breast. Then she pushed me back, removed her bikini top, and threw it on the floor. Her cheeks turned pink. She smiled. I moved my lips around her breast, and she eased me onto my side. I got up to remove my shoes and shirt. I turned around to see Sophia raise her hips and lower her bikini bottom. I froze.

"Are you OK?"

"I-I don't know," I said, feeling torn to shreds. "I don't think I can do this."

"What do you mean?" Sophia's face now crimson. "Did I do something wrong?"

"It is a sin," I said.

"*What?*" She swiftly pulled up her bikini bottom.

"Doing this." I looked away but pointed in the direction of her waist.

I turned back when I heard her get up from the bed. She covered her breasts with one arm and turned her back to me. She tied on her bikini top.

"I just don't want to die poor."

"Are you joking?" She looked at me, incredulous. "You are not! Oh, my God."

"Our master Muhamad—Allah prayed for and saluted him—said, 'Pronounce to those who kill they shall be killed and those who sin shall die poor even after a while ...'"

"Oh, my God!" Sophia's eyes darted around the room.

"Are you upset?" I asked.

"This is the weirdest moment in my life. Ever! Oh, my God!" She tugged on her shorts and pulled the tank top over her head.

"This is the best day of my life."

"Are you kidding?"

I shrugged and before I uttered a word, Sophia said, "Oh, my God. You are not!"

"I don't want to defile your body."

"Please! Stop!"

"Sex corrupts. It is an immoral Western—"

"Stop! Don't say any more."

She opened the door and left.

"Why are you acting like this? Where are you going?" I chased after her.

I knew I was right, but I didn't know how to win her over to my point of view.

She stood on the balcony. I approached.

"You think I am disgusting," she said. "What next? You are going to tell me that the devil sent me to lure you into sin?" she asked, now furious.

The majority of dwellers in hell were women. I recalled the narrative.

"Oh! My God, no!" I said.

"What did you think we were going to do?"

"I just thought ... I am trying to be good to you."

Silent tears rolled down her cheeks. I stood dumbfounded. I didn't know what would comfort her. Should I go or stay?

I apologized again and again. I tried to explain myself. Sophia was inconsolable.

Lights suddenly came on inside the flat. Sophia wiped her tears, turned around, and forced a smile as she walked into the living room to greet her parents.

I stayed where I was. I couldn't move. Mr. and Mrs. Nader approached. Sophia made the introductions. Mr. Nader said that he was pleased to meet me. He directed Sophia and me to sit at the sofa in the living room.

While Sophia looked distraught, I felt empowered. I had seen Western shows where a boyfriend is treated like a family member. Mr. Nader asked me to sit by his daughter in his house.

Mr. Nader sat in one of two maroon wingback chairs facing us.

Walid walked in. He looked like he was thirteen years old. He wore faded jeans and a T-shirt. He shook my hand firmly and sat next to his father. Maha cheered.

"Hi, Rami!" I reached to shake her hand.

She ignored it and gave me a big hug.

"What do you like to drink?" Mrs. Nader asked.

"Nothing. Thank you."

"OK."

That's it?

"Sophia said you saved a boy's life. I can't help but look at you with admiration. Saving lives *is* the act that should be held holy in this country," Mr. Nader said.

"How far along are you in college?" Mrs. Nader asked.

"Um ... I missed classes and lost my scholarship yesterday."

"This damned country ..." Mr. Nader said. "Honorable and smart men like you are falling victim. If you are not in the economy of conflicts, you will wither."

"It is my responsibility. I should have made it to class, no matter what."

Mrs. Nader and Mr. Nader glanced at each other. Their expressions communicated dismay at my self-deprecation.

"What is the matter, baby?" Mrs. Nader asked Sophia.

"Oh! Nothing. You are right, Daddy."

I detected subtle insincerity in Sophia's voice.

A few moments of awkward silence ensued.

"I must go now." I stood up and waited for Sophia to lead me to the door.

The entire family got up for me. I shook hands with the parents and Walid. Maha hugged me again. "We hope to see you soon," Mr. Nader said.

"It will be my honor, sir!"

Sophia walked in front of me. She opened the door and looked down.

"Please know that I love you so much. You are everything to me."

Sophia remained silent.

"Can I see you tomorrow?" I asked.

"I need time."

"Sophia, please ..."

"I opened my heart. I surrendered to you, but you ..." She shrugged. "You made me feel sleazy."

"I want to save the act until we get married."

She took a deep breath and shook her head as if I was naïve.

"Will you get engaged to me if I have a job?"

She stood silent.

"Can I kiss you?"

Sophia turned her head, and I kissed her on the cheek. She didn't react. I walked backwards and pressed the button to call the elevator. Without a word she slipped inside their flat and shut the door.

CHAPTER 19

YOU ARE A GOOD MUSLIM
FEBRUARY – MARCH, 1984

The possibility of having a job soon pacified my father and delighted Mama, but I never said it was with a Christian company in East Beirut. They stayed out of my business, which allowed me to dwell on what had happened with Sophia. I found myself emotionally depleted, and the need to be with her paralyzed me.

For three weeks I questioned my values. I thought I was honoring her, but she felt rejected and humiliated. I should have been more affectionate. Allah would have understood. He knows everything. I love her, and she was his creation.

On the afternoon before the interview, I rode my bicycle to Sophia's building.

"The job interview is tomorrow," I said through the intercom system. I hoped she would ask me up.

After a few moments of static ridden silence, Sophia said, "Do you want to come here tomorrow and tell me how it went?"

"I would love that."

"Great. And Rami ...?"

"Yes, love."

"Good luck."

"I love you."

"I know," she said, then waited for me to disconnect. She still cared.

That evening, I devised the strategy for the interview. In the unlikely event Mr. Deeb rejected me, I would remind him of Caesar's rescue. While sitting at the edge of my bed and in the midst of a silent interview rehearsal, Mama barged in. She swung a smoking incense burner from her fingertips. To complete the ritual, she spun it around my head.

"You are choking me!" I waved the smoke away.

"May Allah pave your way tomorrow! Did you pray?"

"I did," I lied.

"Do you see the connection? Jamil gifted me these rocks from the holy land just in time. It is a sign."

Mama was doing her part by activating a foolproof holy shield around me and relying on Allah for my salvation.

"In sha'Allah!" An Allah response reinforced and expedited the ritual.

I woke up early the next morning. I borrowed a white shirt from my father and wore blue trousers, the only dress pants I had. With a cease-fire agreement in effect for a few weeks now, the Museum-Barbeer passage was open. This time, only Allah would stop me from crossing to East Beirut. I decided to bring my Red Cross badge.

My appointment was at one in the afternoon. If it weren't for all the war hurdles, it would have taken ten minutes to reach Mr. Deeb's office next to the seaport. I decided to allow extra time for unpredictability and leave at eleven. At that moment Nabil and Jamil entered the flat, and Mama left to visit with Hajjeh.

Baba opened my door. "Ya'Allah! Wash up to join us for the noon prayers."

"I can't. I have to leave for my interview in a minute." I shoved past him to the foyer, where I picked up my shoes.

"Allah will have his way with him," Baba told Jamil and Nabil.

He sat at his chair in the family room to pull on his socks.

Jamil stood behind me. "Don't they pray on Fridays? What is the name of the company?" He finished his ablutions, wiping his forearms with the wet towel that Nabil and Baba had used.

"May peace be upon you. Why?" I penalized him for violating a narrative that directed us to greet first.

"May peace be upon you ... Maybe I know someone there."

"You wouldn't!"

"We'll give you a ride after prayer," Nabil said.

"Do your deeds and earn your rewards elsewhere." I covered my dirty secret, pursuing work with Christians, with a verbal attack.

"*Pimp*!" Nabil mumbled.

"*Shh* ... Pray for the prophet!" Jamil silenced Nabil. He turned to me. "There is a lot of tension on the streets."

"They failed to reach an agreement in the Lausanne conference," Baba said. "Take Nabil's offer. Only Allah knows what is going right now. Where is the interview?"

Baba referred to a meeting held in Switzerland—one of the many intended for consensus building between the militias.

"OK," I said to humor him. Instead of warning me of danger, it would be easier to tell me when it is peaceful.

"Where is the damn interview?" Baba asked.

"At the port."

"What?" Nabil said, outraged. Baba leaned forward to inspect my seriousness.

"It is a real job," I said. "Getting promoted to martyrdom is not the top position."

"In sha'Allah you fail!" Nabil said.

"I will be in good company."

"I want to kill him." Nabil jumped up.

"*Shh*." Jamil raised his hand and subdued Nabil.

"I need a job. I want to have a family one day," I said, soliciting sympathy after stabbing into the heart of Jamil's world.

"With the heretic ... Sofa something," Nabil said.

Mama, goddamn it! She must have told them.

"She is not a heretic and her name is Sophia," I said defiantly.

"Sofa."

"She is more a Muslim than many I know. She is more accepting—"

Jamil spoke softer. "'And they will have therein mates perfectly pure, and therein will they abide...' A Muslim sister is more worthy of you. Come pray with us, love."

"'Allah created you from dust, then from a sperm-drop, then he made you pairs ...,'" I said. "*Pairs!* Not prayers."

"'Don't guide who you love, Allah guides whom he wills.' Let him be!" Baba said.

I grew extremely irritable. Each time they resolved to win me over and lost they uttered those words.

At that moment the call to prayer blasted from the minaret. On cue, we mumbled, there is no god but Allah, and Muhamad is the messenger of Allah.

"Are you coming with us or what?" Jamil asked.

I invoked a verse. "'And strive in the cause of Allah as it behooves you to strive for it. ... He has laid no hardship upon you in religion.'"

I opened the door, and just before I closed it behind me, Nabil prayed, "In sha'Allah you fail!"

I slammed the door. On my climb down, I cursed Nabil, Jamil, and Baba, and pitied Mama.

When I reached the ground level, the call to prayer concluded with *Hayya alal-falāh*-the time for work has come.

I felt vindicated, but I had committed blasphemy by pursuing love and work with Christians over prayer. Jamil said the streets were unsafe. I feared dying on bad terms with Allah. It was clearly stated in the Qur'an, "Let not the believers take disbelievers for superiors in preference to believers—and whoever does that has no connection with Allah—except that you cautiously guard against them. And Allah cautions you against his punishment; and to Allah is the returning."

I flexed my index finger, symbolizing Allah's uniqueness and uttered my declaration of faith. "There is no god but Allah, and Muhamad is the messenger of Allah," I said softly, and cleared my conscience.

Jamil, now in the money, had his brand-new 1984 Silver BMW 745 parked in the alleyway. Despicable! I turned to the crossing of the Museum-Barbeer interchange, a half a mile away.

Well before I reached the Barbeer Bridge, I saw the line of cars that stretched from the Museum checkpoint. Hundreds of people walked to and from the Barbeer checkpoint on West Beirut's side. I wore the Red Cross badge around my neck and walked alongside a car, which a soldier allowed through.

"Stop!" the soldier demanded.

I waved the Red Cross card, downplaying the significance of the order.

"Come here!" the soldier demanded.

I wiggled the badge again. He pointed to the ground where he wanted me to stand, right in front of him. I submitted.

"Name?"

"Rami Hadhari."

"The graveyard Hadharis," he scoffed and then passed his finger down a list.

"No."

"Is your name on the list?"

"I am on Red Cross business."

He reached for my badge and flipped it around. "Go renew it."

"What?" I said in disbelief.

Damn! It had expired.

"Return!"

"But, I—"

"If you don't return now, I will have this man there ..." He pointed at a shorter and angry-looking soldier "... give you an unforgettable beating. *Ya'Allah!*"

"I have an important meeting. It is the only thing—"

He cocked and pointed his M16 at me. "*Now,* donkey!"

I had grown indifferent to having a gun aimed at me.

"All right! You are the boss." I calmly turned around and considered running for it. If I made it, however, he would alert his counterpart at the Museum checkpoint.

I walked out of the soldier's line of sight and solicited a ride from one of the drivers. A well-meaning woman said, "Love, passengers' names must be on the list, too."

I straightened up and stared at those who crossed. Some men carried briefcases. Most wore smiles. I needed to be in East Beirut more than anybody else. *I will cross today.*

The Horsh—the fenced-in urban park where Nabil had been burnt by the Israeli bombs—separated West and East Beirut. It was less than a quarter mile south of the Barbeer Bridge. I looked at my watch. Eleven-fifty. I trotted until I reached its fence by noon. The concrete base rose two feet above the sidewalk. Green vertical rods kept pedestrians out. Some bars were bent, but not enough for me to squeeze through. I picked up the pace until I found a wide opening. I poked my head between two bars and scanned the area.

The ground was covered with stubs of charred trees and stumps. Only a handful of pine trees remained green. About a third of a mile east, a wall of badly damaged buildings rose. I feared Christian snipers had taken positions there to defend against the Joint Forces of West Beirut. I retreated and considered the stakes.

This job opportunity was all I had. Mr. Deeb owed me. He had seen me in my finest moment. He would sing my praises for my tenacity after the fallout at the checkpoint. Sophia and her family would respect me for my bravery. "In sha'Allah you fail," Nabil had said.

I leaped through the bars into the horsh. My nerves were frayed. I strained to listen for a warning shot. A car honked. It made my heart lurch. I looked back. A service car driver pointed ahead, his way of soliciting my business.

"Do I look like I need a goddamn ride?" I screamed at him.

"May Allah curse you!" he shouted back.

"And this world. *OK.*"

I turned around and plotted my route based on the thickest tree trunks. I could duck or hide behind the stumps or trees for cover if someone opened fire. I darted to the tallest one thirty yards in. My senses were acute. I listened intently. No one fired. No one demanded I freeze or identify myself. I eyed a tree more than forty yards northeast. I sprang and dove skidding to it.

Clear!

The thrill of progress exhilarated me. I snapped my head from side to side. I took visual snapshots of the path ahead. I blasted into sprints and dove behind stumps. My confidence surged with each success. Just two more stumps ahead. Right before I sprung into another sprint, shots fired. I lowered my head and pressed my back against the stump. The shooting intensified. I stiffened at the sound of each shot. I checked the ground for signs that the bullets had struck. More guns and automatic weapons fired.

What have I done? The weight of my irrational decision sunk in. I could be stuck in this spot for days. Nabil almost got killed here. I would die here. The last person I would have seen alive detested me and I him. My corpse would swell from decay. The dogs would devour my carcass. The years of living in the combat zone came in play. The sound of AK-47s was all too familiar, and the fury of drivers honking signaled their terror. People in West Beirut ran for their life. I ran away for a job.

Perhaps I *am* a rose-picker and a breeze-sniffer.

I crawled on my belly toward the shelter of the next tree. My breaths became shorter and louder. I was sweating profusely. My shoulder muscles burned. I stopped behind the last tree. Now heavier-caliber weapons and rocket-propelled grenades fired, but from West Beirut. The sound of a battle raged. Thirty yards ahead, I saw a concrete wall. Without hesitating I ran with all I had. With five yards to go, I exploded into a sprint and dove at its base.

I took hope from the sound of nearby traffic. Horns and engines revved in all directions. I leaned over and peeked around the tree trunk. Four feet below, pedestrians roamed. I jumped down and blended in with the others. I hurriedly brushed off my shirt and pants between hollering for a service car and responding to a honk. I looked at my watch. Ten minutes before one.

"*Poght*," I said port with a French accent to mask my Muslim background. A driver declined me. I decided to double the fare first and then call out my destination. I didn't risk my life for a job only to save money.

"Where?" the driver asked.

Again with a French accent, I said, "Deeb Shipping! It is next to the poght—"

"Get in."

I jumped in the front seat and glanced around the cab. Just like West Beirut drivers, the car was packed with religious symbols and pictures. Sun-faded cards of Mother Mary and Jesus curved over the vents. A crucifix pendant hung from the rearview mirror, and a black and white photo of a young man covered the speedometer. I reckoned he lost a loved one, my clue to stay quiet.

"May Jesus empower them against each other. These Muslim pigs," the service car driver said. Like his counterparts in West Beirut, the driver continued without a hint of interest from the passengers.

"This is my son." He pointed at the picture bent over the dashboard. "The Muslim pimps killed him in the Market District. The damned barbaric Palestinians want to make Lebanon theirs. We will bury them here. May Mother Mary look after my two other sons. They will not let it happen." The driver honked furiously at a pedestrian at the Saseen roundabout in the Achrafieh area, a half-mile east of our home and worlds apart. "Move, May Jesus run the blood of the Muslim children up to their parents' knees. *Move!*" He yelled.

Oddly, the prayers had no effect on me for I had heard them before from a different cast. I knew how to respond: Long nods of passive approval and insincere hardened features. Only if the day of reckoning unfolded would I say anything.

Five minutes later, the driver pulled over. He pointed at a white midrise. A large marquee covered the entire balcony on the top floor. "Merci," I said.

I handed him the fare, all I had.

The building looked whole. All the windows were paneled. I walked in the well-lit entrance. I saw the sign: Deeb Shipping. Tenth floor.

I pulled the elevator door and saw my reflection in the mirror. I looked disheveled. My shirt and pants were sandy. As soon as the elevator moved, I frenzied into cleaning up. I rubbed the front of my shoes with the back of my pants and pounded my chest and thighs. The elevator stopped. I opened the door into a sunny and expansive reception area. The smell of the Mediterranean scented the floor. I felt energized.

"How can I help you?" A lady about my age asked from behind a long, curving marble-topped counter. I could only see her face.

"I am here to see Mr. Deeb," I flashed a smile.

"Mr. Hadhari?"

"Right! Rami Hadhari!" I approached.

"We thought you weren't going to come."

"Well, here I am!" I comically said.

She didn't appreciate the humor. She looked beneath the counter, picked up a phone, and dialed three digits.

"Gilbert, Mr. Deeb left, but his appointment is here." She paused and then looked up. "How did you get here?"

"Through the Museum-Barbeer crossing."

"But it is closed." She raised her hand and winked, her polite way of asking me to wait while she listened to the other end of the phone.

"I am Dana. It is good to meet you finally. Mr. Deeb mentions your rescue effort and taking charge of that emergency in almost every staff meeting. Please have a seat." She pointed to a large black leather sofa. Magazines covered a wide coffee table in front of it. I sat down and looked around. To the left, I saw the horizon beyond a glass conference room. To the right, past a group of work stations, extended a panoramic view of the Gulf of Junieh.

I picked up one magazine after the other. I soaked up industry jargon. I learned that *NVOCC* meant Non Vessel Owning Common Carrier Company; *FCL*, Full Container Load; and *LTL*, Less Than Load. I memorized the intricacies of "trade lane," "tariff," and "free on board."

Two hours later, Mr. Deeb emerged from the elevator with a fit young man in a business suit.

"Rami Hadhari!" He looked startled.

I swiftly stood up.

"Impressive! How did you make it?" His smile stretched from one ear to the other. He turned to his companion. "Murad! I told you how this young man operates. He is what we need in West Beirut. A go-getter. A punctual businessman with character." Mr. Deeb almost crushed my hand shaking it.

"What an honor." Murad reached to shake my hand as well.

"He was here at one sharp." Dana boasted.

Mr. Deeb thumped my back with one hand and pointed in the

direction to his office with another. "After you! I insist."

We walked down a long passage between work stations in which young women and men smiled at Mr. Deeb.

"Honor me in!" Mr. Deeb directed me inside his corner office. "You, too!" he told Murad.

This is personal, I thought. Perhaps Murad will be my boss.

From Mr. Deeb's office, the view stretched to Mount Harissa, where I made out the statue of the Virgin Mary.

I sat where Mr. Deeb pointed, on a black leather chair. Murad sat next to me and wore a permanent smile.

Mr. Deeb lounged in a high back leather chair behind his large glass-top desk. "You have to tell me how you got here?" He lit up a cigarette.

I explained my adventure and made eye contact with Murad, in case he would indeed be my supervisor.

"This explains the dirt on your shirt and pants."

"Yes. I am sorry."

Murad's smile now irritated me. I couldn't tell whether he admired or pitied me. Mr. Deeb's expressions, however, were all too familiar. He wore the same look of fascination I saw when he had handed me his business card on the beach.

"I am not sure what to say!" Mr. Deeb leaned forward and put his elbows on the glass. "Not one employee in West Beirut reported to me for a month, but you ... you are here. You are one of a kind."

Life, here I come.

"How come you are not in school?"

I briefly explained the ordeal to Mr. Deeb. Before he had the chance to comment, Murad spoke through a smile. "The Murabitoon and other Sunni militias are getting wiped out. The battles are raging in West Beirut as we speak."

In Allah's name, shut up! I thought. I turned to him. "We can't stop each time the thugs battle each other. We have to persevere.

Keep charging ahead. We can't let them dictate our pace." I faced Mr. Deeb. "Right?"

"Y-your punctuality and determination are priceless. They are rare. … Don't you agree, Murad?"

"Of course!" Murad said emphatically.

I expected to be told about the start date and an orientation somewhere. Now Mr. Deeb faltered.

"None of my salesmen in West Beirut booked a dismal LTL since January." Mr. Deeb grimaced. "We are in mid-March now. Nothing—"

"Not only will I book Less Than Loads, I will book FCLs. You know! Full Container Loads," I said, desperate, but focused on breaking down the acronym and throwing one of my own.

Mr. Deeb raised an eyebrow. "FCL! Have you worked in shipping? Never mind, love! You see, I want to hire you, b-but I-I am torn. The US Embassy has been bombed, the militias are wreaking havoc in west Beirut. You heard Murad."

"Here, too!" Murad chimed in. "Everyone is fighting for power." He lit up a cigarette.

Damn Murad! What does Mr. Congeniality know about my pain? I will walk in sewer up to my knees to mine gold for you.

"With all due respect Murad, Mr. Deeb has three choices here." I turned to Mr. Deeb. "You can convert the company into a war venture, shut down and go home, or Murad and I can work harder to book cargo on every inbound and outbound ship in all trade lanes." I turned to Murad. "How else will he make payroll to pay our salaries?"

Murad leaned back as if I punched him in the gut. Mr. Deeb took a long drag and stared at me for a few moments. I didn't know whether I infuriated or impressed him.

"I certainly have no intentions of joining those riding the war wave. But, you see, love, you know! The thing is—"

"I am so embarrassed!" I dropped my jaw. "I forgot to ask. How is

Caesar?"

"Oh, Jesus! This war makes us forget what is important. I *shipped* him to Paris. He is with his uncle. I miss him so much."

"He is a good boy."

"Do you want to stay with us until it is safer for you to return?" Mr. Deeb asked.

Mr. Deeb deflated my resolve. I felt my shoulders drop. My strategies and spontaneous know-how had amounted to nothing. I thought to myself, if a guy whose son's life I saved turned me down, who else would see me through? I had no chance.

"Are you OK?" Mr. Deeb asked.

"Yes, I am great. Thank you."

"What a tough guy!" Murad patted my leg. "You are a good Muslim man."

I stared at his hand until he removed it.

Mr. Deeb insisted on escorting me to the lobby.

"If there is anything else that I can do for you, just name it," he said.

"Please tell Caesar, I said hello!" I fought back tears of misery.

"May the Lord populate the earth with your kind," he said as the elevator door closed.

May Allah hasten my demise and end my misery, I prayed.

Late in the afternoon after three days of fighting in West Beirut, things returned to normal. Baba, now showing signs of frailty, agreed to let me borrow his car if I exchanged the four forty-pound propane tanks and hauled them up to the flat. I dropped off the tanks and went to Sophia's.

Sophia was elated when she recognized my voice on the intercom. This set a favorable tone for our little sojourn. On the other hand, the hostile concierge ordered me to return to the car. Building attendants were known to get aggressive with visitors, forcing them to stay in their vehicles to mitigate the risk of a car bomb.

As soon as Sophia settled into the passenger seat, she leaned over and planted a kiss on my lips. She wore a black skirt and a blue blouse. I drove searching for the perfect spot for us to watch the sunset, where I would attend to our reconciliation. I craved harmony with her.

"Can you park here?" Sophia asked.

I ducked to look out the front windshield at the No Parking sign. It was riddled with bullet holes. "I can't read it."

She grinned.

I parked the car on the sidewalk parallel to West Beirut's sandy shoreline. "We are at war. Who cares where I park?" Policemen on government payroll were fighting on the green line. The idea of violating any law bothered Sophia, while the power of entitlement emboldened me. Why must westernized Christians be so naïve, I wondered. Get real! Rules during a civil war? Not for me.

She lowered her window and took a deep breath. Sophia always found solace in nature. Every time I detected her indulging in a make-believe, joyous world, I felt a demonic drive to jolt her into my reality. Maybe I was resentful because I couldn't recognize and cherish beauty. Either way, our love would be shallow if she didn't understand how I, a Middle Eastern Muslim man, felt.

I leaned over and took in the scent of her hair. Sophia ushered in the scenic backdrop to her five senses, staring at the setting sun until its bottom rim seemed to boil the sea. In the meantime I absorbed the foreground.

Sophia tilted her neck and lifted her shoulder as if to make them meet. "This is gorgeous," she said in English with her American accent. "Look at the sun sinking into the water."

I struggled to understand her words over the sound of the waves breaking on the brown, sandy shore. The colors fused from radiant amber to total darkness all the way to the mountains in the east. The halo of the sun fluttered like a mirage over the horizon.

"You see that?" I pointed at an abandoned car parked on the weed-infested median to my left.

"What about it?"

"It may blow up at any second."

My fears of a probable and sudden disaster gave me perverse pleasure. I always found myself suppressing my joy to keep the evil powers at bay. The fact was that nothing went my way except after a disaster. Even meeting Sophia had taken place in the aftermath of saving Caeser from drowning.

"One day, Rami, you will travel outside Lebanon and see—"

"See people like me drugged or drunk."

"No, you will see that nature is the ultimate beauty."

"Are you serious? Who has time for nature? Let the Americans and the West enjoy nature. I need to deal with survival."

"We all have to do our part."

"I see the devil everywhere and in every human. We might be in the most beautiful country in the world, but the Lebanese are the most savage on earth."

"People are good!" she insisted. "They are just caught up in—"

"Acting on their natural tendencies, slitting each other's throats."

"Why are you angry? *You* are beautiful to me." She reached for my hand and brought it to her lips.

I took hers and held it in front of my face. "This will take a minute. ..."

"What?" She rolled up her window with her other hand.

"I want to memorize the lines on your palm, your fingerprints, the softness of your forearms ... the shape of your elbow. I want this feeling of connectedness to last. I adore the line above your upper lip, Sophia. This! Here!"

I leaned over and delicately placed my lips on hers. I could stay here forever.

Only a few moments to go before darkness set in.

"I am worthless without you," I said.

"I'd like for us to talk about last week," Sophia said.

"Yes, of course. Can I kiss you first?"

She smiled, looking worry free, the way I always envisioned her when we were apart. We kissed. She moaned.

A thin, insulating layer of fog began to form on the windshield, and the car transformed into an incubator. I felt reborn, unobstructed by the madness of the combat zone or its proverbial shackles. The evil spell was dormant!

As I kissed Sophia, I observed the vague outline of a man approaching her side of the car. He wore a light-colored gown. I saw his hawkish eyes prying the windows open.

I recoiled.

"What's the matter?" Sophia whispered.

"This pervert!" I inclined my head in his direction as he curved away, shaking his head and vanishing into the darkness.

As soon as his silhouette faded, I leaned over and kissed her forehead.

Sophia dropped her shoulders. "I feel safe with you."

"I will take care of you. I would give my life for you. Unless, of course, someone put a gun to my head." I laughed and instantly berated myself for my dark Lebanese humor. "You have more maturity and self-awareness than all the women in my entire family, combined."

"That is very sweet. Thank you," she said affectionately. "Tell me more." She took my hand, kissed it, and rested it on her thigh.

"You know! I feel stupid for saying this, but I haven't been with a girl before ... What I am saying is ..."

Sophia now caressed my hand on her thigh to calm me.

I continued, "I am honored that you welcomed me into your world."

"Open the door. Now!" a voice barked outside my window.

I snapped back into my seat.

Flashlights beamed inside the car. Lights swirled around like hornets disturbed in their nest. Hands pounded on the trunk and hood. With the bottom of their flashlights, they hammered on the windows in a frenzy to open the locked doors.

How many are there?

"Open, or I will smash the window! Open now!"

Not for a fraction of a second did I think he wouldn't. Don't escalate, I told myself. Just placate. I fumbled for the door lock and opened it.

"Unlock your door," I whispered to Sophia.

The men yanked open our doors so fast, they bounced back and slammed into the intruders' hips. Men reached in from both sides and unlocked the rear doors. They aimed their flashlights at the backseat, perhaps looking for guns.

There were six of them. They wore light-color gowns. One had draped a black cloak over his and had crowned himself with a black turban. In the reflection of the last glimmer of light from the half-sunken sun in the horizon, I noticed a dark-brown bruise on his forehead. The Seal of Faith lessened my fear of being executed or robbed. Then confusion set in. What would a pious Muslim bruised from countless prayers want with us?

They engulfed the car—one per door, one behind the car, and the man most prepared to fire a round put one foot on the front bumper and aimed at me from the hip.

Their beards reached their chest. AK-47s and ammunition belts strained at their gowns. Their sagging breasts and barrel bellies pressed against the fabric. I figured that like most militiamen, they never ran a mile in their lives.

It dawned on me that they had done this before.

I can handle this, I thought. A few Quranic verses or a couple of narratives, and we'll be on our way.

Sophia looked around as if to calculate options for an escape.

"Is she your wife?" the man with the turban asked.

"No."

"Is she your cousin or fiancée?" he asked sarcastically, his eyebrows raised.

"She is my girlfriend," I said proudly.

Sophia nodded in agreement. "What is this about? What do you want?"

"Do you worship her?" he continued.

"Only Allah is worthy of worship. I just love her."

"Get out of the car, donkey."

"What do you want?" I asked.

"You don't get to ask questions, *you heretic!*" He and another grabbed my T-shirt and pulled me out of the car.

That Seal of Faith on his forehead is the Mark of the Beast, I thought.

"Give me twenty," one demanded.

"I only have five dollars on me."

"Push-ups, dummy! Push-ups."

I obliged.

"This guy is fit. Push-ups are not going to do it," the jerk at the front bumper said.

Damn! What was I trying to prove? I should have wobbled. I stood and rubbed my hands together to shake off the dust and pebbles grooved in my palms.

"What's your name?" another thug asked Sophia. He looked at her, but not at her face.

"I am Sophia Nader." She defiantly tilted her head, looking up at him from her seated position.

No, no, Sophia! I tried to communicate with her telepathically. Play along, please please please. You are not in a position to defy them. You are a Christian girl in West Beirut. Allah, please help me now!

"Nader as in the architect Nader?" he inquired.

Great! This could be our pass.

"He is my father!"

"Does he know you are here defiling your body?"

"Doing what?" she said. "Go ahead! Call him and tell him all about this."

"Sophia, please. Just—"

"What do you want?" she demanded as she stood up from the car. The gunman roughly pressed her shoulders down, and she fell back in her seat.

He chuckled. "Your father will know what happened here when you return to him."

"Get on your knees," the man with the turban told me.

"What are you going to do?" I tried to sound pitiful.

"You have sinned. Since she is a Christian, but we view her as a spoil of war."

"I have not sinned."

"I decide that."

"Who gave you the—?"

"Because we are the enforcers of the absolute truth. We are the sharia enforcers. We *are* Islam!"

"Intercourse is a sin," one said.

"I did not have intercourse with her!"

"Had we not stopped you, you would have fornicated."

"Allah said," I quoted from the Imran chapter, "'Surely Allah knows full well what is in the heart.'"

"So you know the Qur'an."

"And the narratives," I said solemnly. "I am a Muslim. I pray five times a day. I fast in Ramadan. I know the narrative about 'announce to killers that they shall be killed and sinners shall live poor sooner or—'"

"You should be punished for having no kinship with her."

"Are you a Shia?" I asked, propelled by a regrettable feeling of superiority, being a Sunni.

"And you are a bourgeoisie Sunni," the man at the trunk said. "You don't run the show now."

Why is it permissible, pimp, for Shias to marry for pleasure and then quickly divorce, and I can't kiss and hug my girlfriend?

"I am sorry this happened," I said, and flicked a glance at Sophia. "Please tell me what I can do to fix it."

"Shut up, you heretic!"

"A heretic is someone who doesn't believe in Allah. I believe in

Allah, Glorious is He and He is Exalted. And I believe in our master Muhamad—Allah prayed for and saluted him—just like you do."

"Imam Ali is my saint." His voice got louder. "You Sunnis have wreaked havoc on Islam. Muhamad designated Ali to succeed him, but you put three caliphates before Ali, the rightful successor."

"I believe in the four caliphates, including Imam Ali."

"Shut up."

"My girlfriend and I are courting for an engagement," I pleaded. "I am your brother, and you are obliged to pardon me and treat me with peace and forgiveness. Our master Muhamad—Allah prayed for and saluted him—said that by definition, 'A Muslim is one with whom people are safe from physical and verbal abuse.' I—"

"Our master Muhamad this and Muhamad that. Give me the scissors, Shaheen." He turned to me as the concrete dug into my knees. "I will cut out your tongue if you keep talking back."

Two of them laughed.

"Mahdi!" the commander called out to another follower.

"Yes, imam."

Imam! A Shia cleric!

"Bring the whore over here."

When he called Sophia a whore, fear stole my breath. Mahdi grabbed Sophia's right arm and yanked her from her seat. He shoved her around the car until she stood by my side. I turned away so I would not watch her humiliation. I caught two of the men winking at each other as she bent over then straightened.

"Get on your knees, whore," the imam barked.

Depending on where people got caught in the Muslim world, the imam commenced a proceeding, the worst nightmare of two lovers. Those accused of adultery could get stoned to death or lashed on the word of at least four witnesses. There were six of them right there and then.

"The adulteress and the adulterer—"

"Holding my girlfriend's hand is not adultery," I mumbled, fearing his wrath.

"Oh? Our scout tells us you've been doing more than holding hands. 'Flog each one of them with a hundred stripes—'"

"We are not sinners!" Sophia shouted.

Oh, God, please help me! Sophia is all I have left to keep me in check. You do this to me, and I will turn on you.

"You have no sharia authority over me," I shouted.

He cocked his AK-47 and pressed the muzzle to my forehead. "Shut up!"

The others gathered around and stood astride.

"You, too, whore! On your knees."

"Look up, adulterer," the imam ordered. He slowly raised his AK-47, swung it away from me and then brought it around and slugged me on the chin with its wooden butt.

An explosion of pain detonated inside my mouth. Blood splattered. I fell on my hands. A swirl of saliva and blood streamed down and formed a small puddle directly under my mouth on the loose pebbles of the concrete sidewalk.

I pressed my jaw with my left shoulder. Shock fully claimed my legs. Just like I felt each time a mortar bomb exploded in the buffer zone, my calves began to quiver, leaving me disabled on the ground.

"Get up," the imam demanded.

Dazed, my legs shaking, I couldn't.

I crawled backwards, feeling my way to the car.

"Sit." The imam said, pointing at the driver's side.

I climbed up and sat.

"Leave him alone!" Sophia screamed.

"Shut up, whore."

Shaheen grabbed chunks of my hair and chopped them off.

The imam told Sophia to go to the other side of the car. A sharia enforcer sheared off Sophia's beautiful blond hair.

"This ought to teach you a lesson! I don't want to see you here ever again!" The imam pressed the muzzle against my forehead one more time.

"Yes, s-sir."

In contrast to their stealthy approach, the men strolled back to their car as they laughed in victory and gave each other high-fives.

Sophia walked around the front of the car, climbed in, and gently closed her door. I slammed mine, and she flinched. I turned the ignition, and just as the tires rolled, two rounds were fired. On reflex, Sophia ducked, slamming her chin on the dashboard.

I stomped on the brakes. In the rearview mirror, I saw the imam and his AK-47 illuminated by the brake lights, pointing skyward while his crew huddled behind him. They gestured at me to go. When I lost sight of them, I sped up.

Sophia sobbed, staring out her window.

The gearbox between us might as well have been the abyss that I knew would soon separate us forever. My relationship with her had changed. Our love would be tainted by trauma forever. We would never forget this terrifying night.

Like a mist of electrified water sprayed at my body, my skin tingled at the recollection of her declaration, "I feel safe with you." The realization of being emasculated in Sophia's eyes enraged me. I observed my hands on the steering wheel and felt the desire to cut them off.

Enraged, I wanted to inflict pain on myself or someone. A Shia! That would be an ideal target. The Oozae road, a coastline stretch, turned to a slum where Shia refugees who fled south Lebanon after countless Israeli attacks used rubble and sand from the shoreline to build shacks. The area afforded me plenty of targets. I gripped the wheel so tightly, my knuckles turned white. I shifted from fourth to third gear. The engine revved louder. It infuriated reluctant pedestrians.

I want to kill Shias. Here and now!

Fifty yards ahead the headlights shone on a mother pushing a baby in a stroller. She just made it to the sandy embankment in front of the stores on the right side. I blasted a prolonged roar out of the window and steered the car at them. I pressed the gas pedal to the floor. Sophia screamed, "No-o-o!"

"Donkeys!" I shouted as I steered the car back onto the road at the last second, narrowly missing the stroller.

Long minutes of silence in the car ended when I stopped in front of Sophia's building.

"Please look at me, Rami. Please!"

I turned away. I couldn't make eye contact with the victim of my bad judgment.

"Is this it? You want me to leave you now?" Her voice cracked as she opened her door. "OK. Goodbye."

"I am cursed. You shouldn't be with me. I bring misery and death to people."

"Please look at me."

"I can't." I wanted to remember Sophia just as she looked when I picked her up, kissed her, and cupped her cheeks in my hands. I resolved not to commit to memory the image of her beauty sullied by the curse that surrounded me.

When Sophia shut her door, my heart sank. I knew her departing steps could be the last I would see and hear. She walked unsteadily as she crossed her arms and stepped onto the curb. My prospects of seeing Sophia again were nil. Surely, Mr. Nader would put a bounty on my head.

Like I always did, I took off only after she was inside and had locked the entrance door and disappeared into the dark lobby.

My father always said, "Only weak men cry." Sophia was not going to see my tears. But as soon as I was out of sight, uncontrollable tears burned paths down my cheeks. My throat hardened. My manhood had been dismantled.

I couldn't swallow until I reached the Barbeer Bridge. If hell existed on earth, it stretched before me, from the bridge to the Sodeco intersection.

I deserved a severe punishment. Tonight, I shall deliver myself to the altar of the Christian sniper.

For a few moments I stopped the car and pondered my options. The entire half-mile corniche in the combat zone was devoid of life. I stopped my car before the bridge. Blind sniper fire broke the silence, shots that served to remind the Muslim militias and the few families remaining in the area that an imminent threat remained. If the shadow of a rat skittered across the rubble, a fatal round would be fired.

I shifted into first gear and forced the car over the concrete median. The undercarriage protested, and the muffler was bent as the car descended onto the other side of the median, heading into oncoming traffic—if there were any. The lane was deserted before the ramp.

I switched off the headlights and sped forward up the ramp in the wrong direction. I hoped a speeding civilian or militia jeep evading sniper fire with its headlights off, would collide head-on with me.

No luck! No cars around.

After clearing the ramp, I drove the car back over the median and returned to the right side of the road—the side closer to East Beirut, from which Christian or mercenary snipers fired. I turned my headlights on. None of the snipers at the eight intersections I crossed even noticed.

Where are you when I need you the most?

I maneuvered the car around the rubble in the middle of the corniche to avoid a blowout.

Finally I took aim at another object of my anguish, the disease-ridden dogs, those feral beasts that roamed the dead zone and green line and scavenged for fresh human bodies or rotting carcasses.

I focused on a mangy dog crouched in the center of the road. It hopped up, sped away in front of me, and then veered to run alongside the car. I looked down, and it locked its hungry, moon-glossed eyes on mine, its tongue lolling. Then, exhausted, it fell behind and stopped.

In the side-view mirror I saw darker shapes gather. More dogs! But I was almost home.

I pulled into the alleyway. On the tan leather headrest clumps of Sophia's blonde hair shone under the moonlight.

I got out of the car and began the routine: open the entrance door, climb the dark stairways, select the shortest key, and feel for the hole in the lock of the door to our flat.

Mama swung the door open. She held a candlestick in a round, brass candleholder. The glow flickered, but she saw enough to gasp, "Praise Allah, Glorious is He and He is Exalted! What happened to you?"

"Nothing." I brushed past her to go into the bathroom. I dreaded looking at myself in the mirror, fearing that seeing my hair chopped off would remind me of what Sophia must look like.

My mother chased after me. "What happened? May Allah curse the war and break their bones! Who did this to you?"

Allah this, and Allah that! What kind of Allah would allow this? "It is nothing."

"Who did this to your face?"

"You missed my hair." In a way I craved sympathy.

"Oh, Merciful." She shouted into the flat. "Sami! He is hurt. Someone beat up Rami."

"He took the damn car longer than I allowed," he called out. "That's what Allah does to those who defy their parents."

I turned to Mama and wrinkled my face in utter disgust.

"Nabil will find them," she said.

"I don't want anyone to know!" I said.

I washed up as Mama stood in the doorway. I walked to my bedroom and sat at the edge of the bed, then buried my face in my hands.

Mama brought a wet rag from the kitchen sink and pressed it against my chin.

"In Allah's name, what happened?"

"What happened *was* in Allah's name, Mama."

CHAPTER 21

A SO-CALLED MODERATE MUSLIM
APRIL, 1984

I should have snatched the AK-47 from the imam and lodged a round in his skull and then opened fire on the rest. I should have clasped the holy hairdresser's wrist and plunged the scissors through his eye all the way into his brain. I should have spared two of their lives, ordered them to strip naked, fired rounds between their feet, and made them run to their slum. I should have grabbed any opportunity to protect Sophia.

I lay on my bed. In the background, the distant cacophony of war played on. Gun battles and explosions of various intensities erupted. I lit a cigarette. My lower lip stung at the first drag. I put it out, sat up, and sobbed. Needlelike pain pierced my face.

Just then the power came back on. The TV in the family room blared. I kept my room dark. What have I done? I ensnared Sophia in my web of misery. I superimposed my world on the Naders'. She lived in a secure home and attended the gated university. I had to do something to fix it, but what? The only thing I could think of was never to see her again, but that would be impossible. I'd rather be dead.

I went into the family room. Baba clicked his dentures and

munched on mixed nuts as he watched an Egyptian movie on TV. Mama, uncharacteristically, sat quietly across from him. When she saw me, her eyebrows arched. She patted the chair next to her for me to sit. I did. Her chin quivered and her eyes flooded with tears. She breathed in short bursts. I had never seen Mama like this before.

"Oh! Our master Muhamad! Shield my son from your believers and Ali's followers."

"Say Allah, woman!" Baba said.

"Say Allah?" Mama's voice cracked. "Just look at him!" She pointed at me. "What's next? They kill him and use acid to disfigure the girl he loves?"

Before Baba had the chance to commence a tirade, Nabil returned from a holy escapade and opened the door.

"May peace be upon you. What's going on?" He must have heard Mama from outside.

"Glory to Allah! Your timing is stupendous," Baba said glorifying Nabil's arrival.

Mama rolled her eyes.

"Good things, In sha'Allah?" Nabil said.

"Help me with these two." Baba shook his head, displaying disgust with Mama and me.

Nabil unlaced his boots, then walked in and leaned his AK-47 by the TV. He stunk up the flat. If air were visible, a toxic cloud would surround him. He swayed by the coffee table while shooting me a you-are-far-beneath-me look. Then he stopped and stared. "What happened to the rose-picker?"

"Shut up," I said.

"You better show sympathy to your brother," Mama admonished Nabil. Her support had always been a liability, but that night she was a mighty vigilante.

Nabil slowly sat next to Baba, forming an us-versus-them configuration. He groaned to emphasize his hard work in the battlefields.

"For starters," Mama said, "don't you ever call him a rose-picker. Do you understand?"

"Sorry, breeze-sniffer!" Nabil mocked.

Baba coughed a laugh.

"Smelly pimps like you are roaming like rodents," Mama seethed. "They cut his lip and chopped his hair." She turned toward me. "Rami is your *brother*." Mama had a raging glint in her eyes as she turned to Baba and edged forward in her chair. "And your *son*, Mr. Backgammon War Analyst!"

I put my hand on Mama's forearm to calm her.

Baba froze. The white in his eyes glowed.

Nabil looked stupefied. Then he pulled the rosary beads from his coat pocket, threaded them through his fingers, and bowed. "Glory to Allah. The work of a warrior never ends, even at home. May Allah award me the patience." He put the rosary beads on the coffee table and lit a cigarette.

Baba set the bowl of nuts in his lap and resumed chewing cashews and splitting pistachios.

Nabil smirked. "So what happened? Did a Christian hairdresser give you a haircut?" He glanced at Baba for support.

"May Allah curse you, righteous zealot," I said.

"Quiet!" Mama ordered me.

"In Allah's name, how did you earn this?" Nabil asked me.

Baba spat out pistachio shells and tossed them in the ashtray. "He was humping his girlfriend in my car."

Mama turned to Nabil. "When did you become your brother's worst enemy? When did you value the donkeys above him?" She jabbed my arm with her index finger.

"My brothers are donkeys?" Nabil asked mildly.

Mama clamped my arm and shook me vigorously. "*He* is your brother, not those dropouts who take up arms to compensate for their worthlessness."

"I am doing what Allah commands me to do!" Nabil said.

"You and your bearded gangsters twist the interpretation of the Qur'an. 'And blood relations are nearer to one another. ... ' Go look it up in the 'Parties' chapter. You want to be a good Muslim, a good son, a holy warrior?" she shouted, pointing at the street. "Then go find the donkeys who did this to your blood brother."

Nabil stomped on the floor and stood up. "Let us go, rose-picker. We'll find some real Muslims and teach them not to mess with you. How about I start a fight with my *brothers* over you chasing a Christian vagina?"

Suddenly my body was on fire. "You—"

"Tell me, was she any good? Because if she was, then it will be worth it."

Baba tossed more pistachio shells in the ashtray.

I stood up. "Take it back! I am a better Muslim than you'll ever be, talking trash like this."

"Is that so?" Nabil smirked. "Do you pray five times a day?"

"I-I pray."

"Do you fast?"

"I ... I—"

"Heretic," Nabil scoffed.

I felt inferior. "Faith is the one that enlightens the heart and enriches people around you," I said.

"You sound like all the so-called *moderate* Muslims." Nabil formed quote marks with his fingers when he said moderate. "Is she feeding you this sacrilege."

"You branded Islam with savagery."

"I follow the sharia and our master Muhamad's teachings—"

The three of them simultaneously said, "Allah prayed for and saluted him."

"Sure you do," I said. "Muhamad asked that we refrain from shaving to keep us from spending time on our vanity. *You* wear it for show."

"So I should shave to look like you, a homosexual?"

"Stop it! Both of you," Baba ordered.

"Are you insane?" Mama shouted at Nabil.

I built on Mama's momentum. "You and your sharia gangsters should be hung by your balls."

"They should have wiped their asses with you and your—"

"Shut up, both of you!" Mama flung her arms at us.

Nabil's color rose. "You are nothing but a heretic with excuses Allah wouldn't hear."

"Another Allah spokesman!" I scoffed. "Tell me, Mr. Jihadist, is killing people of a holy book a pillar of Islam?"

"It is my *duty*," he said.

I pointed at Baba while I challenged Nabil. "Then is it your duty to hold him accountable for cheating his brothers from their sharia entitlements?"

Baba hurled a handful of nuts at me. "Why you donkey! You got some mouth on you." He turned to Nabil. "Hit him. I said *hit him*."

"That's right! Hit me!" I shouted. "'Islam is a religion of peace and love.'"

"You are the devil's mouthpiece," Nabil said.

"And you turn everything into a holy war. Just like the Phalangists and the Israelis."

Nabil gasped. "I am like the Jews?" He got up and balled his fists. I readied to slug him.

"Sit down!" Mama shouted at me.

"Hit him!" Baba urged Nabil.

"Sit down!" Mama got between us and held on to Nabil tightly. I knew she feared I would get hurt, but she underestimated my rage.

"Sit *down!*" Baba roared, and pointed at my chair. His hand shook.

Mama and I sat down.

Baba jabbed his finger at Mama and Nabil. "They are righteous people," he told me. "But *you!* You chase work with Christians, and you hump a Christian."

I closed my eyes and took a deep breath.

"Repent! Redeem yourself. Look at your brother."

"'Look at your brother,'" I scoffed. "I picked up his victims. I made it through battles and snipers to get to college. I did my part."

"You are weak." Nabil straightened in his chair. "Maybe we should try the Western way with you. 'Tell us how you feel! Tell us about your trauma. Aw, let me get tissues and wipe your tears.' You are an idiot."

"And despicable," Baba seethed. "Fear Allah, damn it! Repent!"

"May Allah curse this hour!" I shouted.

"He will bless you with opportunities in ways you never knew existed, love," Mama said, shifting her support. "Fear him."

Now that Mama crossed over to their side, Nabil lit a cigarette and took a handful of nuts.

"I don't fear Allah!" I pointed at Nabil. "I fear the likes of him."

"How much of this nonsense should we hear?" Nabil turned to Mama. "Get the plunger. I'll unclog the sewer in his mouth."

"That 'sacrilege' spewing girl said she wanted to convert to Islam," I told them. "But your *brothers* ... well, let's just say they didn't close the sale."

Suddenly their twisted faces opened. Baba glanced at Nabil.

"Oh, my Allah!" Mama said. "Bless her heart."

"Glory to Allah!" Nabil said. "Why didn't you say so in the first place?"

"Look at you." I was disgusted with their sudden transformation. "Now she's your voucher to win heaven. Islamists like your son here ..." I looked at Mama and pointed at Nabil "... *they* are Islam's worse enemy. After what those thugs did to her, she will never convert." Having delivered the knockout insult, I got up and went toward the door. "'Only Allah knows what is in my heart.'"

Mama was devastated. "No! No, love! Allah will unconditionally reward you heaven if she converts!"

"I hope she never does." I opened the door and naturally followed a narrative, stepping out with my right foot.

"How will you repent on Judgment Day?" Nabil asked and quickly mocked me. "Let me see ... *hmm* ...'Please, Allah, forgive me. I loved a whore.'"

I pulled myself back through the doorframe, turned, and clenched my fists, ready to crush Nabil's bones. I charged at him.

Mama shouted, "In Allah's name, leave!"

No earthly force could stop me now. I kicked the coffee table over. The ashtray, cigarettes, and the rosary beads flew off. The wooden backgammon board fell from the shelf below. Nabil stood up, and I lunged at him. He fell back. I threw myself on him, pinned his shoulders with my knees, and punched him in the face again and again.

Mama shrieked.

"Don't you ever ..." I slugged him in the mouth. "Ever!" I punched him again. "Call her a whore!"

I got off him and straightened my shirt. Baba stayed quiet. The thought of Nabil reaching for his AK-47 slowed me. I turned away, and he tackled me. We fell on the coffee table, shattering the glass.

"Stop them!" Mama cried out.

"My table!" Baba shouted. "May Allah curse both of you!"

Nabil rolled on top of me. He clamped his fingers around my throat and squeezed. The veins in his forehead bulged. I lashed out, but his chokehold was unrelenting. I tried to shout, but I couldn't breathe. With all the strength I had, I flipped him over. We kicked and threw punches. Nabil landed a blow on my cut chin, and pain shot down my body. He threw punches at my ribs while Mama wailed for Allah to intervene. Then she grabbed him from behind. "In Allah's name! Enough!"

When he wouldn't stop. Mama slammed the wooden backgammon board on the back of Nabil's head.

"May Allah curse your father!" Baba yelled. "My board!"

I crawled backwards, leaned against the wall, and stood up.

Nabil got up and rubbed his bloody knuckles. His chest heaved, and he glared at me. "If you ever lay a hand on me again, I will put a round in your defiled brain." He inspected the floor and located his rosary. He picked up the beads. "All this for a whore!"

I snarled and sprang to punch Nabil's teeth in. Mama and Baba shouted, "Stop it!"

Mama hurried around Nabil to get between us. At that instant he cocked his elbow to punch me, but it caught her straight in her eye. She collapsed on the glass shards and shrieked so loudly the walls echoed.

"Mama! Mama!" I dropped to my knees.

She sobbed. Her elbows and hands bled. "May Allah curse this war!"

Nabil stepped back in confusion.

"Look what you have done to your mother, you animal!" Baba screamed at me. He grabbed me from the armpit and shoved me at the door. "Get the hell out of my house."

I didn't resist.

"Go to your whore." He slammed the door behind me.

CHAPTER 22

LET MY DAUGHTER BE

I felt my way down the dark stairway with one thing on my mind—to see Sophia, and that meant dealing with the Naders' wrath. I turned right out of the alley and picked up the pace. I felt a twinge under my jaw. I passed my fingers over my chin, and it gushed blood.

In the moonlight, I saw roaches scatter. I stomped on as many as I could. Rats scurried. I picked up stones and took aim. The street dogs barked in the distance. I growled through my clenched teeth.

When I reached the sniper intersection, I sprinted across. A sense of determination propelled me on the half-hour walk to the Naders' building. The worst they could do was denying me entry, but I would camp outside their door until they let me in. I would accept their verbal assault, and when they tired, I would apologize to Sophia and each of them profusely.

I rang the intercom.

"Who is it?" Maha asked.

"Rami. I need to get in."

"Rami!" Maha whispered into the speaker. "What do you want?"

"Please buzz me in."

"I have to ask."

My pulse quickened.

Maha muffled the speaker and talked with someone for a minute.

"It is very tense here."

"I know."

"OK." She buzzed the door open.

I pushed in and walked steadily toward the elevator. The concierge first smiled and then quickly transitioned into squints and stares.

I took the elevator up, all the while pacing. Outside the Naders' door I stood and eavesdropped. Silence. I rang the bell once and stepped back.

Maha opened the door. The moment her eyes landed on me, she gasped. "Oh, my God! You are covered in blood."

I inspected myself. Bloodstains and grime coated my wrinkled shirt and pants. "Where is Sophia?" I crossed the threshold and looked past Maha.

At the end of the hallway, Sophia stood next to her father. Behind them, Mrs. Nader and Walid grimly shook their heads at me. Sophia looked ravaged. Her eyes were red. She had bathed and brushed some long strands of hair forward, trying to cover a bald patch at her right temple. Chunks of short hair stood up on top of her head. Wishing I could take all her pain, I forced a smile. She raised her eyebrows and smiled wanly back. Good enough!

"Come in." Mr. Nader looked grave. He inclined his head toward the living room. He led. The others except Sophia followed. She took a few steps into the hall, away from her family's prying eyes. I gave her a gentle hug.

"I am so sorry," I whispered.

She wrapped her arm around my waist. "I am OK. They are not." Her voice was strained. She glanced toward the living room, then quickly released me and led the way.

"There!" Mr. Nader pointed at one of the maroon wingback chairs. Sophia took the chair to my right. Mrs. Nader and Maha sat on the sofa with Mr. Nader. Walid stood, arms crossed, to their right.

Mrs. Nader's eyes widened as she inspected me. She turned to Maha. "Go, love. Put ice in a hand towel and bring it to him."

"I am fine. It is Sophia's pain that I am here for."

Walid shot me a scornful look.

"I will be right back," Maha said.

I stole a glance at Sophia. She wiped her tears and sniffled. A long silence settled. Mr. Nader looked guarded.

"Mr. Nader, I am sorry I brought West Beirut into your home. I caused your family pain."

"Here." Maha handed me a white hand towel. I pressed it to my chin, aware my blood would stain it.

Mr. Nader moved straight to the bottom line. "What do you want to accomplish here?" He clearly summoned all his civility.

"I am here to beg Sophia and all of you to forgive me." I turned to Sophia. "I am truly sorry." Then I glanced at Walid. He looked like he wanted to beat me senseless.

I continued, "It is my fault. I made a bad decision to go into that area. What can I do to fix things?"

"Do you think you can bring these thugs to justice?" Walid asked sarcastically.

"I-I am not sure, but—"

"If we find them, do you think they will be locked up in prison somewhere?"

"I don't think so."

"Let us say we find an influential, good Muslim." Walid rolled his eyes when he said "good Muslim." He continued, "Do you think holding the men accountable will reverse what happened to my sister? Better yet, do you think they would leave my family alone after we incriminate them?" Not yet fourteen years old, Walid spoke more intelligently than my father.

"I think they should pay the price for what they have done," I said.

"Rami," Mr. Nader snapped, "what happened is not your fault or Sophia's." He commenced a short philosophical overview of the breakdown of social justice in the region. I got stuck on "not your fault."

"Who do you think is going to open an investigation in this lawless land?" he finished.

"Pardon me! You said it was not my fault or Sophia's?" I knew I sounded naïve.

"Sophia knows better."

"It is not Sophia's fault!"

"I didn't say it was," he said louder. "I want you to leave her alone for a while."

Exactly what I had gone there to prevent. "Mr. Nader, I dishonored you. I have to find a way to fix things."

"Dishonored?" He snorted. "Everybody makes everything about honor."

"They laid their hands on Sophia." I found myself sinking deeper in guilt to prove my sincerity.

"Listen, Son." He leaned forward and spoke through clenched teeth. "I know what surrounds us. Religious zealots. So-called patriots. And all those who've been persecuted who now persecute others. Do you understand me?"

"Absolutely," I said. Listen and let him vent.

"Most Muslim men, especially in the Gulf, would kill their daughter for fornicating."

"But we didn't—"

"I didn't say you did. Please listen. I have worked hard all my life. I attended the best schools in the world. My professional reputation is known in the major cities around the Gulf and Europe. Do you think for one moment I would lose my mind or act like a savage because Sophia might have had sex? My honor, my soul, have nothing to do with a hymen. If you think otherwise, then you have us all—including my daughter—figured out incorrectly."

What kind of immoral man are you? I thought, shocked. I suddenly saw the entire family as Westernized beyond redemption, but Sophia remained holy. Mr. Nader continued. I tuned in and out.

"Not for one moment think that we are unaware because we don't live in the combat zone," he said. "We get it. We see all those in the inferno from the outside in. They all seek spirituality in their places of worship and act barbarically on the streets. My heart is bleeding out for my daughter. *You* being here today to apologize *is* honorable."

"Thank you," I said. I shifted into a more upright position.

"Now will you honor my request?"

"Which request?"

"The only one I made tonight. Let my daughter be. For at least four weeks."

The family watched me intently.

"In sha'Allah!" I said. Only if the earth stops spinning, I thought. Allah might will for me to see her sooner.

Mrs. Nader shook her head in disapproval.

"God willing?" Mr. Nader asked incredulously.

"We want *you* willing!" Mrs. Nader's eyes flashed. "I want you to leave my daughter *alone*. Forget that she ever existed. Can you get that through your head?"

Maha wrapped her fingers around Mrs. Nader's hand. Mrs. Nader continued, "You have done enough damage to this family. You are way out of your league with us."

"Mommy! Please!" Sophia said.

"I know. I am nobody," I said.

"Please stop!" Sophia sobbed.

I turned to Sophia. "Please look at me. You know I would do anything to protect you. I *tried*. But he cocked an AK-47 and planted it on my forehead."

Maha gasped.

Mrs. Nader looked astonished. "What? My God!"

Obviously Sophia had not told her family everything that had happened to us.

"That's enough!" Mr. Nader stood. My time was up.

Sophia stood, and in front of her family, she hugged me and sobbed in my arms. I dropped my head over her shoulder and gently stroked her back. Her anguish stabbed me a hundred times.

"Go!" Mr. Nader stretched his arm to herd me out. "It is late."

Walid grabbed my arm and tugged.

I released Sophia and followed Mr. Nader. Walid bumped into my heel.

At the door, I turned around. "Mr. Nader, I love your family. I hope you accept my apology."

"You are one of *them*," Walid said.

I saw the ambush in the making, but not the timing. "The only difference between you and them is that you were on the receiving end this time."

"That's enough," Mr. Nader said indecisively.

"Had this happened to *your* sister, you would smash our door down with your brothers, and God knows what you would have done in the name of retribution and honor."

"That's enough, Walid." Mr. Nader opened the door. As soon as I stepped out, he said, "Tonight has changed everything."

"What does that mean?" I asked.

"Good night." He closed the door.

I felt like retching. As strongly as I loved Sophia was as low as I sank in grief over losing her.

Battles raged in West Beirut. My room felt darker and the walls closer. I chain-smoked. Sophia wouldn't have liked it.

Before that fateful night and in spite of my chronic failures, I always believed I was capable of creating a good life. Sophia's presence in my world supported that hope. But now I felt lost and helpless.

Two weeks later, at noon on a Friday, as I stared into space in my room, Mama raised the volume on the radio in the family room. She wanted to hear the pre-prayers Qur'an recitals. Moments later I heard Baba and Nabil discuss their options of mosques for that day. They left right away. They liked to rub shoulders with the early birds. I came out. Mama had gone into her room.

I lit a cigarette and turned down the transistor radio on the coffee table—the replacement from the penthouse. Minutes later the athan came on. As it always did, it ended with, "*Hayya alal-falāh.*" The call, for the time for work has arrived, enraged me. The thought of striving to see Sophia, however, soothed me.

Mama came out of her room. She raised her devoutness a few notches on Fridays. She wore a white hijab that draped down to her chest, and she tucked a prayer rug under one arm. She looked exactly like Hajjeh. She unrolled the rug, facing east, and hustled to the kitchen, where she fired up the smoking thurible. She returned swinging the incense container from side to side while praying under her breath.

I put out the cigarette and went onto the balcony. She followed. I wished she could read me, like Sophia did, and leave me alone.

"You must go pray. Allah will pave your way."

"Mama, please. I beg you. Let me be." I stared out at the ravaged buildings across the corniche.

"Go shave. You are starting to look like your brother!"

I took a deep breath. Maybe as a parent Mama would have a valuable perspective on Mr. Nader's statement. "What do you think Mr. Nader meant when he said, 'Tonight has changed everything'?"

"Maybe he is thinking that since you were seen in public ... you know ... doing it—"

"In Allah's name, we were *not* 'doing it.'!"

"Maybe he thinks you two should get engaged. You know; His honor is at stake."

My expectations to hear inspirational words vaporized.

"Go and find out. It will be a change we need in this family."

"He made me commit to stay away for four weeks."

"He didn't mean it."

"How else should he say it to mean it?" I turned around and looked past Mama realizing that indeed the Naders were out of my league.

"I'll ask her." I walked past Mama to leave.

How much worse can it get? I wondered.

"May Allah be with you. .. and pray *istikharah*," she suggested I perform a consultation prayer to receive inspiration from Allah.

I was in a near frenzy of nervous energy. I stole Baba's car and sped off toward Sophia's building. I parked next to the long and steep stairway directly across from the building and I waited.

I smoked, paced, smoked, stood, smoked, sat, and smoked some more, waiting until Sophia emerged from the building. When she did at last, she looked as glamorous as the first time I saw her. I fell in love with her all over again. She wore a navy blue beret—a fashionable solution to conceal her chopped-off hair. The concierge of her building almost bowed to her. She pressed her books against her chest and turned toward the university gate in a life-as-usual manner. As soon as she disappeared around the corner, I left the car and trotted behind her. I didn't have the courage to break my commitment to Mr. and Mrs. Nader two weeks early.

She entered the campus, seemingly unaware that I even existed in the same city. I had expected she would look for me. I didn't give up. I returned to the car and waited.

A few hours later, Sophia came through the university gate. My heart fluttered. I sank in my seat. Then I left the car and walked in her direction. She suddenly stopped. I wanted to be caught, but I felt dumb. She smiled and marched toward me. Her disarming expressions pulverized my doubts for violating the agreement, and I stayed put.

"How did you grow your beard so fast?" she asked.

"I miss you. I can't live without you."

"We need to talk."

"Of course we do."

"This is really serious, Rami."

"I know!"

"We are leaving to America."

"What? You can't be serious! When? For how long?"

"Next week. For good."

"No! No! No!" I pulled on my hair. I spun around. "One week? This is impossible."

Sophia reached to hold my hand. "Remember I mentioned to you that when we were in the mountains Daddy got an offer from one of the top architecture firms in Boston?"

"B-but you are going to school."

"I am just killing time." She tugged on my hand. "Let's walk."

My desperate need to cling to the present overrode my desire to move. "Marry me." I freed my hand.

Sophia looked bewildered, and then tears gushed from her eyes.

Before she could respond, I continued, "I'll do anything, everything you want. We can go to Saudi, Kuwait, or, or I will get a job and enroll in school. I can do it! You know I have it in me. Say you will."

Sophia took my hands. "I can't." Her voice cracked.

"What do I need to do to make you stay?"

"I have to go. I will miss you. You know I love you."

"What am I supposed to do in this dump without you?"

"I will write. I promise."

"Write? You must be joking."

"Mama said it wouldn't be easy."

"For you or me? To hell with your mother. Your father, too. Damn this world. May Allah curse everything!"

I yanked my hand from hers and hurried back to the car. I didn't know what to do or say. I was enraged that no apology in the world or mansion erected in Sophia's name would ground the Naders in Lebanon.

"What about me, Rami? Huh?" Sophia called out.

I slammed the car door shut and wrapped my fingers around the steering wheel. My eyes could see but one direction for my life, emptiness. I screeched the tires past Sophia. Twenty yards later, I slammed on the brakes. I was confused and angry, but I knew I had to make every last moment with her pleasant. I had to control myself. She approached and knocked on the passenger window. I nodded, and she slid in. She twisted forward, eager to make eye contact with me, and I saw her tears. "I am sorry." I kissed her.

She playfully pushed me away. "You've been smoking! Smoking will kill you."

"Not soon enough." I wasn't in the mood for jokes. "Please give me a few moments to process things."

I put the car in gear. Sophia took my hand, placed it on her thigh, and swept my hand with her thumb like a windshield wiper. I drove down the hills to the Corniche Bahr.

"The sharia donkeys ruined everything," I said.

"This is not your fault," she blurted. "Daddy and Mommy said that wise and able parents should never let their children live where people apply their beliefs and interpretations of religion to the law."

"Thousands live here."

"That doesn't make it right! Daddy says he let his plans to emigrate drag on too long."

"Will you come back? Ever?"

"We will keep the flat and the chalet and one car. You know what that means?"

"The flat and the chalet will be pillaged and the car will be stolen."

She punched me playfully on the arm. "No! We will be back to visit."

We arrived in front of the tower of the American University beach where Sophia and I first met. She said, "Let's take a walk."

I pulled over, and we got out of the car. I felt jittery. Even in their absence, the sharia jury, judge, and executioners now dictated how I displayed my love for Sophia. I scanned the area—no armed and gowned men in sight. I lit a cigarette and held her hand. She pressed her hip to mine. We walked slowly.

"Let me see what you like about this." She reached for the cigarette, took a shallow puff, and coughed comically. "Disgusting!"

"If I stop smoking, will you stay?"

She wrapped her arm around my waist and hugged me. I admired her audacity. She had moved on. Her mind had already traveled to the Free World.

We walked for an hour. She said that she would love me forever. She would remember me until she died, even if we never saw each other again. That helped a little, but nothing Sophia could say or do would sooth my anguish.

"Can we leave the car here and walk back?" Sophia wanted our time together to last, too. For a second, I feared Baba would return to find the car missing. To hell with him, I thought. Every moment with Sophia was invaluable.

We strolled in silence until we reached the bottom of the steep stairway across the street from her building. I swept Sophia off her feet and climbed the one-hundred-yard stretch. I stopped frequently, but not to breathe. I leaned on my knees and played up the exhaustion to win my rewards, kisses.

Sophia's mother shrieked from the balcony. She had apparently been pacing herself into a nervous bombshell.

Sophia waved gaily to her mother. "She gets too worked up over nothing."

Mrs. Nader was the least of my concerns. Actually I found her actions comical. She whipped her arm around and around, ordering Sophia upstairs like a cowboy spinning a rope to lasso a calf.

Sophia and I walked into the entrance. I held her tight and rocked her.

"I must see you tomorrow," I said into her fragrant hair.

"I will be locked down until we leave." She pointed up with her eyes. "They are getting more paranoid by the minute."

Mrs. Nader came on the intercom, demanding Sophia come up immediately.

"I better go." She pushed me back.

The concierge became Mrs. Nader's watchdog. "Ya'Allah! Come on."

"Leave us alone," Sophia shouted at him.

He retreated to his quarters.

"I have to say goodbye. When do you leave?"

"Next Monday."

"What time?" I asked.

Sophia stood on her toes, and we kissed. Then she dashed into the elevator.

Chapter 23

I Will Always Love You
May, 1984

Late that afternoon and right after I dropped Sophia off at her apartment building, I visited the Middle East Airlines office. It was two blocks away on the street level. I stared at the model Middle East Airlines aircraft displayed behind the massive glass storefront. That airline was the only remaining carrier operating in and out of Lebanon. If only I had money for the airfare, a visa, and a college degree, I would leave this dump on a one-way ticket.

Deep inside the store, a cigarette dangled from a travel agent's mouth, while he shuffled papers behind a counter. Next to him, a younger lady sat at her desk. Recessed lights reflected off her heavily made-up face. Sophia never wore makeup. She was a natural beauty.

Judging from the strained look on the agent's face, I had to have my act together before opening the glass door. Hearing muffled shouts, I looked up. The agent gestured to me to go away. I opened the door, and before I could say anything, he said, "We have no change. May Allah be with you!"

It never crossed my mind that I looked like a beggar. I marched forward.

"All flights to Africa and the Gulf are full," the woman at the desk said. She assumed I was a laborer.

I put my elbows on the counter. "Will the flight to America leave on time next Monday?" I asked, hoping to hide my ignorance in the travel world.

The man snorted. "There are no direct flights to America." He plastered a comical smile on his face. "Ya'Allah, go, love. May Allah be with you!"

I had to get the time and date of the Naders' flight. I directed my words to the lady behind the desk. "My girlfriend will leave for Boston next Monday. There was shelling when I was on the phone with her. There was shooting. Her father hustled her away from the phone. They had to take shelter. We got disconnected before she could give me the flight information."

"Oh! Poor soul! May Allah curse this war!" She lit a cigarette. "Are you going to follow her?" she asked, moving around her desk, eager to hear more.

"Of course! But you know how it is with this damned fighting!" I shrugged, projecting disappointment. "When is it going to end? May Allah break the fighters' bones!"

The man took a drag while staring at me with distrust.

"I just want to know the departure time, please!"

She said, "The only flight west on Monday goes to Heesrow. It will leave at nine at night."

"Heesrow?"

"*H-e-a-t-h-r-o-w,*" she spelled the airport name. "It is in London."

My heart resumed pumping. "Thank you! Thank you!"

"I hope you see her," she said warmly.

"It is all in Allah's hands now," I said, summoning every ounce of sincerity for the finale: "Can I have a cigarette?" I asked her coworker.

He mumbled incoherently and tossed one across the counter.

Sophia had quoted her father, saying, "The only flawless thing about West Beirut is lawlessness." I figured he would take every measure to mitigate West Beirut's risks and leave early for the airport.

At five in the evening the following Monday, I stood in the living room and begged Baba for his car. Lucky for me, Nabil was away, riding high in the fancy BMW somewhere in the city. Mama avoided seeing me humiliate myself. She stayed in the kitchen.

"I know I never was the good son. I let you and everyone down over and over. It is all my fault."

As far as Baba was concerned, I had finally succumbed to the lowest rank on the inferiority ladder. He shifted in his chair. While he played out his act, I suddenly realized why he never threw me out. He feared my uncles would catch the news of the fallout. They would rejoice and find all Baba's enemies to say, "Allah has his way with corrupt Muslims. Even his own son disowned him."

Baba popped his knuckles and looked far and deep as if to demand the attention of an orchestra before conducting a symphony. Then he transitioned to a look of deep concern. He dabbed his forehead and took too many long breaths.

"Just give him the goddamned keys and let us have dinner," Mama demanded as she brought a tray with pita, assorted cheeses, and strained yogurt.

Without a hint of a smile, I whisked the keys from his fingers and dashed out of the flat. I plunged down the stairway three steps at a time.

The streets were mostly empty. As soon as I took the turn to the Upper Basta, I gunned the car up the hill into West Beirut, toward Sophia's building. I sped through every gear.

On the two-way street in the Verdun area, about half a mile from Sophia's building, a dirty camouflage open-top pickup truck appeared from nowhere. It hurtled past me. In the truck, two men wore kufas around their necks. They were Palestinian fighters. The soldier in the back spread his legs on the flat tailgate and clenched the grips of a Dushka, a high-caliber Russian machine gun.

When the hell did they crawl back into West Beirut? I wondered.

The driver careened the truck in front of my car. I swerved right, determined to pass. I gunned the engine and made a hard right. He accelerated and cut me off. I slammed on the brakes. The car bounced over the sidewalk. The undercarriage scraped loudly. Two schoolgirls sprinted to dodge the collision. The car skidded to a stop only a foot from hitting them. The girls pounded their fists on the hood and spewed profanities.

I put the car in reverse and snapped my head back, intent on fleeing. I had no idea what I had done and what my punishment would be, but I had no time to answer for a crime. I had to get to Sophia. As soon as I shifted to first gear and looked ahead, the Dushka man swung his weapon around, tracing my speed with the muzzle. One round from that beast would pulverize my skull. The driver fired two rounds from his handgun into the sky. He jogged toward me and fired once over the car roof. I killed the engine.

As my chances of seeing Sophia evaporated, I grabbed the steering wheel and began pounding my forehead on it. May Allah curse your revolution, I prayed.

"Get out of the car. Now!" the gunman yelled.

I kept pounding my head on the steering wheel. Pain distracted me from the anguish of missing Sophia.

"We have a nutcase here, Abu Nidal," he shouted with a Palestinian accent to his comrade.

The guerilla fighter opened my door, grabbed my shirt, and hauled me out. I was limp. I didn't care what he did with me. If they wanted the car, they could have it. Worse-case scenario, it would be OK to take a bullet, but not in my legs. I needed to run to the Naders' building after these madmen were done with me.

"How much fuel do you have, donkey?" He called me a donkey just like the Phalangists on Black Saturday.

"Drain what you need," I said coldly. "Make it quick." I shoved past him, kicked the rear tire, and leaned on the trunk, turning my back to them.

On the other side of the road, four disheveled teenaged boys wearing plastic slippers, shorts, and torn shirts stood next to a tire store and watched. Past them, older kids had cleared a landfill wide enough to make a soccer field. They continued their game.

"You are one rich, arrogant bourgeoisie," he grated.

I crossed my arms and stared away from him.

"Bring a canister," he ordered his comrade. "We are at war for *you* while you are taking a joyride," he said in my direction.

I watched the soccer game. "I am worthless. I am nobody. Spare your breath. Take the fuel."

"They all say that when they see the barrel of my gun," he boasted.

I heard the fuel lid open. I turned around. Abu Nidal, the Dushka man, put a five-gallon canister capped with a yellow cloth on the ground. He removed the fuel cap and fed a long, transparent, narrow hose into the tank.

"Leave some for me. I have to make it to the airport," I said matter-of-factly.

The soldier didn't like my disregard. "Maybe I should put a round in your big head right now."

"Like I care." I leaned inside the driver's side window, shamelessly ignoring him, and reached for my cigarettes.

"What are you doing, donkey?"

Silently I retrieved the pack and lit one. "You want one?" I offered.

"No," he snapped.

I smoked while Abu Nidal worked. He sucked the air from the other end of the hose. As soon as fuel emerged, he jerked the hose from his mouth and plugged it in the nozzle of the canister. His handgun, shoved between his belt and pants, glistened. As the gasoline trickled down, I couldn't believe I had once aspired to be a

Feda'ee-a Palestinian guerilla fighter. At that moment, I prayed for Israel to finish them off.

Abu Nidal hunkered down by the canister while the driver paced. On my side of the street, the reactions of the public varied. Some drivers slowed to watch. Others accelerated, fearing an escalation. Some shot me looks of pity. A warmonger shouted, "Teach the donkey a lesson."

On the other side of the road, one driver blew the horn and then shouted, "Leave the kid alone! May Allah break your bones."

Abu Nidal shouted back, "Pull over, donkey."

Tires squealed as my supporter made a run for it.

Abu Nidal's comrade unleashed his rhetoric. "We do your dirty work. We fight your wars. All you do is stand on balconies and cheer. Now you want us out. It is not up to you, Beiruti Sunnis, dogs!"

"I am for the revolution," I told him. "The second thing after learning I was a Muslim was to support Palestine."

He turned to Abu Nidal and mocked me in a singsong voice. "I am for the revolution." He looked at me. "You sold your vote to the Zionist politicians. When it came time for you to fight, you prayed in fright." He stalked off to his truck.

"So what's new?" I asked Abu Nidal.

"We are going to crush every Jewish skull ... butcher their mothers and wives. Say Allahu akbar!" He made no eye contact with me.

"Sure. Allahu akbar," I mumbled lest I be shot for sympathizing with the Jews.

I devised contingency plans to catch up with the Naders, while Abu Nidal focused on the rising level of gas in the canister. I considered walking behind him, snatching his handgun, and firing a round in his ass. Then I would take aim at the driver, order him to stand in the middle of the street and drop his pants, and then I would lodge a bullet in his balls.

"Switch! Switch!" the driver shouted as he returned with another canister. Fuel gushed over the sides of the first one.

Abu Nidal calmly plugged the end of the hose with his thumb and then inserted it in the second canister.

"Where do you live?" he asked a moment later.

I relaxed muscles that I didn't realize I had tensed. "My name is Rami Hadhari. I live in Ras El-Nabeh."

The driver heard. His face opened as if he saw light beaming down on me and heard angels reciting the holy Qur'an. "Why didn't you say so, love? May Allah reward you for supporting us against his enemies!"

I shrugged in response to his worthless change of heart.

"Only heroes live in Ras El-Nabeh," he continued. "Let's go, Abu Nidal. Leave some for our brother."

Abu Nidal picked up the canister. They left.

Damn you and the entire Arab world for this brotherhood! The car started. The low-gas warning light glowed.

The Naders recoiled when they saw me in the entrance of their building.

"Rami!" Sophia screamed and broke away from her family.

I hugged her and spun her around. The rest of the Naders and well-wishing neighbors ceased to exist. I held Sophia, the remnants of my world, tight.

Mr. Nader whipped me into reality. "We must go!"

I released Sophia reluctantly. When her feet touched the ground, she blushed and walked back to her mother.

"Here, let me help." I walked toward the last suitcase. Walid stood next to it as if dreading the lift. Its sides bulged. "Hi, Walid," I said in English.

He didn't flinch. Mrs. Nader and Mr. Nader looked indifferent. Maha waved silently.

I picked up the heavy suitcase and bounced it off my leg to the sidewalk. Sophia walked along. If I had eyes in the back of my head, I'm sure I would have seen Mrs. Nader's revulsion and Walid's confusion about whether to hate or pity me. In my mind's eye, however, I saw Maha touched by the romantic moments unfolding before her.

"There are two cars in our convoy," Mr. Nader said.

On the street, the cars idled. The concierge took the driver's seat of the Naders' Buick LeSabre, a large American car. Only the wealthy owned American cars. He had the headlights on. "We are full," he said. "Go there."

I set the suitcase on the sidewalk by the first car, a silver Renault. There, Sophia introduced me to her uncle. He bypassed the handshake and went straight for the suitcase. He hefted it on top of others, now above the window level in the backseat.

Mrs. Nader, Maha, and Walid climbed in the Buick's backseat.

"All right! Have a good life." Mr. Nader walked around the front of his car.

"Can Sophia ride with me? One last time?" I asked, gesturing toward my father's car.

"No," he said firmly, then opened his door and watched us. He waited for her.

I gave Sophia a hug, not a farewell embrace. I whispered in her ear. "I will follow you to the airport."

"How did you know we were leaving now?"

"Allah! He tells me everything." I unearthed every last bit of humor I could muster to make her last moments with me fun. She smiled. Inside, I wept.

"I am going to follow you," I declared to Mr. Nader and crossed the street to my car.

"Rami!" Mr. Nader yelled behind me.

Welcome or not, I will follow you! I thought.

"We're going by the seaside!"

Seaside, the route that fringed the shoreline, was the farthest from the combat zone, with the last turn available to the airport. He had chosen it to avoid potential trouble.

Mr. Nader unknowingly disabled me. The very idea of taking a seaside route for safety was terrifying. Nine years before, on Black Saturday, the ticket agent on the public bus promised me and the other passengers safety ... before the Phalangists marched us to the killing field.

I stood across the street from Sophia, but spun around as far as my body allowed.

"Well?" Mr. Nader inquired, out of patience. He had his arms open, waiting for a response.

Before I could utter a word, Mr. Nader blurted, "Are you going to follow us or not?" He got in and slammed his door. Sophia's uncle started his Renault in the front. The convoy moved away.

The desperate desire to hold Sophia one more time propelled me. I scanned the area for signs of a massacre: civilians wailing, smoke bellowing, guns firing, or sirens howling. Nothing. The Naders' car engine revved at the top of the hill. They veered left and disappeared.

I flung my car door open, hopped in, and peeled out. I caught up with the Naders right before the Hobesh police station, almost a quarter mile ahead. Sophia was looking for me. When she saw me catch up, she waved happily, knowing we would be together one more time.

"I love you," I said under my breath. She saw me. She mouthed, "I love you, too."

We snaked down the steep, curvy one-way street by the light-house. At the bottom of the hill, we turned left at the Military Beach Club and drove alongside the shoreline. I locked my eyes on Sophia's blond hair. Almost every minute she turned and waved. I concealed my grief with a smile.

We climbed the Rawsheh avenue. There, my car coughed. My worse fear almost materialized. I clutched the wheel as if to transfer my energy to the engine. I eased off the gas pedal. The car resumed. I had no money for a service car to catch up with the Naders. They most certainly would not pick me up. As we went downhill, I put the car in neutral, and when the road leveled, I shifted straight to higher gears. Just before the climb to the Airport Corniche, I caught sight of the sunset, an image that would always remind me of the self-nominated sharia enforcers who triggered the Naders' exodus.

The convoy turned right at the corniche. I merged into traffic, pinning my eyes on the Naders' cars. Drivers honked and cursed. One man shouted, "Turn on your headlights, donkey!" I did. One mile to go.

The car stalled. I kept it rolling while my eyes darted between the ignition key, dashboard, and the Naders' convoy. I pumped the gas pedal as if to resuscitate it.

I turned the ignition key. The starter screamed, but the car wouldn't run. All the red lights lit up on the dashboard. I looked out. The Naders had vanished. When my car slowed almost to a stop, I slammed the handbrake and flung the door open, abandoning it across the street from the Al-Rasoul Al-A'atham Mosque. I raced toward the terminal almost three-quarters of a mile away.

I knew the Lebanese army checkpoint segregated travelers and their luggage from well-wishers, but did they enforce a no-pedestrians rule? I ran at full speed and slowed only to catch my breath.

A circus of lights came into view—red brake lights from the cars lined up at the checkpoint, flashing on and off at the pace of passage. On the other side of the road was the rush of headlights coming in my direction out of the darkness. My vision blurred by my tears. I ran into the middle of the road to get a long view of the line of cars. There were around fifty of them weighed down by heavy loads of suitcases. All of the occupants had acted on the decision of a life-time—to leave and probably never look back.

I sprinted alongside the queue, gulping exhaust fumes, searching for the Naders. I feared they had already gotten through. About three cars before the checkpoint, I saw them. I broke into a dead run and released a piercing yell. *"Sophia-a ..."*

The brake lights on the Buick went out. The concierge drove closer to the checkpoint. The Naders were next. I reached the back of the car and slapped the trunk. Sophia was the only one who didn't jump in terror. She flung her door open, dashed out, and threw herself in my arms.

I gasped for air while she kissed me frantically. Walid shouted from his window. "Come on! We are next."

The uncle cleared the checkpoint. The concierge stopped.

I held Sophia tight. "I will always love you. I will never forget you, no matter what happens."

Cars honked in protest. The soldier yelled at the Naders to approach.

"Sophia! We have to go!" her mother screamed.

Suddenly Mr. Nader was at my side, and his arms snaked around his daughter. "Put her down!" He tugged forcefully, and I let Sophia go.

She sobbed. "I love you, Rami."

Mr. Nader whisked her away. A high-pitched whistle seared my ears, and the world spun as the Naders cleared the checkpoint.

Sophia glanced out the back window at me one last time.

"Just hang on, love," I mumbled. "I will see you again." But I knew I was only fooling myself.

My heart ripped into shreds. I had never known such pain. The lump in my throat finally burst into sobs. I held my face in my palms and walked back into nothingness.

CHAPTER 24

I AM THE DEVIL

I turned around and began the walk home. About six miles later, I gripped the concrete railing of the Barbeer Bridge and looked around, considering my options: jump over the rail and die or let the street mongrels end my misery. On any other day, my senses went into laser-sharp focus, alert for moving objects and animals. That night, not one explosion detonated near or far. Perhaps I had missed a raging battle, or the civilian-killing machinery had taken a break. It didn't matter.

I wished someone would walk by, if only to recount my final moments for my mother. My mother! Oh, my Allah! I couldn't do this to her. I reconsidered my options. The thought of a typical witless, sardonic Lebanese comedian repulsed me. "Jump! Say Allah! Ha-ha-ha."

Damn you, Lebanon! Damn you, Palestine! Damn you, Israel! Rage fueled me to fight for survival. I resolved not to become another victim of the anguish that wreaked havoc on the world. I planned my route to evade snipers and mortar bombs. I reckoned that at night, snipers would miss me at the first three intersections. Then I would turn at the building with the collapsed balconies, walk through an alleyway, a vacant lot, go around a schoolyard concrete wall, creep under sand barrels, and walk quickly to my residence.

But first I had to get past the dogs under the destroyed building.

I took the ramp of solitude and entered into the zone of despair. I trotted at the first two intersections, fearing the snipers would take aim. They didn't. At the third intersection, I opted to walk, crouching, to make myself harder to shoot and to sneak up on the dogs and not awaken them. I collected two handfuls of stones as ammunition.

Regardless of how lightly I crept, pebbles cracked under my feet. The full moon wrapped me in a feeling of safety and yet exposure. My shadow slithered over the concrete rubble, remnants of the bombed-out building. There, its parking lot had become a graveyard for charred trucks, Jeeps, and cars. I entered the range of the carcass feeders. I scoped my path.

I strained to listen. I heard scratching from under one of the large black trucks then muffled barks. The first and likely the hungriest dog emerged. Vicious barks came from the pack. A gruesome, hyena-like dog approached me. Its eyes glowed. It leaned forward and growled. More dogs appeared in the median and behind me. They slowly approached.

I wanted to scream for help, but the nearest living beings would be in our flat a quarter mile up the corniche.

Sniper shots and the *whoosh* before explosions had prepared me for sudden jolts. My reflexes were honed. In a fraction of second, I could dive for my life. Tonight, though, a dive to the ground would only make me easy prey.

The mongrel lowered its head. It thrust its body forward and sped toward me. The rest followed and then slowed about twenty yards away. They formed a semicircle. Their barks grew vicious as more than twenty dogs converged on me.

I shuffled backward. From shoulder level, I hurled one stone, then two and three. My weak demonstration intensified their barks. When they approached and barked louder, I turned, hunched over, and broke into a sprint. I heard their nails slip on the asphalt from their explosive start.

Only one thought consumed me—to outrun the beasts. Adrenaline powered my legs. I pumped my arms and sliced the air. I raced over gravel, shrapnel, fragments of cinder blocks, and bomb craters. I leapt to clear patches of asphalt. My wide-open eyes made tears flow to my ears. I feared falling. I groaned in terror. The shortness of breath burned my lungs. I prayed for salvation.

I heard their nails scratch the asphalt as they closed on me. I couldn't run any faster. I had envisioned dying a hero! Please, not like this!

On instinct or stubbornness I stopped and pivoted to face my demons. The dogs skidded on the asphalt. Small puffs of dust flew off their forepaws. My hunters stood motionless. I squatted and locked eyes with the leader, the closest.

I stretched out my arms and then got down on fours. I roared and leapt closer. I felt my scalp tingle and the hair on my body stand up. I made claws of my fingers, swung my arms like a bear, and roared.

"*I am the devil!*" I screamed.

Just like that, the lead dog turned his head away from me, and his body followed. I jumped from side to side to intimidate the rest of the pack. One by one, they followed him.

When the last of them withdrew, I reverted to my human form. As I walked, I pretended they didn't exist. I snapped around to yell at them, "Don't even think about it!"

After one hundred yards I strode into an alleyway. Gunshots echoed between the bullet-scarred buildings. Not one sound of life complained from the sudden noise. I arrived at our building. There I saw the glow of the candlelight in Mama's kitchen. The onset of relief.

With shaking hands I traced the indentations on the key for the entrance door. I entered and locked the door behind me. Safety in darkness, at last! The only sound was my rapid breathing.

I had celebrated the demise of Jews and the execution of Christians and had aimed my weapon to kill them. I had lost myself in the savagery. Sophia had grounded me with her calm and beauty. She tamed my aggression. Now that she was gone, I had one more thing to do. I needed to get out of this hellhole.

CHAPTER 25

JESUS ON THE CROSS
MAY – NOVEMBER, 1984

I wrapped my fingers around the wrought-iron bars, and stared into the dark alleyway. I pounded my forehead on the metal to inflict pain on myself. I caught sight of Jamil's BMW out of the corner of my eye. The fancy car infuriated me. I stopped and climbed up to the flat.

"Come on! Show yourself!" I screamed into the dark stairway. I challenged the holy ghosts to reveal themselves.

"Rami?"

"Love? Is that you?" Mama yelled down from the third floor.

Her voice jolted me. "Who else?" I confirmed. I drew comfort in the dim reflections of the flickering candlelight on the second floor.

Her slippers scuffed the landing outside the flat. "I've been worried sick about you." Her voice was strained. "What took you so long?"

My pace exceeded my desire to be there. I reached her level. Mama held up the candle and squinted, inspecting me, just in case I had earned another beating somewhere.

"You look pale." She reached to touch me.

"I can't do this anymore, Mama. I just can't. If I can't get out of this shit hole, I am going to kill myself."

"Oh Merciful! Suicide is haram!" She paused. "Is she gone?"

Depleted, I nodded.

I followed her slowly. My feet grew heavier. Mama walked into the flat first. I dreaded going in. Inside, Nabil and Baba played backgammon. They monopolized the lantern.

"Damn this world. Damn this life," I mumbled and took off my shoes.

"Here comes the angel of misery," Baba said. "Where is the car?"

I had no way of dodging the question. With no power or warfare, the sound of the engine would be heard from the Barbeer Bridge, a quarter mile away.

"Did you hear the dogs? They almost mauled me."

Mama gasped. "Oh Merciful. I heard their barks."

I wanted to go the bedroom, away from Baba's inevitable eruption, but I had to answer him. I dropped into a chair.

"You pimp! Where is my car?" Baba held the dice in his hand and glared at me.

Nabil turned his body, crossed his arms, and waited for the answer. Mama stood in the middle. I wondered where Jamil was.

"I am fine. Please don't work yourselves up over me," I said. "I parked it a half a mile after the airport roundabout—"

"May Allah curse you!" Baba pitched the dice at me.

"Palestinian thugs!" I shouted in resentment. "They drained the fuel. They fired at me. What would you expect me to do?"

Mama got up to fetch the dice. Nabil pushed himself away from the backgammon board, got up, and sat next to Baba.

"Go get the car," Baba ordered Nabil.

"At your command," Nabil said submissively.

"Hurry before the Shias strip it down to the chassis." Baba said.

"May Allah forgive you for demeaning other Muslims." I stood up to leave.

"Shh ..." Mama handed Baba the dice.

"Congratulations on the new backgammon board," I said before I cleared the living room.

Nabil said, "You should start praying again."

I turned around and stared at him with disdain.

"Seek his blessings. The dogs are his work." He pointed upward with his index finger as if sharing a profound revelation. Nabil had copied Jamil's gestures.

His pronouncement ignited the little energy I had. "OK, Mr. Resident Cleric. I seek your wisdom. Explain this—the mongrels fled from *me*." I pounded my chest. "I terrorized the monsters. They scrambled. Now, Cleric, does that mean I defied Allah or that He protected me?"

"Allah has control over all his creations." He stood, picked up the rosary beads and lowered it around his neck.

"So Allah commands you *and* the dogs?" I asked pretending to be fascinated.

The redness of Nabil's eyes glowed even in the faint light.

Mama gasped and looked at Nabil. "Oh Merciful. He didn't mean that," she said, hoping to suppress his anger.

"*Shut up!* Donkey!" Baba shouted. He slammed the new backgammon board shut and hugged it.

Mama darted toward me, and herded me toward my room.

"Don't call me *donkey*! May Allah curse this family," I said over my shoulder while Mama pushed.

"You keep asking for it," Mama hissed, and shoved me into my room. "Lock your door."

"Blasphemous!" Nabil shouted.

"*You* said 'they are his work.'" I protested.

"Pimp! Heretic! Where did the whore go?" Nabil shouted and paused.

I maneuvered around Mama. As soon as Nabil saw me, he said, "To the land of Satan, sin, and sacrilege! Your death is *halal*, lawful."

Somewhere along the way—maybe in the bunkers or the Qur'an

study circles—Nabil had given himself the authority to issue a *fatwa*, a legal ruling.

"Where is your master?" I asked.

"*Allah* is my master," Nabil said.

I snorted. "Jamil!"

"Go to your room. For Allah's sake and yours, stop!" Mama said.

Baba put the backgammon board at his side.

"Is he in Europe with prostitutes?" I asked rhetorically. "Oh! I am sorry! My mistake ... Allah allows holy warriors to hump non-Muslim women. They are but the spoils of war—"

"Have some decency." Mama glared at me.

"You pimp. Watch your mouth," Baba said.

"Answer, Cleric. Where is Jamil?"

"In Monaco," Nabil said reluctantly.

I burst out laughing. "Monaco? Ha! Where have I heard that before? I see it in *your* future. I see naked women bowing before you. Takbir!" I mocked.

Baba stood up, took two long strides, and slapped me with all he had. He lost his balance with the momentum, and I scrambled to catch him before he fell. I was twenty-three years old, and he still felt empowered to hit me.

Mama shouted, "Get in your damned room. *Now*."

He mumbled prayers for my demise as I helped him into his chair. I stared at Nabil. "Happy now?"

"Your blood is halal!" Nabil roared.

Mama swiftly clamped my shoulders and turned me to face my room. "He will kill you. Don't you understand? He will kill you."

"He is a coward." I reached over Mama and raised my voice. "I *am* the real Muslim. You were Othman's donkey. Now you are Jamil's donkey. They say talk, you bray. They say 'with Allah we are victorious,' you kill civilians. You are nothing, but a war criminal." Suddenly I loathed myself for skipping prayers and fasting.

Nabil approached, and Mama released me. Cold and deliberately, he slammed into me on the way to his room. "Don't go anywhere," he said through clenched teeth.

Mama screamed, "Rami, leave!"

I went back into the living room and sat down. I crossed my arms over my chest and waited. My heart thumped. "Where did he go?" Baba asked.

"To his room. Do something," Mama urged Baba. Then, she released the loudest shriek I ever heard in my life. Baba pressed both palms against his ears.

On his way from the foyer, Nabil cocked his handgun. A round flew out of the chamber. For an instant our eyes locked as he leveled the gun on my face. He approached and pressed the muzzle to my forehead.

Mama shouted, "In Allah's name! Put it away!" She swung her arm up and down but didn't touch Nabil.

In my peripheral vision, I saw Baba watch for my reaction.

Mama slapped her cheeks and wailed. "Ya Allah, where are you?"

I kept my eye on Nabil's trigger finger. I tensed my neck and shoulders and leaned into the muzzle slowly and defiantly. Then I carefully tried to stand up.

Nabil's eyes were icy. The expression on his face was diabolical. "Sit down."

Will my obituary say "martyr?" I wondered. Suddenly my fear of failure, anguish over my faith, regrets, and worries about the future lifted. I exhaled and drifted into indifference. I closed my eyes. "Shoot."

I heard a noise. I opened my eyes. Mama leaned her weight on Nabil's arm, trying to press it down. He transferred the gun to his other hand and balled his fist to slug her.

"*Stop!*" Baba shouted. "May Allah curse all of you! Put the gun down!"

Nabil obeyed. Mama collapsed.

I made my decision. I would go to the United States embassy to seek a visa, even if I died trying.

Car bombs became the assassination weapons of choice, after the Shias, Druze, and communists—they formed an alliance with the Syria—annihilated the Sunni militias. They were detonated mostly in Sunni enclaves regardless of the citizens caught in the middle.

Um Muhamad, Husam's wife, died in a car-bomb explosion while buying pita outside a bakery. Mama wept for days. I cried with her.

In late September 1984, a few weeks after Um Muhamad's death, Husam came to visit before the Friday prayers. Between sobs and curses at Muslim and Christian militias and the Palestinians and Israelis, he explained the circumstances of his wife's death. "I ran out of the house as soon as I heard the explosion. She lay there on the sidewalk. Women and children were screaming and men on the ground moaning. It was chaos. There were earlobes, hands, and feet on the pavement. Pieces of flesh stuck to the storefront."

I had grown indifferent to graphic details.

"She was buried in a mass grave," Husam said solemnly, "somewhere by the Sabra mass grave. I-I just don't know where to pray for her."

Mama, Baba, and Nabil quoted as many popular Qur'anic verses as they could to comfort Husam. While they eulogized Um Muhamad, I silently prayed for an American visa.

At noon, Husam, Baba, and Nabil went to the mosque. I stayed behind. I followed Mama out to the balcony, where she hung laundry on the lines. I shared with her my new and final aspiration.

"In sha'Allah. Whatever is in the book for you" was her response. It irked me. Did she see me as a chronic loser with high ambitions? Maybe I had blown the trumpet for her salvation one time too many. I had said I would shred her dishwashing gloves and get her a maid one day. Maybe she tired of my antics. I feared I had become a burden to her.

"You don't understand. I want to leave forever. If they give me the visa, I am out of here."

"In sha'Allah."

"That's it? In sha'Allah!"

"Both embassies were bombed. You haven't heard about Awkar? It was yesterday."

Mama referred to the explosion that claimed the US Embassy annex in East Beirut. Eleven people were killed and ninety-six injured.

"I will go to Damascus," I told her. "If I make it to America, I will send you money. I will send after you. I will take care of you."

Mama smiled sadly: "'Those who believe and those who emigrate and strive hard in the cause of Allah, it is these who hope for Allah's mercy.'"

"I will prosper and provide for you," I said.

"Count on Allah!"

"I will go in October. Let the Americans calm down a little about the Lebanese."

Mama shrugged. She promised to keep my quest a secret.

Another flicker of hope finally glowed. My mind and soul had already left for America.

When power resumed and no one was home, I glued my eyes to American television shows. One time Mama sat next to me, and we watched *First Blood*. She read the subtitles with fervor. What happened to John Rambo in jail unnerved her.

"I don't know about America!" She lit a cigarette. "What if a policeman did this to you?"

"It is just a movie!" I said.

"The entire town is not a movie. What if they know about Nabil? The Americans know everything."

"OK! You are right. Beirut is better in all ways!" I joked.

"Why don't you see Husam? He knows shipping and travel. His son traveled before. He will keep your secret."

"Great idea."

Mama went into the kitchen. I picked up a cigarette and marveled at the prowess of Rambo, an American veteran in distress.

That afternoon, October 5, 1984, I rode my bicycle to Husam's flat. After a warm welcome and his commitment to confidentiality, I revealed my plans.

"You will need a passport before you go to the embassy. For that you will need two photos. ..." Husam studied my face. "Thousands of applicants get rejected. Most are Muslims."

"I don't know where to start or where to go," I said.

"There is a young man. His name is ... um ... Fuad. The Americans rejected his visa request a few years back. He made it his calling to aid all visa seekers. That is his way of retaliating. Anyway, I play backgammon with his father. He is our local notary."

A notary public was empowered to create and endorse low-level legal documents. Husam told me where to find Fuad.

"Tell him that I sent you, or you will have to count your fingers after a handshake with him," Husam joked, and then on my way out, he shoved two hundred-dollar bills in my shirt pocket.

My heart melted. I felt a sudden burning in my eyes. I reached for Husam's hand to kiss it. He jerked it away and gave me a hug instead. I hugged him tighter.

"Rami Hadhari," I said, reaching out for a handshake.

He stared at my hand and sized me up.

"Husam sent me. He says hello."

Fuad twitched a short-lived smile under his thick mustache and slowly reached for my hand without disturbing his pochette, a

French-fashioned handbag that hustlers and French wannabees tucked under their arms.

"The graveyard Hadharis?"

"Uncle Husam said that you can help me with a visa to America."

In his mid-twenties, Fuad lived on commissions from the bribes of citizens paralyzed by the bureaucratic maze requiring a date stamped on even the simplest documents by government employees. He talked fast, his version of flexing his intelligence. I fought the urge to punch him.

After he collected his consulting fees up front—a whopping one-hundred dollars—we agreed to meet every morning at eight for three weeks outside his father's store. On the first day, he removed keys from his pochette. "For the padlock." He pointed at the shop's roll-up metal door. I unlocked it and lifted it while he lit a cigarette.

When Fuad turned on the fluorescent lights, they flickered, and the transformers clicked for a few seconds before the sterile light shone. The dingy office looked, smelled, and felt like the fetid basement garage in our building.

Fuad walked toward the back of the store. The poster of the Christian Maronite president, Aziz Gemayel, hung above his father's desk. As with all government agencies, he had no choice in the matter.

Fuad returned with a broom and held it out with a straight arm. "Sweep outside."

When I finished, he told me to take out six stacked plastic chairs and arrange them for two backgammon matches on the sidewalk. Fuad had enslaved me. It crossed my mind that I had paid him to work for him.

"You are doing great. Sit." He pointed at a metal chair in front of his father's desk, which he walked around to take his father's chair. Red and black inkpads lay under a round rack full of stamps. Two wire-mesh bins bent under a load of papers.

Fuad tutored me in the world of the Americans-their mind games and trickery. During the first two days, I fought the urge to ask him: if you are so good at knowing what it takes to win a visa, why couldn't you get one yourself?

On the third week of documents trickling in and behavioral training for the interview with an embassy counselor, Fuad leaned forward and said, "Your passport."

Jubilant, I snatched it from his hand. I flipped the pages and smelled the cover. The feel and scent of freedom was finally within my reach.

"Your folder is now complete," he said. It was at nine in the morning on October 31, 1984, when Fuad threw a manila folder on the desktop and said, "Now I'll tell you exactly what to say. Listen carefully. If you want a visa, you need to be clever."

By saying clever, Fuad meant cunning. Master Muhamad permitted deception as a means to save one's life. I had resolved to commit suicide should the Americans deny me the visa; therefore, lying was halal.

Fuad pulled one document after another from the folder. He presented me with an employment letter, bank statements for the entire year of 1984, an identity card, and official high-school transcripts from the top school in West Beirut. All were in English. My achievements dazzled me.

"The Americans objective is to find holes in your story. When they fail, they want to see how desperate you are. Act like you don't give a shit. If you show an atom's worth of desperation, kiss freedom goodbye! If you plead, you're done. You follow me?"

"Yes, sir!" He was in my age group, but I found myself humbled.

"Do you have a cross pendant?"

"Of course not," I said resentfully.

"Here." He pulled a gold-metal crucifix pendant from his front shirt pocket.

"I can't afford that," I said.

"It is fake gold. Give it back to me after your appointment. The Americans don't like jewelry, but Jesus on the cross goes a long way. Are you with me?"

Nine years before, Husam told me to deny being a Muslim should I get stopped by a Phalangist. I had stuttered, and the vicious militiamen herded me onto the slaughter field. Now I snatched the chain with a vengeance.

"Atta boy! Talk like a Christian. Lighten up on the vowels. The Americans won't know your religion from your name."

"I didn't realize that," I said, impressed with Fuad's insight.

"Shave the morning you walk into the embassy. Not the night before. When you stand across from the visa counselor, button your shirt up to here." He tapped under his neck. "Once, they rejected a guy because he rubbed his chest hair with mousse. Idiot! The Americans don't like hair."

"I am not hairy."

He rolled his eyes. "Let's move on. If they ask if you have friends in America, what are you going to say?"

"I have many."

"None!" He shook his head in disappointment. "You are there for a quick visit. If they think you know someone, then they will assume you will stay. They don't want you to stay."

"But I want the visa to find—"

"Forget about that Christian girl. I already told you a hundred times." He spread a stack of glossy travel brochures on the desktop. "Pick the one that speaks to your heart."

I selected the pamphlet with the Statue of Liberty on the cover.

"Perfect!" he said. "What is the purpose of your trip?"

"Tourism."

"How long will you stay?"

"Fifteen days."

"Who will you visit?"

"No one."

"Where will you stay?"

"At this hotel." I pointed at a hotel inside the pamphlet.

"Excellent." He handed me a fax copy of a hotel reservation in New York.

"Read it." He wiggled his index finger.

"I am booked from November 26 through December 9?" I put the paper down. "I can't afford that!"

He threw up his hands. "Why must all my clients be so dumb?"

"Can we do this without the insults?" I asked, annoyed.

"Listen, love," he said with elaborate patience. "I will cancel the booking on the evening of your return from the embassy. Please ask me why I chose those dates."

"OK. Why?"

"Because the day after Thanksgiving is the biggest shopping day in America. Not only you will be touring, but you will be spending money on shopping. The Americans want your money."

"OK!"

"'OK?' It is brilliant! You should go to the embassy and interview on November 12. Not before, not after."

"Yes, sir."

"Do you have a job?"

"Of course!" I slipped out the forged employment letter.

"Are you married?"

"I have a girlfriend!"

"Will it tear your lips to smile? In Allah's name, show some joy when you mention her, so they'll know you'd be miserable without her."

I nodded.

"Where is she?"

"In Beirut. We are sort of engaged." I smiled sheepishly.

"Excellent. You have nice teeth. Show them." He rubbed his hands together. "We are making progress."

Suddenly his demeanor changed. "Damn. I forgot to get you a college degree." He blew his breath in my face. "Your file is demanding. It will cost you!"

"What degree?"

"I can get you a Business Administration degree from the American University of Beirut. That one is two hundred dollars. One from the Beirut Arab University is fifty dollars."

Fuad said that an American University degree was the ace in the hole. After a round of pleading and begging, he agreed to furnish one for fifty dollars.

"Give me your passport!"

I pulled it out of the folder.

"This is the fun part. Watch this." Fuad threw the passport on the floor, got up, and stomped on it a few times.

"What are you doing!?"

"Do you want to go to America or not?" He picked it up, licked his thumb, vigorously rubbed the gold emblem, and then scratched it with a fingernail until it partially faded.

"How much do you have on you?"

"Twenty dollars."

"That will only get you a stamp for Turkey. We need you to go to Greece as well. Give me the twenty."

"That's all I have." I handed him the last bill from Husam.

"That is all right. We are almost done." Fuad took three rubber stamps from the rack, and then he flipped the lids of the inkpads, opened the passport, and made impressions with loud thuds. He adjusted dates on one stamp and resumed stamping.

"There! You have been to Greece and Turkey. You left on these dates." He turned to the pages in the very back. "And you returned on these dates. Memorize them."

"What is that all about?"

"To show the Americans that you are well traveled." He handed me the battered passport, "and that you return to Lebanon from your travels."

"Now, my friend ..." He leaned forward, and his eyes glowed. "You are visa worthy!"

CHAPTER 26

DESTINATION: AMERICA
NOVEMBER, 1984

On November 12, 1984, right after midnight, Husam dropped me off at the Cola Bridge, just like Fuad had instructed. There, long-haul service cars operated between West Beirut and Damascus.

The night was chilly, and I wore a thick coat, obeying Mama's pleas to do so. I had secured my documents in a maroon leather port-folio with sharp brass corners and held it close to my chest. Husam paid the driver $100 for me to ride alone, straight to Damascus. We kissed on the cheeks and said our goodbyes. Over the sound of the engine, he prayed for me to win the American visa.

The driver mumbled prayers and put the car in gear. "It used to take under ninety minutes. May Allah break the bones of the Syrians and the militias. Now it is a five-hour trip." He accounted for the numerous checkpoints of village vigilantes and warring factions.

The route was mountainous and treacherous. Our headlights alerted the thugs to our approach. They dashed to the deserted checkpoints to receive us. When confronted by more aggressive militiamen, the driver used me as comic relief. "He wants to be first in line at the America embassy," he said, chuckling, but no one laughed with him. They let us pass.

We reached Dahr El-Baidar, the highest elevation point in our journey inside Lebanon. There, the Syrian army had settled with tanks, trucks, and troops. Two hundred yards before arriving at the checkpoint, the driver rudely ordered me to sit up straight and smile. He dimmed all the beams and turned on the car's interior lights as he rolled up to the soldiers.

As the car neared the checkpoint, my throat tightened. I remembered how Syrian soldiers had dragged my uncle-by-marriage from his car and beaten him in front of his wife and small sons. The interior lights in his car had malfunctioned, and the soldiers assumed Uncle was defying them when they demanded he switched them on.

I pressed myself against the seat. I dropped my shoulders and contrived a smile.

At the last second, the driver pulled out a cigarette pack from his shirt pocket.

"Where are you going?" the soldier asked, disgruntled.

"In sha'Allah, Chtaura," the driver lied. He named the most populated village in the Bekaa valley, six miles down the steep, dark, and curvy roads, probably to avoid further questions. "Please." He offered cigarettes to the soldier.

The soldier snatched the pack. "*Get the hell out of here!*" he barked the verbal approval of passage and flung his wrist for us to move.

Down the narrow roads, I stared out to my right into darkness.

The driver interrupted my thoughts. "Give me your passport." We had cleared the Lebanese customs and arrived at the Syrian border. He left the car to fill out the forms to enter the country. Twenty minutes later, he returned with a smile as if we were privileged with the honor to enter the industrialized world.

We drove into Damascus at five in the morning. The car entered a roundabout and climbed the gently sloping Hay Al-Kazzazeen Street. A wide grassy median divided the four-lane road. The area was clean and quiet.

"There it is." The driver pulled over before another roundabout and pointed to a building on the left side of the road: "United States of America Embassy."

In spite of the darkness, the three-story building glowed like a snow-white mountaintop in a desert. Two Syrian guards sat on stools next to a glass booth outside. They warmed their hands at a fire inside an olive-oil drum. I guessed that the Americans had few security concerns in Syria, as the building was behind a four-foot-high concrete wall without barbed wire coiled atop or below. The entrance was a head-high, wrought-iron, double-wide gate.

"Are you sure?" I asked, looking for the American flag. I had expected to see countless dreamers already lined up to claim their turn.

"Ya'Allah, love. That is it. See?" He showed me a flagpole sticking out of the second-floor balcony. "Get out now before we have to deal with them." The driver inclined his head toward the Syrian guards.

I picked up my portfolio and slid out. My senses were hyper alert. All the surrounding stores were closed, and for a city known for its diesel engines and mopeds, all I heard was the crackling of the fire across the street, next to the booth. I left my body and saw my world unfold.

I jogged across the two-lane road toward the square aluminum-frame booth immediately to the left of the wrought-iron gate. The upper half was glassed-in, and the bottom was covered with white panels. Its size reminded me of the bathroom where Grandmother's body was washed before her burial.

I noticed paper signs posted on the booth. I figured I would go to get information.

One of the Syrian soldiers snapped to his feet, picking up his AK-47. "State your business," he demanded.

"I am here to apply for a visa."

His comrade emerged, swinging his weapon around his shoulder. "Beiruti, ha? Of course you are. Where else would you go? You bombed all the embassies. Stand right there."

My dialect was a dead giveaway. He pointed at a spot before the glass booth. I obeyed.

"Stop pushing him. May Allah curse you! He is first." The soldier pretended to address someone behind me. They high-fived each other.

I forced a smile and then saw a sign in Arabic and English, taped to the glass booth: VISA APPLICANTS ACCEPTED HERE FROM EIGHT TO NOON, MONDAY THROUGH FRIDAY. CLOSED SATURDAY AND SUNDAY. Americans made rules and followed them. I prayed they enforced the hours and acceptance of applications as well. My worries didn't subside.

Am I a dead man walking or a free man in the making?

I stepped back and paced. I pressed the portfolio under my arm and plunged my hands deep into my coat pockets. I felt the crucifix. I pulled it out, stared at it for a moment, and returned it.

Time moved slowly. I rehearsed Fuad's lines silently, but I felt conflicted. Maybe I didn't have to lie. I was different—I was the real deal. I had nothing to hide. I wasn't a war criminal like Jawdat, one of Nabil's friends whose specialty was to set Othman's victims on fire. He got a visa.

At seven in the morning, pests descended from various directions on foot, bicycles, cars, mopeds, and public buses. I braced myself against a metal bar in the embassy gate. Between seven-thirty and eight, the place was as jammed as a pita bakery in West Beirut. Anarchy at America's door disappointed me. I expected order. How could they allow chaos to break out on their doorstep? If they did that, how would they be able to distinguish me from the criminals?

People jammed the sidewalk, huddled on the median, and unfolded chairs on the other side of the street. It looked like it was a routine. Some applicants shoved me with sharp elbows. Others pushed to uproot me. I turned the corners of my folder into a weapon and poked them back. I tightened my grip around a bar in the gate and stood as close to the booth as I could. I held on until my knuckles turned white. As I waited, I told myself to envision a positive out-come, being with Sophia.

A US soldier finally emerged from the embassy. I let go of the gate. He handed off an Arab man to the shortest and meanest Syrian guard and then retreated behind the gate. I jumped in front of the booth. The guard escorted the Arab man into the back of it, where a door opened. I wondered why an Arab staffed the booth.

The Syrian guard walked up to my right and faced out. "Listen up, everybody," he shouted. "I don't want any disorderly conduct. This is not Lebanon. You understand? This is Syria, the free. Sign up here." He pointed to the window at the booth. "You better stand in line or I will whip you."

Fuad had told me what to expect. Suddenly people surged forward, and the onslaught for claiming turns ensued. But I had already pressed my body against the window.

Two Syrian guards stood next to the booth and two on each side of the gate. A minute later the shorter and meanest looking guard walked inside the booth. He and the attendant talked in close prox-imity. They grinned sadistically. People behind pushed me against the glass. I leaned back with force.

At eight-fifteen, the ruckus grew even louder.

"Let us in!" a man shouted. He looked to be in his thirties.

"Shut up, you Lebanese donkeys," the Syrian guard next to me shouted.

He turned to the US soldier and shrugged with the look of: if not for me, they would devour you. The soldier nodded.

The booth attendant slid the window open. "What is your name?" he asked me.

"Rami Hadhari." I sounded eager to please and ready to build a long-term relationship.

Without looking at me he asked, "What is your business here?" He scribbled my name on a voucher pad.

"I am here to apply for a visa."

The air got thicker and my breaths, shorter. The Syrian guard inside the booth stepped out. "Move to the side. We will call you when it's your turn."

I froze. "But I am first?"

The guard poked my gut with the muzzle of the AK-47. "Move, donkey!"

"But how am I going to hear my name over all this?"

"One more word out of your filthy mouth, and you will never set foot inside, mule!"

I retreated while glancing at the mighty US soldier. He looked unconcerned. My body temperature soared. I wiped my forehead. Despite the cold, my shirt stuck to my back.

Ten minutes later, the Syrian guard relayed the booth attendant's calls for applicants. Each time a name was shouted out, the respondent almost fell over himself in his rush to the gate. Using names instead of ascending numbers allowed scammers to call people out of order. I figured the order of calls corresponded with the payoff amount. I had only enough for the fare to Beirut. I resigned myself to my fate, which the crooks held in their hands.

The pandemonium didn't let up. I heard prayers to Allah to expedite a turn. Others jostled me while they complained about waiting for their loved ones who were taking too long to emerge from the embassy. The remaining visa seekers craned their necks in anticipation.

An old man wearing a kufa yelled, "May Allah burn the Americans in hell!" From about thirty feet away he demanded the attention of the US soldier. "You American!"

The soldier looked up.

"Yes, you!" the man continued in Arabic. "This is our third time here. If you don't give my son a visa today, I will kill you. *Heretic.*"

Third time? I panicked. Why three? Had they shown early but

still not gotten in? The possibility of being turned away and having to go through all this again made me feel sick. The soldier turned to the Syrian guard for an interpretation. The guard shrugged.

By 11:43, I feared I was caged in the open and denied freedom inside. I fixated on the guard who had shoved the muzzle in my gut, the dealmaker. I begged Allah to order the guard to move aside. There had to be a way to impress upon the attendant in the booth to let me in.

I hoped fervently that an American somewhere would demand an audit of the sequence of applicants. Nothing! With time running out, the men around me complained loudly. Some shouted ideas to improve efficiency.

How typical, I thought. We create processes to fit our personal needs only to blow them up after we are done or others have mastered them first.

"Ya'Allah! Get us in!" Cries urging the guards multiplied. The mass of people churned.

A black US soldier emerged from inside the embassy. He must have been over six feet, four inches tall. He held his assault rifle in his hand and wore a handgun. He looked angry. Those who were agitated subsided.

When the soldier went back in, tension escalated to a new level. The man with the kufa chanted, "We want in!" He punched the sky. The shout instigated a roaring wave of chants. Panicking, I prayed the unruly would behave and the loudmouths shut up. I hadn't traveled to Damascus to take part in a revolution or a protest. What if the embassy closed its doors in response?

The standing US soldier looked tenser. The four Syrian soldiers unstrapped their AK-47s. I saw two put their fingers in the trigger guard. The mob closed ranks. I got shoved into the wrought-iron gate. I turned to the US soldier and threw him the look of that said, 'I am being crushed. Help me!' He ignored me.

I looked around. Syrian pedestrians and drivers stopped and shot us looks of scorn. We, the Lebanese war victims, had it coming.

The short, mean Syrian guard ran out of patience. With less than seven minutes remaining before the embassy closure, he cocked his AK-47 and shouted, "You Lebanese donkeys! You earned your demise!" The lead Syrian guard aimed from the shoulder. The shouts subsided. I hid in plain sight to avoid guilt by visual proximity.

Three minutes before twelve, despair struck. My shoulders sagged, and grief paralyzed me. I felt like slitting my wrists.

At 11:58, the Syrian guard called another name. I stared at the responder with utmost resentment and glared at the Syrian guard.

I fantasized about springing forward, tackling the guard in charge, snatching his AK-47, and killing him and his comrades, then handing the weapon to the American, dashing inside the embassy, and shouting, "I am a refugee! I seek political asylum!"

"Rami Hadhari!" the soldier shouted. "Rami Hadhari!"

I started. "I am Rami Hadhari! I am here!" I cried out. "I am Rami Hadhari!"

"Show yourself."

I plowed through the frenzied crowd.

"Step aside, mules!" the guard screamed at them, and waved his weapon. Without it the mob would have crushed him. The crowd became subdued, but the angrier applicants didn't budge.

With the Syrian soldier now on my side, I carved my way through the people with the pointy brass corners of my portfolio. I elbowed and bumped everyone in my path. I stood before the US soldier, gasping for air and awaiting instructions.

"This way, please," the US soldier said without a trace of emotion.

From that point forward, time flew. Things moved fast. I had nothing to fight over. It was peaceful.

The black soldier approached. "Sir! Please put the portfolio here," he said robotically and pointed to a table. "Empty your pockets."

I quickly took out my keys, pendant, and coins, and then he rummaged through my portfolio. When finished, he returned all the documents to their original order. After patting me down, he said, "Thank you. This way please." His tone was firm. His eyes were fierce. "You are welcome!" I smiled. I followed him up to the first floor, my back straight and chin up.

He made way for me to enter first and stayed at the door. "Please have a seat, sir." He pointed at a bank of attached chairs—four rows of five chairs each.

Three people sat quietly. In my world outside the embassy, only lethal force could get a Lebanese brain surgeon to shut up even during surgery. Inside the embassy, people acted politely. Just before I took a seat, an American civilian lady assigned me number 127.

I sat in the first row and scanned the room. A photograph of the Washington Monument hung on a wall. Ahead and to the right was a row of three glass-paneled cubicles, where consular officers interviewed candidates. The consular officers were out of my line of sight, but I observed two applicants in the midst of an interview. At the first booth, a man in a shiny blue suit, white socks, and black shoes crossed his ankles as if he had to urinate. He dropped a paper. He snatched it up and apologized profusely. He pressed his palms together under his chin as if praying for mercy. The act nauseated me. Have some dignity, I thought.

At the second, a chubby woman wore a hijab and spoke loudly in Arabic, mixing it up with "bleeze" and "sank yu."

The third booth was vacant.

In the waiting area and two chairs to my right, a nondescript-looking man in his mid-fifties sat next to a woman. I could see only her feet. The man leaned forward to gawk at me while the woman maintained a submissive posture. She was half his age. Her skin was dark. Two rows behind, a young man with a thick mustache wore a cross over his suit jacket. He looked frightened.

The US soldier from the gate entered and approached the woman who assigned the numbers. He pointed at me and said, "He is the last one," then left.

I took a deep breath in and slowly exhaled. Last, but in.

"Number one twenty-five," the lady called.

"That is you," the nondescript man told his companion. The young lady got up. "Remember what we talked about," he threatened. The clerk pointed her toward the far cubicle.

From the middle booth, the veiled woman, looking dejected, walked toward us. "My nephew just died in a car accident. All I want is to be at his funeral!"

When she got in front of me, she probably expected a look of sympathy, but I turned away. Fuad had told me that the most frequently used story was a death in the family. She should have consulted with him first. When the woman reached the exit, she jabbed the soldier's chest with her index finger and in Arabic said, "Death to the whore," referring to the consular officer. "Death to America!"

The guard braced his weapon and shook his head in disgust. I'm sure he had seen this reaction and heard these incomprehensible insults countless times.

"One twenty-six," the lady called.

I was next. A wreath on my grave tomorrow or a visa on my passport today. My heart thumped.

No one moved. I looked at the man next to me, inquiring if it was his turn. He shook his head.

"Serving one twenty-six," the lady repeated louder.

I turned and watched the cross-wearing man behind me jump as if a bombshell exploded next to him. In a flash his demeanor changed from terrified to joyful—his game face. The caller pointed at the middle booth, exactly where the woman with the hijab started her rant.

If I end up in the middle booth, how will the consular officer see me? I dreaded the encounter.

The remaining man leaned over. "I already live in America. I am trying to take my wife to our new home there." He pointed toward the cubicle with his thumb. "It is our fifth trip here. The idiots are torturing us. They can't tell good from bad anymore. In sha'Allah a good outcome this time."

"In sha'Allah!" I whispered, and looked in the opposite direction. I saw through his scam. Fuad told me that some married men returned to Lebanon to take live-in maids back to America under the pretense of being a wife. They only cost $150 per month.

Suddenly I felt disgusted with myself. I was not like the others! I was not a cheat!

"Death to America!" the man who wore the cross shouted. He turned from the middle booth and stomped out. He yanked the necklace off and threw it on the floor. The American guard stood taller as the man stormed out.

The outbursts against the Americans lowered my hopes even more. The wide range of deception would have disheartened even the most forgiving of all saints and made them suspicious of even the angels. I had invested money, time, and practice in my story.

I had to get the visa to survive. It was my only chance to rewrite my life on my own terms. I had envisioned myself being the calm and quiet guy, in a house of my own, with classical music playing as I sat at my desk overlooking a manicured lawn. In my dreams, I entered a world where success was based on ethics and proper dealings, not bribes and scams. My vision of success included marrying Sophia, having joyful children, unassuming friends, and warmhearted neighbors. I aspired for an environment where I would be valued for my good character, not on the strength of my aggression. I wanted to leave West Beirut, the four square miles of a lesser world. I aspired to be measured by my merit, not my religious affiliation. I was ready to take on the frontier, but I sat panicked. I had to control my anger. I had to exert the utmost self-control and let my visualization of a life in America lift my spirits.

The dark-skinned woman emerged from the booth and faced her man. She glowed. He looked up at the ceiling and at the length of his breath said, "Thank Allah. Always thank Allah!" He finished with force.

He put his hand on my shoulder. "Good or bad, no matter what happens, always thank Him."

I recoiled. I took deeper breaths. Any second now, the woman would call my number.

My mind left my body. I went under water. Sophia followed. She pulled me toward her and then threaded her arms through mine. I wrapped my arms around her waist. We drifted deeper. Her hair floated. Sunrays beamed through it. She pressed her lips on mine. I moved my hands up and cupped her cheeks. She released me and swam to the surface.

"Number one twenty-seven."

The call to destiny. It was my judgment day. I decided there would be no lies, no cheating. I picked up the portfolio and walked slowly toward the clerk. My name is Rami Hadhari. I am number one twenty-seven, and I am not a scammer. In the Qur'an, Allah said, "... this is a day when *only* the truthful shall profit by their truthfulness ... that indeed is the great triumph. ..."

I stood before the caller. She pointed at the middle booth.

The consular officer was a petite blond woman wearing large, white-frame glasses. Only her head and shoulders cleared the counter. She looked angelic. There was an opening at the bottom of the glass panel.

"May peace be upon you! Do you speak English?" She spoke through a round hole in the glass. Her soft voice and accent reminded me of Sophia.

"Hi! Of course! Happy Thanksgiving." I smiled.

"You jumped the gun, but ..."

"Jumped the gun?" What does that mean? I didn't mean anything by it. I prayed I had not insulted her.

She continued, but I was unable to comprehend her words, so I smiled sheepishly.

"Passport, please!" She stuck her hand out and waited.

I pushed the passport through the slot. I saw a mug full of pens and two stamps encased with chrome—the kind that didn't need ink pads.

"This passport has seen better days!" she said, studying it.

Damn you, Fuad!

She opened the first page and inspected my photo. I stared at her nose for a moment. Just like Sophia's. My heart melted. She glanced at me to match the picture with my face. Then she flipped to the next page to examine the expiration date.

"What is the purpose of your trip?" she asked the patented question.

"Visit," I said calmly.

"Where?"

"Boston."

"Who will you visit?"

"My girlfriend."

She shot me a look of suspicion. "What is her name?"

"Sophia Nader." My pulse quickened.

"How long will you stay?"

"Two weeks. Um ... it really depends on how well her mother will receive me."

She grinned.

"Does your girlfriend know you want to go?"

"Not yet. I promised I would, though."

"Does her family know you plan to visit?"

"I hope not. They will move again!"

She chuckled. I wasn't joking. She hesitated, looking between two stamps, considering, while I held my breath. At last she reached for one, flipped to a blank page on the passport, and with a thud inked my passport with her verdict. She picked up a pen and scribbled over the stamp.

"Safe journey back to Beirut," she said with an unreadable face. She folded the passport and shoved it through the slot.

"Thank you." Afraid to ask for her decision, I put the passport in the portfolio. I would look at her verdict at the time and place of my choosing.

Outside the embassy, the unruly rejects and the visa hopefuls lingered needlessly. Some stared at me with inquisitive eyes. I reciprocated with dull looks.

Five minutes later I threw myself on a chair inside a restaurant located by the Hay Al-Kazzazeen roundabout. From my seat, I saw the panoramic view of the street. I put the folder on the table and stared at it.

"What can I get for you?" the waiter asked.

"Oh! Right." I snapped from my stupor. "May I have a *sigarah*?" I asked for a cigarette.

"Of course!" He pulled one out and lit it for me.

"Hot tea, please," I ordered.

The waiter left. I opened the portfolio. My heart raced. I took a long drag. I stared at the passport for a while and then finally reached for it. I closed my eyes and took a deep breath. The waiter returned with the tea. I put the passport down again. My hands shook. I tried to take a sip, but sloshed tea on myself. I put the glass down and picked up the passport. I flipped through the pages.

The United States
Of America
Nonimmigrant Visa
Issued at
Damascus

Below, today's date. In a box titled *Classification of Entry,* the consular officer struck through *Multiple Entry.* Next to it, she wrote and circled "1."

I was thunderstruck. When Sophia would see me at her doorstep, she would scream for joy.

I continued reading. Under *Valid for Entry Until,* the officer wrote January 12, 1985. An orange adhesive label dated November 18, 1984, signified the earliest I could enter America. Only six days from now.

My eyes stung. I had not slept for almost two days and hadn't eaten much. Since Sophia had left, all the hours were odd and days dark. But now energy crept into my muscles, nerves, brain, and heart. I went to the restaurant's glass wall and peered out at the embassy.

The visa extinguished all the despair that I had bottled up and all the anguish that had devoured me from the inside out. No longer limited to those four square miles, my life suddenly had value, and I cried.

CHAPTER 27

TAKE CARE OF THE BUILDING
NOVEMBER – DECEMBER, 1984

Unable to understand the English stamps and because obtaining a visa requires a near miracle, Mama needed a lot of convincing. "Mama, it says it right here." I pressed my index finger on the visa stamp. "One entry. Look." I turned the passport around. She froze for a moment and then released a deafening, high-pitched trill of triumph, her tongue darting from side to side.

I had heard that sound only during wedding celebrations on Egyptian soap operas. Luckily, it was a chilly night, so the windows of the occupied flats were shut, and with the electricity on, radios and TVs were humming. The visa became a new secret that Mama and I shared. Should my father and Nabil find out, they might take the passport and shred it.

I had entered the flat at nine-thirty that night. I was cold, tired, and hungry. Mama said that Baba was upstairs, playing backgammon with Abu Muhamad. Nabil was out, location unknown.

After the celebration, Mama rolled hallum cheese and cucumber slices into a pita and served me hot tea. Suddenly I was too tired to finish my sandwich. I ate half, downed the tea, and then went to my room and collapsed on the bed.

I woke up in my clothes and shoes at ten-thirty the next morning.

I kissed Mama and told her that I would find out about flight schedules.

At eleven, I pushed open the glass door of the travel agency and went straight to the female agent, Samira. Instantly her coworker, the male agent, wore a scowl. She jumped to her feet. "Did you find your fiancée? Did you say goodbye? Say you did."

"I did. May Allah grant you longevity! It was a sad day, but I am ready to follow her."

"No visa, no booking," the male agent told me.

I ignored him and presented Samira with my passport. "How soon can I get to Boston?"

She flipped the pages until she saw the visa. She turned and glared at her coworker as if to say, "I told you so."

"Would you like a cigarette?" the jerk offered.

"No, thank you," I said before thinking. I hadn't smoked since I laid eyes on the visa stamp.

"Samira, Ya'Allah dear! See what you can do for our friend!" He turned to me. "Please sit. Tea, coffee, water? Anything?"

"Nothing," I said, cherishing the shallow transformation.

"You know the airport is closed," Samira said.

"When will it open?" I asked. I had always considered airport closures trivial. That day, I felt the world collapsing.

"Only Allah knows." She leaned forward and whispered, "Since the Shias, Druze, and communists wiped out the Sunnis, we are under their mercy." She pointed at her co-worker with her eyes.

Samira referred to the few days in West Beirut when more than ninety people were killed and more than 350 injured—the clashes that started when I interviewed with Mr. Deeb and during the weeks that followed.

She straightened up and resumed the business talk. "All flights from Damascus are full. You'd need to wait for months. Oman, Jordan, is just a day's trip by car. Your best option is flying out of

Oman."

"How much will it be?" I asked.

"Twelve hundred dollars," Samira said nonchalantly. "Should we book it?"

"I ... um ... I have to think about this. I thought I could just leave from Damascus." I tried to fold skin in my forehead, masking my poverty with pensiveness. I stood up. "When I buy, it will be from you. I promise you that."

She smiled widely.

At noon, the clouds dissipated. It was chilly. I walked in the sun to feel warm. I got home around one in the afternoon. Baba made the usual loud noises behind his bedroom door. Nabil was out. Mama smoked at the kitchen table, facing the sink.

"You should stop smoking," I said.

"What did you find out?" she whispered.

"Flights leave on Wednesdays and Fridays. I want to go next Wednesday."

"That soon? How much?"

I told her.

"Oh Merciful!" Neither Mama nor I had seen that kind of money.

"Husam will lend it to me."

"Say he does. Where will you go?"

"I saw a really nice doghouse in a magazine ... in one of those backyards in America." I leaned and whispered, "I have three months to get the money and go, or I will lose the visa."

"What's all the whispering about?" Baba asked from the kitchen doorway. He had been eavesdropping. He did that often.

"Oh Merciful," Mama snapped. The chair squeaked under her.

He wore a gray dress shirt tucked into his maroon sans belt pants, which were lifted to his belly button.

"I haven't seen you wear these shoes since our wedding," Mama said as she sized him up. I looked down. He had used white shoe polish to paint his black moccasins, as if to make believe he had more than one pair. The shoes glowed. He looked down to admire his new look.

"We are out of pita." Mama flashed me a wink.

I hid my smile. Nice! If Baba went to the pita store, he would stand for over an hour fighting for a turn!

"For you, I will go to the end of the world!" Baba put his hands in his pockets and wiggled the pants up a little more.

Mama gaped in bewilderment. I heard him, but I didn't believe my ears. I wondered, what exactly did Baba do in his room behind the locked door? Each time he came out, he appeared puffed up, self-congratulatory. He looked at me. "Ya'Allah. We will buy cake, too." He inclined his head toward the doorway, motioning me out. He whistled on his way out to the foyer.

"You go with your father. Ya'Allah!" Mama melted with the rare affection and pushed me out of the kitchen.

Baba shouted, "Ya'Allah!" from the stairway.

I moved slowly. "I don't want to," I whined to Mama.

"Allah will open new doors for you."

"If only he'd lower his pants ..."

"Shame on you." Mama grinned.

I chased after Baba. He had just reached the entrance. He was seventy-six years of age, and his pace was now reduced to putting both feet on each step before venturing down to the next. At the ledge into the alleyway, I saw him grip the iron bar at the entrance door to climb down. His head bobbed. In that moment, I felt an enormous flow of sympathy for him. I rushed to his side.

"Take my hand!" I reached for his.

"No!" He recoiled and turned around. "I know what you are doing. I saw you with your mother. 'And know that your possessions and your children are bait.'"

Here we go again. Each time I unearthed a sentiment, he crushed it with the assumption that it was to win him over for an inheritance.

"May Allah grant you longevity!" I wished I could be more sincere.

The pita shop was across from Othman's old stores at the bottom of a midrise building, which were now Jamil's headquarters. Maybe we would see Nabil there. I had avoided that side of the neighborhood since my momentous humiliation, or salvation, more than eight years before. I walked at Baba's pace until we arrived at what had been Othman's grocery.

Baba and I stopped. I stared at two faded posters of Othman, displayed on both sides of the front door. Under the pictures, an inscription designated Othman saintly and granted the company of our master Muhamad. In the meantime, Baba surveyed the pita bakery.

Across the street and past the sniper-ridden intersection, pandemonium had erupted in front of the bakery. Baba and I would have to duck under sand barrels to avoid getting shot—a routine, low-risk maneuver everyone in the combat zone took.

Abu Ali, the pita-store owner, had had a concrete wall erected, running the length and height of the storefront, with a small window elevated four feet above the street. Through that window, Abu Ali handed pita to customers and took their money. I watched the shoppers wave cash and shout for bread. He brought a stack of pitas to the window, and the crowd surged forward, pushing and shoving. The younger adults had no chance to get to the front. Like me, they were taught to respect the elderly, who elbowed them remorselessly.

Abu Ali screamed, "Back up! Shut up! Get in—"

An explosion echoed. Everyone ducked and became silent. I had heard faint explosions that morning—nothing unusual. But this explosion sounded near. The pita customers used the sound to pressure Abu Ali.

"Abu Ali!" they shouted.

"For Allah's sake, hurry!"

"They are getting closer!"

I saw a woman raise her small child high, above the others. He clutched a bill in his little hand as she inched him closer to the window.

"Go get Nabil!" Baba said. "He will get you past the peasants."

"*Me*," I snapped.

"Go on! I will wait."

I needed to dodge the throng of angry, stinking customers. I peered into the lingerie boutique that Othman once looted and turned into his headquarters. Young and elderly men, all armed, congregated or leaned against the walls.

I squinted through the glass to look for my brother. Muhamad and Basel, Abu Muhamad and Kifah's teenage sons, sat across from Jamil, exactly where Nabil and I once sat across from Othman. Jamil projected himself majestically. I shuffled into the store.

Jamil had been ranting. He sat upright, chin held high, and eyebrows raised. Nabil stood behind him, wearing a scowl.

I waved for Nabil. Jamil noticed and paused. His eyes were red. He and Nabil flicked a glance and ignored me. The boys didn't flinch. I waited.

Jamil resumed his talk. "'... whoso does evil and is encompassed by his sins—those are the inmates of the fire; therein shall they abide. ...'" The boys shuddered.

"You don't know Allah's ninety-nine names, do you?" Jamil asked rhetorically. "Do you think Allah, the all-hearing, all-seeing, and all-knowing doesn't know that you skip prayers and that when you pray, you are not absolutely connected to Him? He knows you play soccer and think about girls."

The boys looked frightened.

"And you, Basel. I thought you would be different," Jamil went on. "I thought you would knock on my door every day. I thought you do whatever it takes to uphold Allah's message that nullified all before."

"Takbeerat!" a man shouted.

"Allahu akbar," everyone but me echoed.

"Don't let your brother die in vain." Wearing a look of utter disgust, Jamil threw himself back in his chair.

Basel glanced at Nabil for help. In turn, Nabil put his index finger on his lips for the boys to be quiet.

At that moment I wanted nothing more in the world than to see a bullet strike between Jamil's eyes. I was furious.

"You are alive only because Allah allows you to be," he continued, his voice dark with threat. "Allah, the giver of death, the avenger, and the oppressor, could snuff out your life in an instant. You hear?"

"Yes, Imam," the boys said, subdued.

Jamil had not studied at Azhar, the most celebrated school to educate clerics, nor had he attended an Islamic seminary. It only took a beard, a kippah, and a few memorized verses to impress these young boys. I detested him and pitied the children, who slouched over and looked at the floor.

Jamil would continue to describe the vast opportunities for the boys to save Islam. When they died, Jamil, like Othman, would travel to Saudi Arabia, Kuwait, Iraq, and Libya to solicit funding. The more martyrs, the more funding.

"Allah also said, 'Do not transgress. Surely, Allah loves not the transgressors,'" I said, looking at Jamil.

Nabil darted toward me. "You have no goddamned business coming here." He held me from the armpit and shoved me out.

"Let me go, damn it. Your father—" I turned to look for Baba. He stood at the fringe of the mob circle, and I pointed at him with my thumb. "He wants you to get the pita."

A louder explosion echoed. I flinched.

Nabil snorted. "You are still a scared cat."

"That was incoming," I said defensively.

"I am busy now. I will be there in a few minutes! Now go!" He flicked his wrist in the direction of the pita store.

I walked under the barrels and relayed the message to Baba.

"Then you go in." He gave me enough to pay for one bundle and shoved me into the circle. I snatched the bill and plowed through the weakest, those on the perimeter. The stench of body odor suffocated me. I turned around and darted out, gasping.

"Get back in there!" Baba shouted.

"No! There should be a line."

"You think you are in Amer-rka?" he mocked.

If only you knew, I thought.

"I will go to the pastry shop and get the cake," I said, determined to leave.

"Four pieces only. I want money back."

Tell me something I don't know, Tightwad, I thought.

I left him contemplating his pitch to Abu Ali. I knew his tactic. He would start acting classy, and when that failed, he would erupt. Once Nabil showed up, Baba would get a lot more respect.

Gardenia, the pastry shop, was fifty yards down and across the street. As soon as I reached it, I heard a gunshot. I looked back at the pita store. A man waved a gun. He fired another round over Abu Ali's window into the concrete wall. People screamed, but quickly resumed their calls for bread. Infuriated, Abu Ali stretched from his waist out through the window and waved his arms. I heard him shouting.

"Abu Ali has it coming," said the pastry-shop owner, Abu Maher, now outside. We both watched the confusion.

A whistle came from the sky. A puff of smoke. A deafening explosion. A blast of heat struck my face and sucked the air from my lungs. I ducked as glass shattered. My ears rang. A small car took off out of the thick, swirling cloud of dust.

"Oh, my Allah! Baba!" I cried out.

Abu Maher locked his arms around my chest and dragged me into his shop. My feet didn't touch the ground. "They come in twos! They come in twos!" he shouted in my ear.

We crouched behind the low concrete wall between the kitchen and the serving area. We peeked out as shrapnel rained down. The hot bomb fragments bounced on the asphalt, pierced cars, and smashed windshields. On the street, men, women, and children fled past the store, covered in blood and dust. Women and children cried. Men screamed, "Allahu akbar!"

"Oh Merciful! Oh Merciful!" Abu Maher whispered.

"I have to get Baba! Oh, my Allah! My brother might be there, too!"

"Stay!" He grasped my arm and pulled me down.

A man on the street cried out, "Where is everybody? *Help!*"

Another explosion. My shoes vibrated from the force. More windows imploded from the blast. This time the display windows of the pastry shop shattered. I bolted.

Abu Ali shouted behind me, "The shrapnel! Wait! The shrapnel!"

I turned left and burst into a sprint. Across the street from the pita store, two cars were ablaze. The acrid stench of fuel and smoldering tires was suffocating as I ran through the thick black smoke. A man staggered from the dust. He carried a child over his shoulder and ran in my direction.

"Get back!" someone yelled. I slowed and burrowed my nose in the crook of my elbow. Twenty yards to the store, I felt terror. My throat hardened, and my lungs constricted. My calf muscles trembled, and I struggled not to collapse. I stepped up on the curb toward the store. The smoke from the bombs slowly dissipated, but the billowing black plumes from the smoldering car tires remained thick.

I was horrified, but I couldn't cower. What if a few seconds were all I had to save Baba? What if he had last words, and no one heard them? I summoned every fiber of my being to hold steady.

I reached the pita store. Abu Ali's corpse dangled out of the window from the waist down. A small child covered in blood and dust crawled out from beneath a mound of bodies. "Mama!" he shrieked.

Twisted, contorted bodies lay scattered across the street and sidewalk. Some of the injured thrashed about, moaning and crying for help. I searched the fallen, recognizing no one and then Baba's white shoes appeared. The world went silent. My legs wobbled, but I pressed on. I collapsed to my knees at his side. He lay on his back at the curb, his head hanging over it onto the street. I slid my hand under his neck and gently raised his head.

"Baba! Can you hear me?" I leaned to press my ear to his chest. His heartbeat was faint.

He opened his mouth to breathe.

"Rami!" Nabil shouted. "Are you OK?"

I looked around. Nabil was crawling all the way from Othman's store.

"*Baba!*" Nabil slid his arm under Baba's back and tried to help him to sit, but Baba could not. A pool of blood had formed beneath him.

"Oh, my Allah!" He embraced Baba, and his tears gushed. "Baba," he wept. "Answer me!"

Baba's cheeks twitched. He opened his eyes and squinted into the sun.

"I got you, Baba. I got you," Nabil wept. Then he turned and screamed over his shoulder, "Someone get a car!"

"Z-Rami ..." Baba's voice was weak and scratchy.

Nabil and I leaned forward. "I am here! What, Baba, what?" I asked.

"T-take c-care of ..."

"Yes, Baba?"

"... the b-building."

He drew a breath, exhaled, and was gone.

I froze. Grief and rage tore at me. I glanced at Nabil. He gawked at Baba. We were both stunned and, for once, for the same reason. The constant guilt for my inadequacies and knots in my stomach over my failures vanished.

Nabil slowly laid Baba down. His features hardened. I knew that look—he was furious. He stood up and walked away.

"Nabil!" I shouted.

He stopped, and I ran to him and hugged him. "We have each other!"

He sobbed. His body shook as he clung to me. Then he took a step back. His eyes were dark with pain. "Did he just say to take care of goddamned building?"

I nodded.

Nabil wiped his tears and shook his head sadly.

I looked at him, then back at our father. Everything was different now. Everything.

Emergency workers were descending on the scene, and sirens wailed in the distance. Two Red Cross vans converged in front of the bakery. Eight workers jumped out of the vans. Mona commanded the crew. She, Jerjes, and I had buried Palestinians after the massacres two years before.

"Mona!" I shouted.

"Oh, my Allah!" she screamed. "Are you OK?" She sprinted toward me.

"Please! Help." I pointed at Baba. "My father. Please see what you can do. Hurry."

In a few seconds, Mona, two others, and Nabil put Baba on a stretcher and loaded him into the van. Nabil jumped on the rear bumper and held on to the roof as the van sped off.

Five minutes later, I broke the news to Mama. While she crashed on the sofa and bawled without constraint, I was struck by my luck at surviving another close call. Hajjeh and Um Muhamad, hearing Mama keen, rushed into the flat and held her hands. They talked Islam and Qur'an from then on.

For me, it was business as usual. My lack of emotional response terrified me. I wondered if shock had numbed me. I feared I lacked compassion. The only sympathy I had was for Mama suffering the loss of someone who cared only about the building.

Husam joined us later that evening. Having heard about Baba from Nabil, he had composed the obituary and scheduled the funeral service and burial. He requested my approval. I granted it blindly.

Aunt Najat arrived after dark. She knew what to do but had nothing to say. She pulled out her Qur'an cassettes, inserted one in our tape player, and so began the marathon of Qur'an recitals.

"Thank you for coming," I leaned in close and whispered in Aunt Najat's ear.

She took a deep breath. "He is my brother. Your uncles will not be here or at the graveyard."

"Makes no difference," I said.

"*Helfo*, they swore, you know!" she said, ruling out a change of heart.

"It doesn't matter." I loathed them for lumping Nabil and me with Baba in their vindictiveness.

Mama and I stayed up all night. She cried whether sitting up or lying down. I took a bath and changed clothes. As soon as I got out of my room, Mama demanded I flip the cassette on the player. "I don't want a second to go by without the Qur'an. Do you understand?" she shouted at me.

"Yes, Mama."

Nabil returned around seven the next morning, looking pale,

dirty, and tired. Deep circles had formed under his eyes. He was still covered with blood. He hugged Mama and wept. She went off again as if hearing the news for the first time.

Nabil took a shower and went straight to bed. I woke him up three hours later.

"It is time," I said.

Only Nabil, Husam, and I attended the funeral prayers. Jamil was a no-show. He must have concluded that Baba didn't draw a crowd. There were no speeches or eulogies. There was no fanfare. We left the mosque and rode in Husam's car behind the hearse. The driver parked at the cemetery and said, "I will help."

He and Husam pulled the coffin out. Nabil and I ducked under it from the back, and we raised it to our shoulders. Husam and I ended up on the same side.

Atop the Bachoura Graveyard steps, the two guards first looked on and then approached to help. The older guard looked familiar. He got between Husam and me, on the right side of the coffin. "May Allah have mercy on your dead!" Then, as we climbed the steps, he respectfully asked, "Who is the deceased?"

"May Allah grant you longevity! He was Sami Hadhari," Husam said solemnly.

The guard looked perplexed. In the middle of the climb and while the pallbearers on the other side were oblivious to the whispered exchange, the guard strained his neck as far as he could and asked me, "Are you his elder son?"

"Yes. Watch your step," I warned him.

"The very Sami Hadhari!" The guard left the coffin. The weight almost crushed my collarbone in the short climb up the steps. He faced the coffin and said, "Glory to Allah! We are going to bury the Hadhari behind the 'Graveyard Hadharis.'" He formed two-finger quotes on both hands and looked bedazzled.

The entire left side of the coffin rose above Nabil's head. Baba's body shifted and slammed into the panel on my side. We stopped. "Shut the hell up or get the hell out of here," Nabil demanded, supporting almost the entire weight of the coffin.

"Pray for the prophet, everyone!" Husam blurted, to ground everyone in the moment. He climbed up, forcing us to follow.

"May Allah pray for our master Muhamad," we said, and moved to the gravesite.

Nabil requested that we wait a little while before burying Baba. We stood side by side and waited for mourners.

They trickled in—Abu Muhamad and his son Muhamad, Kifah and his son Basel, Zaki, and Jamil and his clan. Then I saw Tufik and Hasan from the American University cafeteria, Elias, Jerjes's father, Simone, and three other volunteers from the Red Cross. Nabil had spent the entire night searching for and notifying all those whom I had befriended over the years. That made my eyes teary.

The notary from Husam's neighborhood attended. Fuad, his pochette tucked under his arm, fetched eye contact with me. When our eyes met, he raised his eyebrows, asking what had happened at the embassy. I looked away, denying him the answer, thinking of all the money I had paid him to advise me to lie.

I turned to Nabil. Our eyes met. The unspoken words united in the space between his eyes and mine. "Thank you." I wrapped my arm around his shoulder.

Nabil slowly put his arm around my shoulders. In the meantime, the grave diggers lowered Baba's shrouded body. I saw a small object bulged through the cloth over the chest area. I whispered into Nabil's ear, "Do you see that? What is it?"

"His transistor radio. I put in new batteries," Nabil said nonchalantly.

I took a step back and stared at him to gauge his sincerity. In response he closed his eyes, smiled as wide as he could, comically taking pride in his gesture.

"Oh, my Allah," I said under my breath, and snickered involuntarily. I put my hand back across his shoulders.

Nabil turned to me and chuckled.

"*Shh* ..." Husam leaned forward and shot both of us a look of reproach then shook his head in disbelief at our levity.

Nabil and I shared a laugh, untimely, inappropriate, but one that laid a new bridge across a gulf that we instantly crossed.

CHAPTER 28

TWO JUDGMENT DAYS
DECEMBER, 1984 – JANUARY, 1985

Grief paralyzed Mama. She sat in Baba's spot on the sofa, wept, and chain-smoked. After a week, she looked haggard and spent. Nabil and I rarely spoke, but we had agreed to spare Mama Baba's last words. As for me, I refrained from talk of inheritance or immigration. I knew it would be heartrending for Mama to lose me to America on the footsteps of Baba's terrible death.

On Tuesday morning, a week after Baba's burial, Husam visited with us at the flat. The sharia dictated that Mama shouldn't be around men for 130 days unless she was pregnant. I overruled it, and Nabil acquiesced.

When Husam came into the family room, Mama did not stand to welcome him. It was a sunny warm day in December, and I opened the doors to the balcony, wishing to clear the stale air of grief.

Husam broached the topic of inheritance. "We need to certify the inheritance with the Islamic Courts." He was experienced with the legalities of death. "It is seven-sixteenths for each of you." He glanced at Nabil and me and then turned to Mama. "And one-eighth to you."

Mama took a drag from her cigarette. She was indifferent.

"What exactly did we inherit to divide?" I asked Mama and Nabil. They looked as if a layer of fog formed between us. They glanced at each other and then squinted at me. "Forgive me, Mama, but we all know Baba didn't do things exactly by the book. And he had a slimy lawyer. Remember him? The will guy? You remember-when Grandmother died?"

I shifted my gaze to Nabil. "I think we need to check with him before we make a move. We don't know what Baba owned or owed."

I prayed that Baba had rewarded Nabil for his years of loyalty and obedience.

Husam conceded the point. We decided to go, and I found the attorney's address in Tarik El-Jadidah, a Sunni enclave.

Nabil and I kissed Mama's hand and followed Husam out. We rode in his car to the attorney's home, and around noon I rang the doorbell. Nabil, the tallest of us, stood next to Husam and faced the door.

The attorney answered, wearing oversized boxer shorts and a dress shirt. His thin, hairy legs were grotesque, and his bulging belly hung over his crotch. A cigarette dangled from his mouth.

Nabil blurted, "You didn't attend Baba's funeral. He paid your fees, didn't he?"

The attorney froze.

"May peace be upon you," Husam said, and quickly turned to Nabil. "Say Allah."

"Allah," we all said.

Husam continued, "They are Sami Hadhari's sons."

"Oh Merciful! What happened?" The attorney instantly transitioned to condolences and unrelenting hospitality. "Honor me in. I insist. In Allah's name." He flung the door open and introduced himself as "Professor Jalal."

Nabil snorted. "'Professor!'" he said under his breath.

Jalal showed us in. The furniture in the living room was gaudy. Nabil shoved past Jalal and sat on a wingback chair before anyone else took a seat. I admired Nabil's boldness for bypassing the formality of waiting for Jalal to tell us where and when to sit. The attorney hadn't earned my respect, either. Jalal showed Husam and me to an ugly red-velvet sofa. We maneuvered around a marble-topped coffee table.

"I am their mother's cousin." Husam shook Jalal's hand before taking a seat. Like Nabil, I dropped onto the sofa and skipped the formalities. Husam sat at my right side, closer to Jalal.

"Please have a smoke." Jalal offered an assortment of cigarette packs in a bowl on the coffee table.

"Let's get to it," Nabil said firmly.

At the conclusion of hasty prayers for Baba's soul, the attorney said to Nabil, "Your father wrote a will. I'll get it." He got up. "You know, he always sang to his own tune."

Nabil, asserting himself as the fierce son, got Jalal's attention. "Just get the will!" he said through clenched teeth.

"Of course!" Jalal said, looking intimidated. "At your command. Ya'Allah! I will be right back." He turned and shouted into the flat, "Ya'Allah, woman! Cover up! Tea for four."

Nabil helped himself to a cigarette and puffed away. Five minutes later, Jalal returned, wearing pants and carrying a tray of hot tea. I saw a thin folder tucked under his arm.

He groaned as he laid the tray on the coffee table. "I assume you are the firstborn." Jalal tried to hand the folder to Nabil. Nabil didn't move.

"I am. Rami." I reached for it.

Jalal shifted his gaze to me. "Oh! Glory to Allah! I thought—"

"Get on with it." Nabil was now on the edge of his seat.

"Love, Rami, I have done great work for your father. Anything you need from me—"

"In Allah's name!" Nabil squeezed his fist and groaned as if making an effort to control his rage. "Spit it out!"

Husam quoted the Qur'an. "'Allah loves those of you who are patient.'"

Nabil took a deep breath and then expelled it.

"Here." The attorney straightened and handed me a document. I glanced over it. It was littered with stamps and signatures.

"It is all *yours*," Jalal said. "He left everything to you."

Nabil and I quickly exchanged a look of shock. I turned to the attorney. His face glowed with anticipation—I might be a new client. He waited for me to respond with happiness.

I looked at Husam. His face was ashen.

For a split second I wanted to celebrate the way Baba had valued me, but my resentment for excluding Mama and Nabil grounded me. Nabil averted his eyes when I turned to him. His heart was most certainly torn to shreds.

He fell back in his chair and smiled wickedly. "It is all coming together now."

"What do you mean?" Jalal asked.

I knew what he meant. In Nabil's world, it came down to that moment of truth between Baba and him. Our father had called him a zero on the left side of the numeral, right before I became worthless. I opened my mouth to say something, but I didn't know what to say, so I held my peace. I would deal with our father's blow later, when my brother and I were alone.

Husam cut the silence with a protest. "Unbelievable!"

"May Allah have mercy on his soul!" Jalal said, contriving a smile. "He was different." Then his eyes shone. "As of last year, he had almost four-hundred-thousand dollars in the bank. I suspect it is more now. You know how he is—forgive me, *was* ..." He made a fist. "Stingy."

400,000 dollars! My heart raced.

"You are being kind," Nabil said sarcastically. I was sure he could think of many harsher things to say.

My mind raced. We lived in terror and encountered death almost daily. We could have lived somewhere safer.

Jalal continued, "Love, Rami."

"Who? What?" I snapped from my daze.

"That is the only document I have. Bank statements and such should be at your home somewhere."

Husam dropped Nabil and me off at the alleyway entrance. No one had said a word in the car. Anything Husam might have said would have been an intrusion into areas that were solely between Nabil and me. I admired Mama's cousin for understanding that. I put the key in the lock of the entrance door but couldn't turn it. How was I going to face Mama? What would I tell her?

I removed the key and turned to Nabil. "Let's go."

"What now?"

"Let's perform the noon prayers at the mosque before the muezzin calls for the afternoon prayer."

"Are you joking?" Nabil looked perplexed. I had turned down his requests to accompany him to prayers countless times over recent years.

We walked in silence to the mosque. We performed ablutions side by side and prayed shoulder to shoulder. Right before saluting the angels to conclude the prayers, my mind traveled to the future. In an instant I knew what I needed to do. Nabil and I retreated to a column, where I leaned toward him and looked into his face.

"May Allah accept your prayers!" I said.

"And yours."

I got straight to it. "I won a visa to America!"

Nabil's eyes almost popped out of their sockets. "What? How? When?"

"Before Baba was killed. I have to leave before January 12, or I will lose it."

"Are you going to leave me and Mama?"

Me? I melted.

"I am going to give everything to you."

"What are you talking about?"

"The entire inheritance."

"You are?" Nabil's eyes became moist. He stood taller, as if hope stiffened his spine.

"Everything," I confirmed. "You don't want it?" I asked playfully.

Nabil evolved into a no-nonsense man. "Since you lost your scholarship, I thought our family had no chance at anything. I accepted that you had become ... you know, a dependent. I'm sorry," he said with subdued dignity.

I put my hand on his shoulder. "It is OK."

"And I am just a combat-zone fixture. Inside the city and everywhere else, I am worthless—"

"That is not true!"

"So now you want me to be like him." Nabil pointed in the direction of the graveyard. "A landlord." He wrinkled his face in disgust. "If the war ever stops, I will become a policeman and use the money to bribe my way to a post guarding our neighborhood. Then if I see a politician, I will kill him with my bare hands."

"Pray for the prophet," I uttered to appeal to his sensibilities.

"I am a degenerate."

"Stop, Nabil!"

"Baba cared only about the goddamned building and his money."

"And I almost got kidnapped and killed defending it from the militiamen. Remember that day Mama saved me?"

Nabil nodded. "You just made me realize something." He closed his eyes, and his features twisted in pain. I feared that when he opened his eyes, he would explode. "Baba saw me as nothing but a goddamned live-in guard for his building. What the hell have I done? I've thrown away my life for his approval."

Nabil's insight shone more light on what Baba had done to our family. I was speechless.

Tears filled Nabil's eyes. "I thought his last words would be, 'Rami, take care of your mother and Nabil' or ... or ...'Nabil, you honored me.' Damn the building! Damn the money! Damn this entire country!"

I clamped his arms and shook him. "Stop torturing yourself."

"I am enraged, but you, you sit there composed. You had him figured out."

"I have grieved his loss many times over. That day I cleared the Barbara checkpoint was the end of Baba and me. Right then I understood that he placed all else above his own family. He hemmed in our world and made us believe it was whole. When I met Sophia, my world expanded. I felt hopeful. She is the best thing for me. One day you will fall in love and understand."

Nabil's face opened, and he cracked a wry smile.

I continued, "You don't have to live like this anymore. I want you to take some money and buy a flat deeper in West Beirut. Go to the Rawsheh area. Face the Mediterranean. Will you do that for me?"

"Of course." Then he dropped his head and looked conflicted. "You are going to America. It is the land of sin. Sophia is a Christian. Don't you want to be saved?"

"From whom?"

"To enter His kingdom."

"The only saving I need is from people who are trying too hard to be saved."

"But when we die, we have to answer for our deeds and sins."

"Do you think I am a bad Muslim?"

Nabil's lips were a thin white line. He stared at the altar for a moment, glanced at the pulpit, then looked up at the dome. He turned to me. "Do you remember what we learned in Islamic studies about judgment day?" His tone was solemn.

"Which part?"

"Allah is first. Our parents are second. Do you remember why that is the case?"

"They will be horrified. They will be herded into long lines where people are weeping and sinners are shaking. Everyone will be on his own."

"Right! Mama and Baba will forget we ever existed. It will be all about their salvation. In the eleventh hour, parents will stomp on their children. ..." Nabil continued, describing the horror of the Day of Reckoning. Never before had he talked with me so passionately to make a point. I was eager to hear what he had to say, to understand him better.

"You see how I am looking at it? Are you with me?"

"Yes. I am. More than you think," I said with a smile.

"You had two judgment days, and you shone. You got your visa, but you stayed to make sure Baba received a proper burial. And today, in the bleakest time, our family's day of reckoning, you awarded me and Mama everything. Allah and our master Muhamad—Allah prayed for and saluted him—didn't ask this of you. Not in the Qur'an, nor in the narratives, is there any obligation for you to forgo your wealth for a brother. *You* grace Islam."

Nabil's words broke down every wall I had erected to defend myself from him. He had my soul in his hand.

"You know my decision violates the sharia." I grinned.

"How does it feel?" he asked jokingly. Then he said, "We have to tell Mama his last words. Anger will dry her tears."

"Joy will have a longer lasting effect. A new home will make her happy. A new way of life will erase bad memories." I reached and hugged him. We got up. Nabil's ankles popped. I never knew that about him. We had lived under the same roof, but worlds apart.

After Nabil and I explained to Mama the inheritance and my

decision to overrule the will, she planted kisses all over my face and Nabil's, then began a frenzied search to find Baba's documents.

Nabil and I spent the next two days analyzing papers and calculating expenses and our income. When Nabil detected an error I made, I complimented him. During our due diligence, we found out that Baba was taking payments from Tony for the flat that we occupied. Nabil notified Tony to stop sending money. I admired him for that. Gone were the days when Christians' money and property were spoils of war.

We also figured we spent around $400 and took in over $2,460 a month. When we finished sizing up all the assets, we found more than $410,000 in the bank. Nabil, Mama, and I were excited and disgusted at the same time.

"How could he have had so much and let us live like this?" Nabil frowned. "Mark my words, Mama, we are leaving this shit hole."

That's my brother, I thought.

Mama lit another cigarette. She smoked and stared into space.

The atmosphere in the apartment became peaceful. Our morning rituals changed. Mama, Nabil, and I woke up around the same time. Gone were those days when we tiptoed around while Baba slept in or napped. We greeted each other in the mornings and evenings. Each time Nabil left the flat, he kissed Mama's hand. We had breakfast together at the kitchen table. We actually talked—no more fighting. Nabil gossiped about girls in the neighborhood. I concealed my amusement when he asked about Mona at the Red Cross. Mama reminisced about Audette and her husband, Tony, a subject that would have triggered Baba's insults.

Like they always did around Christmas time, Muslim merchants copied their Christian counterparts in East Beirut and slashed prices. Nabil and I took Mama shopping. She had been wearing the same black dress and a white hijab for over a month. Nabil drove. Mama sat in the front, and I took in the view of my family in harmony. I insisted that Mama wear home what she had bought at the store and leave her other clothes in the store's trash can. Nabil agreed.

Mama emerged from the fitting room looking more glamorous than I had ever seen her. On the way home, Nabil played a tape of the Qur'an, and Mama switched the station. She tuned to foreign music and then turned and grinned at me. Nabil shrugged. Another spell was broken.

While the Christian militias fought each other for dominance in East Beirut, I scheduled the transfer of assets to take place in our flat. Within two days, Husam, who by then knew I had received a visa, the notary, his son Fuad, and another witness paid us a visit to execute the documents. Before each time I signed my name, the notary asked me, "Are you sure you want to do this?" In turn, I looked up at Mama and Nabil and smiled.

Mama looked radiant. Nabil held her hand. Husam was proud. Fuad looked antsy. He must have agonized over suppressing his urge to call me a dummy. The notary closed with: "May Allah populate this world with the likes of you." Husam shot me the unmistakable Middle Eastern look of respect, a squint, a head tilt, and a smile, with an open palm.

The business completed, I asked Husam to stay while the others left. I turned to him. "Thank Allah for you in our lives, Ammo Husam." I called him "uncle" affectionately. We retreated to the kitchen to have dinner.

"I think it is time for me to book a flight," I said, looking at Mama.

She knew it was coming, but the declaration still unnerved her.

"Nabil and I will take good care of your mother," Husam said.

"I am surprised you didn't say 'the building,'" I said before thinking.

Nabil laughed. "That was a good one!" he said.

"What was that about?" Mama and Husam asked simultaneously.

"An inside joke," I said, finding joy in the secret Nabil and I shared.

The ride to Oman, Jordan, would consume a day. I decided to pack on Wednesday night, ride in a car all of Thursday, and be in Oman first thing in the morning on Friday, January 4.

Nabil helped me pack the one suitcase. Mama walked in and out. She brought me packages of needless trinkets, which Baba hoarded and never opened. Suddenly we heard Mama scream from her bedroom. "Rami! Nabil! Oh, my Allah! Come here! Now!"

Nabil and I darted from my room. Our shoulders collided in the doorway. Mama sat at the edge of Baba's bed, holding a wad of cash.

"Where did you get it?" I asked.

Nabil reached and snatched the money. He counted frantically. "Two thousand dollars!" he shouted.

"*Shh!*" Mama said. "The neighbors will hear you. I found it under the headboard. Let us flip the damned mattress."

Mama stepped aside.

"This way." Nabil's eyes glittered. He gripped the corner, stood the mattress on its side, and then threw it at me. I dropped it, and a stash of bills fell off the foot of the bed. Mama yanked the pad off. Nabil pointed at a slit in the lining in the middle. He ripped it apart with vengeance. A thick layer of cash covered the wool under the head and foot of the bed.

Mama and Nabil picked out the bundles of bills and tossed them to me. "Count, for crying out loud! Count!"

"There is more!" Nabil said. "I see more in the padded wool!" He stuck his arm inside and strained.

"Go to the kitchen. Get me the longest shish kebab skewer," Mama ordered him. He ran out of the room and returned in a flash.

Mama sat on top of her bed. She said, "Pull out the wool and pile it here." Nabil scooped wool with both hands. Mama fluffed it with the skewer. White particles floated. Stacks of cash emerged. I counted. Our hearts fluttered. By the time we were done, we counted $52,200.

"All that scratching behind the closed door," I said, resentfully. "He was stuffing the mattress with cash."

"Instead of cotton up his you know *where*, we should have stuffed this." Nabil rolled a hundred-dollar bill between his thumb and forefinger.

I cringed.

Mama pointed the skewer up and humorously wrinkled her face while spinning it around. We broke into hysterical laughter until she suddenly stopped. "May Allah have mercy on his soul!" she said.

"Amen!" we said solemnly.

What we lacked during Baba's lifetime, we found in his death, joy.

At nine the next morning, Mama, Nabil, and I sat in the family room and sipped coffee. My brother put my suitcase and backpack in the foyer. We waited for Husam and the taxi. Horns blared downstairs. It was time to leave Mama, Nabil, and an entire way of life. They stood up.

Suddenly it all felt real. It was no longer an aspiration or a dream. My stomach knotted. Was I doing the right thing? Guilt and an uncertain future gripped me. Nabil and Mama stood motionless.

I scanned the flat for a last look. I stared at my family. They managed to smile. A wordless outpouring of emotions flooded my eyes, smothered my heart, dampened my ambitions, and intensified the agony of separation. My tears gushed.

Nabil walked over and extended his hand. He pulled me up. We heard a knock on the door. Husam had arrived. Mama let him inside and whispered greetings as if to protect the sanctity of the moment.

Husam hugged me tight. "You are doing the right thing. Everything will be just fine!"

I nodded. I took a deep breath and walked to the foyer. Nabil picked up my suitcase, Husam the backpack. They waited outside. Mama and I followed.

Um Muhamad, Abu Muhamad and their children, and Hajjeh, Zaki, and Muhamad stood on the landing between the third and fourth floors.

"May Allah shield you and award you success," Abu Muhamad said, followed by Zaki.

I waved and then turned to Mama. I whispered, "I am not going to America only for me. I will send for you and Nabil."

Mama sobbed and embraced me. "I don't want anything from you. I ask Allah for you to find what you are looking for."

The heat of her teardrops on my shoulder weighed heavier than my guilt at leaving. She breached my wall of detachment, the one I had strengthened over the years. I stayed in her arms for as long as I thought she needed. My enthusiasm for leaving waned. The more she cried, the more I realized that my departure was everlasting. I stroked her back.

"You deserve a better life," she said. "May Allah shield you!"

Mama and I slowly let each other go. I held her elbows; she held mine. She scanned my face, committing me to memory.

Footsteps pounded up the stairs. The taxi driver picked up my suitcase and mumbled apologies. "Forgive me. I need to get out of here. Don't mind me. Only lunatics live in Ras El-Nabeh. I am sorry."

Nabil hefted my backpack.

"Let us go, love." Husam nudged me gently.

"Drive safely!" Mama told the driver. "You pull over when you hear explosions or shots fired. You understand?"

The driver stopped at the landing. "He is not the first and won't be the last one out of this hell-hole! Fifteen million Lebanese are abroad and only two million here!"

Some comforting words. I thought about Sophia.

I kissed Mama on her cheeks one more time and hurried down before I changed my mind. Husam followed.

The taxi was a yellow 1980 Chrysler Regal. A bumper sticker read MY OTHER CAR IS A CAMEL!

I rolled my eyes. Nabil grinned. The driver opened the trunk and tossed my suitcase in. "Easy, damn it," Nabil shouted.

"Sorry! Sorry!" The driver went to his door and waited.

Nabil swung the backpack into the trunk and then turned to me. He looked grief stricken. "Be careful. It's a crazy world out there."

"I will be fine." I embraced him. "I have one last favor to ask."

"Just ask."

"Rami!" Mama yelled from the kitchen window. "Put your money, passport, and airline ticket in your front pocket." I looked up. Above Mama, the rest of the neighbors stuffed their heads through their windows and waved. I unzipped the backpack and obliged Mama one last time.

Nabil handed me an envelope stuffed with cash. "This should give you a good start!" His eyes were moist. "I wish you were not leaving. I wish we could start over, so that we never would have lived in this hell. I wish we had never met Othman—"

"Enough, love." I reached to hug him.

"I think about the two boys every night. You need to know that I have not killed anyone since. What was I thinking! I was dumb ..." Nabil cried on my shoulder. He collected himself and pushed me back. "What's the favor?"

"Please save Basel and Muhamad from Jamil."

Nabil paused. "I will. And I will write to you about my plans. Things will change around here."

"They already have."

The driver walked back and slammed the trunk.

Nabil dropped his hand on the driver's chest. "Get in the car. *Now*," he ordered.

The driver retreated to his door, all the while glancing warily at Nabil. I looked up. Mama smiled and sprinkled rice from the window.

Nabil walked me to the front passenger seat. I climbed in. He laid his hand on my forearm and said, "I love you, Brother!"

THE END

A Personal Request

You traveled to a whole new world and returned safely. You are not experiencing jetlag, but surely, you are now in a higher plain of awareness. *I need your help.*

If you found my novel worthy of your time, intellectual, and emotional investments, please take a few moments to write a review either on Amazon, Barnes & Noble, or Good Reads. Your opinion carries the potential to inspire others to seek more knowledge.

I look forward to reading your feedback.

Sincerely,

Sam Wazan

Authors' Note

My father, Wafik, did the best that he could with what he knew. Like most fathers and his cousin, the former prime minister of Lebanon Shafic Elwazan, Baba believed that the dove of peace in Lebanon needed both wings to soar: The Christians' and Muslims'.

There were countless times that I wished Father resolved to provide a secure home for my brother, four sisters, mother, and I. In retrospect, fighters shifted their loyalties unpredictably; therefore, security was elusive. May Allah have mercy on his soul!

My deepest love and respect go to my mother, Samira. In spite of her ranking in family and society, she remained true to thoughtfulness and kindness. Now that I am through writing the novel, I will make up for my short-changing her with affection. Quit smoking, Mama!

My heartfelt regrets go to my brother Walid, who is *nothing* like Nabil. I overlooked his struggles being the second son. He and I had ambitions in a dysfunctional world, which we thought was whole. His kindness and fragility forced his departure from our flat for two consecutive years. He had resolved to pursue safety and a social standing on his own terms. We lost touch then, but here in the US we rebuilt our bond on a more solid ground. Onward, love!

To those of you who believe that I have exaggerated my portrayal of some Middle Eastern Muslims, Christians, or Jews: I pray that you will never experience wars to be compassionate. Yes! Many of the faithful prayed viciously and acted barbarically. Let us stop the cycle!

I made changes in dates and events and left out countless tragedies. Where I needed to add a checkpoint, I set one up. When I needed to start a battle, I scheduled one.

Finally, any resemblance to persons and events, that are real or imagined, are provisionally coincidental.

I hope you enjoyed the journey.

ACKNOWLEDGEMENTS

I am forever indebted to my wife, Megan Coffey, for her bottomless support and priceless friendship. She is able to deal with the Lebanese gene of risk taking. She is the rock that stabilizes the household and keeps the family on course. She took a chance and married me almost twenty-one years ago, when my accent was much stronger and potential highly questionable.

In the quest for the perfect word or a way to put my thoughts into text, I frequently shunned my sons, Beck and Zane. I am sorry for closing the home-office door and hanging a virtual but forceful "Do Not Disturb sign."

My special thanks and heartfelt joy to Laurie Rosin, the best editor a new writer can ever hope for. I needed her guidance in the magical world of fiction. She honored me with her help and graced me with her delivery. I cherish her generosity with time and care in her responses. When I experienced despair, she resolved to make me proud of my work and encouraged me to stay the course.

Many thanks to my family; Husam, my brother in-law and sister Mona, who for decades dedicated themselves to the affairs of the family in Lebanon; their beautiful and brilliant children, Lama, Lina, Layal, Zeina, and Muhamad. Thank you, Lama and Lina, for refreshing my memory with jokes and play on words.

I am thankful to my eldest sister Maha for her affection and support, my sisters Manal and Diana for their continued timely and efficient attention to my personal business in Lebanon, and for just being delightful sisters. I am thankful to my sister in-law, Liliana Jimenez, for believing in my abilities to produce this novel.

Most notably thanks to Ralph Voltz, the efficient and talented graphics designer and illustrator. He came in at the last minute and responded to emails and phone calls in a timely fashion. Ralph: you are in a league of your own.

Thanks to Malcolm Lowe and Day Hixson for reading the proof copies and providing me with valuable feedback.

My utmost respect, admiration, and gratitude go to Terry K. Gilliam. I am very lucky to have met him—a brilliant man, who enriched my life on multiple levels. TK was a heavenly intervention in my journey in the USA. His emotional intelligence and intellect in the world of creativity and problem solving equipped me to see conflict resolution from an entirely new and functional perspective.

I want to thank Carlos Salum, who gave me the opportunity to take my thoughts public during one of his events. His diverse audience rewarded me with encouragement to stay the course with my message.

It has been my honor to meet peace-driven individuals in various places of worship and nonprofit organizations. I met them in mosques, churches, temples, and various centers such as Covenant Presbyterian Church, Providence Baptist Church, Temple Israel, Temple Beth El, Mecklenburg Ministries, and last but not least United Religions Initiative. I am grateful to the founders of the Charlotte Cooperation Circle, namely Pat and John Moore, for nominating me to be on the Global Council.

Finally, I want to give my cousin, Ziad, a *big* thank you. I arrived to Chicago unannounced and helpless, but hopeful. He picked me up from a motel and hosted me in his home until I found my way.

GLOSSARY OF TERMS

Abu: Father of.

Allahu Akbar: God is greatest.

Baba: Father. Daddy.

Fatwa: Decision. A legal ruling in Islam.

Halal: Permissible in Islam. Halal is most frequently used for food, but it also applies to a range of rulings in Islam such as a physical relation. What could be halal between a husband and wife is haram between unwed couples.

Haram: Unlawful in Islam. It is used to give a religious undertone to a forbidden act. Alcohol is haram in Islam.

Hijab: (1) Booklet of inscriptions from the Qur'an. (2) A scarf women wear to cover their hair.

In sha'Allah: God Willing. The most loosely used term in the Islamic culture. It could mean many things such as: Yes, no, maybe, whatever, I don't agree, I agree, a polite ending of the conversation, or agree to meet another time without a time and date commitment.

Jihadist: One in pursuit of proselytizing Islam. The term is misunderstood by some westerns and Muslim militants.

Jinn: Holy ghosts. They can be good, evil, or benevolent.

Ka'aba: The black cube in Mecca, which pilgrims circumnavigate during pilgrimage.

Kufa: A patterned scarf, that some Palestinians wear. Arafat, the chairman of the Palestinian Liberation organization, often wore it.

Mama: Mother. Mommy.

Narrative: After the Qur'an, Muhamad's narratives are the second source of rulings in Islam. They address matters of jurisprudence. Some narratives serve to explain Quranic rulings. Committed narrative followers are primarily of the Sunni denomination.

Phalange: Al-Kata'eb . A predominantly Maronite Christian militia.

Phalangist: Al-Kata'eb member. A member of the Phalange militia.

Ras El-Nabeh: The combat-zone where the Hadhari tower is located.

Service car: A shared taxi. (*sur-vee-s*). An inclusive means of public transportation allowing drivers to accept passengers along a route.

Shahadatayn: Declaration of faith. It is the first pillar of Islam and a requirement of non-Muslims to enter Islam. "There is no god but Allah, and Muhamad is the messenger of Allah."

Sharia: Islamic law. It is derived from the Qur'an and narratives. In some situations, the scholars issue a fatwa for a ruling.

Shias: Muslim sect followers. They are aligned with Ali, prophet Muhamad's cousin and son in-law.

Sunnis: Followers of the Sunnah of the prophet Muhamad.

Takbir: The call to chant Allahu Akbar, God is greatest, once.

Takbeerat: The call to chant Allahu Akbar, repeatedly.

Um: Mother of.

Ya Allah: You Allah. Pronounced Ya then Allah. It is used to whine about something. It is used like "why me?" in the USA.

Ya'Allah: It is a culturally overused expression used by Muslims, Christians, Jews and other religions. It means; OK, Let us go, come on, coming, move, hurry, go, get out of my way; it proceeds a command like sit, stand, eat, drink, etc. The enunciation, hand, and head gestures signify its meaning.

An audio version will be available in April, 2014

www.samwazan.com

LIST OF CHARACTERS

Abu Ali: Bakery owner.

Abu Maher: Pastry owner.

Abu Muhamad: A Muslim Syrian and a neighbor in the building.

Abu Sharif: Sharif's father.

Ahmad: The boy who died on Black Saturday.

Audette: Tony's wife, a Christian neighbor in the building.

Ayda: Rami's mother.

Amin Gemayel: Bashir's brother in the Phalange party.

Basel: Kifah's younger son.

Bashir Gemayel: The chairman of the Phalange Party.

Caeser: Rescued boy at the American University beach.

Dana: Mr. Deeb's receptionist.

Elias: Jerjes's father.

Farook: Othman's brother.

Fuad: The visa trainer.

Ghazi: A Shia villager outside the American University beach.

Hajjeh: A female neighbor, who performed pilgrimage.

Hasan: A cashier at the beach-cafeteria at the American University.

Husam: Mama's cousin.

Jalal: Baba's attorney.

Jamil: Rami's cousin and Najat's son.

Jamila: The employee at the registration office.

Jerjes: Rami's Christian friend at the Red Cross.

Kifah: A Palestinian refugee and a neighbor in the building.

Maha: Sophia's sister.

Mahdi: One of the sharia enforcers.

Manal: Kifah's wife.

Murad: Mr. Deeb's sales manager.

Nabil: Rami's brother.

Najat: Rami's aunt and Jamil's mother.

Othman: The neighborhood grocer.

Pierre Gemayel: The founder of the Phalange party.

Rami: The protagonist.

Ramzi: Rami's eldest uncle.

Riyad: Kifah's son.

Robert Deeb: Caeser's father.

Saba: The doctor who treated Rami.

Sami: Rami's father.

Samir Geagea: A leader in the Phalange Party.

Samira: Travel agent.

Shaheen: One of the sharia enforcers.

Sharif: Rami's friend in middle school.

Sophia: Rami's girlfriend.

Tufik: Cafeteria manager at the American University.

Tony: Audette's husband, a Christian neighbor in the building..

Um Muhamad: A neighbor in the building.

Um Sharif: Sharif's mother.

Wafik: Abu Muhamad's youngest son.

Walid: Sophia's brother.

Yehya: Abu Muhamad's middle son.

Zaki: Hajjeh's husband and a neighbor in the building.

Book Club Questions

1. Which one word describes Rami? Why?
2. What role did the mother play?
3. What motivated Rami and Nabil to pick up arms?
4. Why did Nabil grow to be a militant radical?
5. Did Jamil know about Othman's assassination?
6. What made Rami transform to a defiant moderate?
7. How did Sophia change Rami?
8. What did Rami expect to find in America?
9. How do parents contribute to radicalizing their children?
10. How did the environment contribute to producing radicals?
11. How did religion shape each of Baba, Mama, Rami, and Nabil?
12. How do people of faith transform into remorseless killers?
13. What are the root causes of violence?
14. How do you view religious violence now?
15. How do Middle Eastern militias and citizens view Americans?
16. How does the Israeli-Palestinian conflict affect the Middle East?
17. What can we, in the West, do differently to catalyze peace?
18. What will it take to build peace, now that you read the novel?
19. What can average western citizens do to derail the wrong?
20. What does it mean to be a moderate Muslim?
21. Is it possible to use religion to end wars?

Invite Sam to your book club. Email to **bookclub@samwazan.com**
Suggest questions or send responses to **author@samwazan.com**

About The Author

Sam Wazan is a fifteen-year combat-zone survivor of the Lebanese civil war. He is a grassroots catalyst for peace, founder of Parenting For Humanity, and a Global Trustee at United Religions Initiative. He is a Senior Management Consultant utilizing his skills to forge authentic relationships with workers on all levels and from various cultures to catalyze breakthrough results. His expertise—in facilitating, for problem solving, innovation, and action planning—rewards his clients with a sustainable competitive advantage.

www.samwazan.com

34918527R00220

Made in the USA
Lexington, KY
24 August 2014